"Rindge's prim[...] [...]ers into both biblical film and [...], along the way, Rindge also [...] [...] many of biblical scholarship's tr[...] [...]cret, the son of man, the move from the [...] [...]e proclaimed, and the historical Jesus). The last t[...] [...]apters alone are worth the book's price as they provide a hermeneutic by which readers can create their own new conversations with the manifold ways that bible and film interact (Bible in Film, Film as Bible, and Bible and Film/TV). Although a primer, Rindge's book, particularly its penultimate chapter, suggests exciting new scholarly possibilities."

Richard Walsh, *Methodist University, USA*

BIBLE AND FILM

THE BASICS

Bible and Film: The Basics is a concise, accessible, and illuminating introduction to the study of Bible and Film. The book introduces non-specialists to the essential content in Bible and Film, and to some of the most common and important methods Bible and Film scholars use. Questions asked throughout the book include:

- How do films (re)interpret and illuminate biblical texts?
- How do films appropriate, reconfigure, and transform biblical texts?
- How does a film's treatment of biblical texts help interpret and illuminate the film?

This book examines various types of interplay between film and the Bible. The theme of 'Bible on film' is explored through Hebrew Bible epics including *The Prince of Egypt* and *Noah*, and Jesus films such as *The Last Temptation of Christ* and *Son of Man*. The theme 'Bible in film' is analyzed through films including *Mary Magdalene*, *Magnolia*, *Pulp Fiction*, and *The Book of Eli*. Films that 'reimagine the Bible' include *Ex Machina, mother!*, and *The Tree of Life*; unusual Jesus figures in *Pan's Labyrinth*, *Dogville*, and *Donnie Darko* are also explored. 'Film as Bible' considers films such as *To the Wonder*, *Silence*, and *Parasite*. A conclusion examines television shows such as *Dekalog*, *The West Wing*, *The Handmaid's Tale*, and *God on Trial*.

With a glossary of key terms and suggestions for further reading throughout, this book is an ideal starting point for anyone seeking a full introduction to religion and film, Bible and film, Bible and popular culture, and theology and film.

Matthew S. Rindge is Professor of Religious Studies at Gonzaga University, USA. For six years he chaired the Bible and Film section in the Society of Biblical Literature.

The Basics

For more information about this series, please visit: www.routledge.com/The-Basics/book-series/B

BIBLE AND FILM

THE BASICS

Matthew S. Rindge

LONDON AND NEW YORK

First published 2022
by Routledge
2 Park Square, Milton Park, Abingdon, Oxon OX14 4RN

and by Routledge
605 Third Avenue, New York, NY 10158

Routledge is an imprint of the Taylor & Francis Group, an informa business

British Library Cataloguing-in-Publication Data
A catalogue record for this book is available from the British Library

Library of Congress Cataloging-in-Publication Data
Names: Rindge, Matthew S., author.
Title: Bible and film: the basics / Matthew S. Rindge.
Description: Abingdon, Oxon; New York: Routledge, 2021. |
Series: The basics | Includes bibliographical references and index. |
Identifiers: LCCN 2021001278 | ISBN 9780815392224 (hardback) |
ISBN 9780815392231 (paperback) | ISBN 9781351199759 (ebook)
Subjects: LCSH: Bible—In motion pictures. |
Bible films—History and criticism. | Motion pictures—Religious aspects.
Classification: LCC PN1995.9.B53 R56 2021 | DDC 791.43/6822—dc23
LC record available at https://lccn.loc.gov/2021001278

ISBN: 978-0-8153-9222-4 (hbk)
ISBN: 978-0-8153-9223-1 (pbk)
ISBN: 978-1-351-19975-9 (ebk)

Typeset in Bembo
by Newgen Publishing UK

For Michael Rindge,
brother and best friend.

CONTENTS

FIGURES

ACKNOWLEDGEMENTS

My thinking about Bible and Film has been influenced and shaped by Richard Walsh, Robert K. Johnston, Rhonda Burnette-Bletsch, Tina Pippin, Robert Seesengood, Adele Reinhartz, Caroline Vander Stichele, Craig Detweiler, Jeffrey Staley, and David Shepherd. I thank them for their wisdom and insights over the years.

I am grateful to Rebecca Shilabeer at Routledge for her enthusiastic support of this project from its conception, and her steadfast patience with me while I worked on and completed it. I thank Amy Doffegnies for communicating with me over several months, and graciously handling multiple requests and details. Emma Craig handled the production process, Andy Soutter oversaw copyediting, and Francesca Hearn helped see it to completion. The book would not exist without them.

I thank Richard Walsh and Adele Reinhartz for their helpful and instructive feedback on the manuscript. This book is better because of their suggestions. All faults, of course, are mine.

My students at Gonzaga University, where I created and have taught "Bible and Film" since 2009, have been valuable learning partners. I thank them for sharing parts of this journey with me.

In 2009, Richard Walsh (along with Jeffrey Staley) welcomed me into the "Bible and Film" section in the Society of Biblical Literature, and mentored me while I served on the committee and later served as Chair. I am grateful that he has remained an invaluable mentor, colleague, and friend.

I thank my children, Andrew and Sophia, for the joy they have given me.

I thank Stephen King, whose *On Writing* helped me at a crucial time, and I am grateful to Nike Imoru, who encouraged and cheered me across the finish line.

Michael Rindge has been a better brother and friend than I deserve. With joy and gratitude I dedicate this book to him.

INTRODUCTION

If, as film critic André Bazin claims, "cinema has always been interested in God," it is also true that cinema has often been interested in the Bible.[1] This book introduces readers to the academic study of Bible and Film. Located within the broader umbrella of Religion (or Theology) and Film, Bible and Film is an interdisciplinary field concerned with the interplay and multiple intersections between Film and the Bible.

Scholars of Bible and Film employ dozens of different methods and approaches. While this book cannot do justice to all these various models, it does illustrate a broad range of diverse ways of thinking about how Bible and Film intersect. I hope this book demonstrates that constructing conversations between films and biblical texts has the potential to illuminate both the film and the biblical text. One of the goals of creating a dialogue between a film(s) and a biblical text(s) is to enrich our understanding of both the biblical text and the film.

Each chapter examines a select number of films rather than treating a larger number of films more superficially. Exploring a smaller number of films in greater depth provides a clearer and more concrete sense of what "Bible and Film" analysis entails, rather than a theoretical discussion about the field. Whether such a choice is more beneficial, and whether I succeed in doing so, is left for the reader to decide. Each chapter concludes with a list of recommended books and articles, allowing readers to pursue certain topics of interest in greater depth and detail.

The book's chapters reflect distinct and diverse ways of understanding how film and biblical texts can be placed into a mutually critical and illuminating dialogue. Two chapters engage the most common type of Bible and Film analysis: overtly "biblical" films that present or retell biblical narratives (the Bible "on" Film). Chapter 2 examines five Hebrew Bible epics (*Samson and Delilah, The Ten Commandments, The Prince of Egypt, Exodus: Gods and Kings,* and *Noah*). Chapter 4 discusses 12 Jesus films (*Intolerance, The King of Kings, King of Kings, The Greatest Story Ever Told, Jesus of Nazareth, Il Vangelo Secondo Matteo* [The Gospel according to Saint Matthew], *Godspell, Jesus Christ Superstar, The Last Temptation of Christ, The Passion of the Christ, Son of Man,* and *Last Days in the Desert*).

Films can also incorporate biblical texts by explicitly citing or alluding to the Bible or including biblical characters (the Bible "in" Film). Chapter 6 analyzes six films that feature biblical characters (*Mary Magdalene*) or cite or allude to biblical texts (*Pulp Fiction, Magnolia, Dead Man Walking, Hacksaw Ridge,* and *The Book of Eli*).

In addition to the Bible "in" or "on" film, films can also reimagine biblical texts by adapting them into contemporary contexts (Bible "reimagined" in film). Chapter 3 analyzes six films that reimagine Hebrew Bible texts (*Ex Machina, mother!, A Serious Man, The Tree of Life, Leviafan* [*Leviathan*], and *The Zero Theorem*). Chapter 5 explores six films that reimagine Jesus; three films offer traditional Jesus figures (*The Green Mile, The Matrix,* and *Jésus de Montréal*), and three films depict unusual or atypical Jesus figures (*Donnie Darko, Dogville,* and *Il laberinto del fauno* [*Pan's Labyrinth*]).

Films can also function as biblical texts (or biblical genres) even if they do not explicitly cite or allude to biblical texts (Film "as" Bible). Chapter 7 examines films that function or operate like the biblical genres of lament (*To The Wonder, Silence*), prophecy (*The Girl in the Café* and the films of Ava DuVernay and Spike Lee), parable (*Dogville*), and apocalypse (*Parasite*). Chapter 8 examines two areas of inquiry that will become more significant in the future of Bible and Film studies: (1) "non-biblical" films (Bible "and" film) and (2) television. Far from being hermetically sealed off from one another, the boundaries between some of these chapters are porous and permeable. Several films can belong to more than one of the above categories.

The twin goals in these chapters is to illustrate the different ways of understanding the relationship between Bible and Film, and to show how films and biblical texts can be illuminated by placing them into a mutually critical conversation. In addition to analyzing films on their own terms and in their own voice, the focus is on how films appropriate and reconfigure biblical texts, and how this interpretive activity illuminates both the film and the biblical text. The book demonstrates how films and biblical texts can be (re)interpreted as a result of placing them into mutually critical dialogues.

NOTE

1 Bazin (1951), 1.

FOR FURTHER READING

Rhonda Burnette-Bletsch, ed., *The Bible in Motion: A Handbook of the Bible and Its Reception in Film* (Berlin: De Gruyter, 2016).
Cheryl Exum, ed., *The Bible in Film—The Bible and Film* (Leiden: Brill, 2006).
Adele Reinhartz, *Bible and Cinema: Fifty Key Films* (New York: Routledge, 2012).
Adele Reinhartz, *Bible and Cinema: An Introduction* (New York: Routledge, 2013).
Richard Walsh, ed., *T&T Clark Companion to the Bible and Film* (London: Bloomsbury, 2018).

HEBREW BIBLE EPICS

One of the most common types of "Bible" films are **Hebrew Bible** epics. By 1916, over 110 films based on the Hebrew Bible had appeared. Plots rife with conflict, violence, and sex make Hebrew Bible narratives ripe for cinematic treatment. Few Hebrew Bible films are based on non-narrative literary genres such as legal material, psalms, prophecy, etc. Early Hebrew Bible silent films include *Adam and Eve* (1912), *Joseph in the Land of Egypt* (1914), *The Chosen Prince* (about David and Jonathan) (1917), and *The Queen of Sheba* (1921). Later "**talkies**" include *Noah's Ark* (1929) and *Lot in Sodom* (1933). Several films were made about Salome (1908, 1910, 1918, 1923, 1953, 2002), and D. W. Griffith's *Judith of Bethulia* (1914) was the fourth film about Judith.

This chapter explores the rise of the Hebrew Bible epic (examining Cecil B. DeMille's *Samson and Delilah* and *The Ten Commandments*), the animated musical *The Prince of Egypt*, and two relatively recent films (Ridley Scott's *Exodus: Gods and Kings* and Darren Aronofsky's *Noah*). In addition to analyzing and discussing the salient themes in each film, I will illustrate how these films take distinct approaches to treating Hebrew Bible texts. The cinematic treatment of Hebrew Bible narratives illustrates how films not only appropriate biblical texts but also reconfigure them. This chapter illustrates how films can illuminate biblical texts, and how biblical texts can illuminate films.

RISE OF THE HEBREW BIBLE EPIC

Director **Cecil B. DeMille** is synonymous with the **biblical epic**, a cinematic spectacle whose large budgets produced ornate and lavish sets, dozens of elaborate and colorful costume changes, scores of speaking parts, and hundreds (or thousands) of extras. These extravagant spectacles are what many people think of when they hear "Bible film." DeMille, whose mother was Jewish and whose grandfather was an Episcopal priest, made four films based on biblical texts: *The Ten Commandments* (1923, 1956), *King of Kings* (1927), and *Samson and Delilah* (1949). Two other DeMille films deal explicitly with religious themes—*The Sign of the Cross* (1932) and *The Crusades* (1935)—and the Bible informs many titles of his other films: *Male and Female* (1919), *Forbidden Fruit* (1921), *Adam's Rib* (1923), *Feet of Clay* (1924), and *Madam Satan* (1930).

SAMSON AND DELILAH

Many consider *Samson and Delilah* (1949) the first true biblical epic. This was the fourth film on the subject (*Samson et Dalila*, Ferdinand Zecca, 1902; *Samson*, J. Farrell MacDonald, 1914; *Samson und Delila*, Alexander Korda, 1922), and four films on Samson have appeared since (Lee Philips, 1984; Nicolas Roeg, 1996; Corina Van Eijk, 2007; Macdonald and Sabloff, 2018). With a $28 million domestic gross, the film earned Paramount more money than any film since DeMille's *The Ten Commandments* (1923). Although its opening credits claim that the film is "based upon the history of Samson and Delilah in the Holy Bible, Judges 13–16," the film differs in significant ways from the biblical text. Such **redaction** can reveal important values and commitments of the filmmakers. Just as authors of biblical texts adapt their source material (e.g., Chronicles and Kings), so too do films reveal important tendencies of their creators when they depart from the biblical text upon which they are based.

DeMille's introductory narration to the film states that tyranny "grind[s] the human spirit beneath the conqueror's heel. But deep in man's heart still burned the unquenchable will for freedom." This will for freedom is a "divine spark" that can alter "the course of human events," and allow one's name to "survive the ages." Samson, DeMille continues, is just such a man whose "bold dream" is "liberty for his nation," a nation held in bondage by Philistines for 40 years. A dominant framework in the film, this theme of freedom from tyranny surfaces in the film's opening scene when an old man tells the story of Moses demanding that Pharaoh free the Hebrews.

A Philistine soldier throws the old man to the ground and forces him to bow to him, illustrating the contemporary bondage of the Israelites under the Philistines, and foreshadowing the same yearning for freedom the Hebrews had under Pharaoh. The post-World War II context, and emerging Cold War between the US and Soviet Union, is a fitting frame for understanding this tale of freedom from tyranny.

In typical DeMille fashion, the film spices up sensual elements, creating a series of romantic triangles that the book of Judges lacks. In Judges, Samson takes a Philistine wife (for political reasons), who is later given to his companion, has sex with a prostitute, and falls in love with Delilah (Judges 14:4; 16:1, 4). In DeMille's version, Samson is smitten with the Philistine woman (Semadar) for reasons of love, not politics. Semadar is courted by Ahtur, and her sister Delilah is in love with Samson. Miriam, a Danite (the word Jew or Israelite is never mentioned), also loves Samson. Samson opts to wed Semadar, but Delilah schemes to have Semadar betray Samson and marry Ahtur. Samson refuses to take Delilah, and she is so scorned she vows to destroy him. DeMille once quipped, "Give me any two pages of the Bible and I'll give you a picture." His pictures just happened to have extra doses of sex and romance. The **Hays code** prevented DeMille from displaying overt nudity, but it did not keep him from spicing up the biblical account.

The most striking change the film makes to Judges is to turn Delilah into a sultry siren who orchestrates Samson's downfall as revenge for scorning her. In Judges, Delilah's only "fault" is that she cooperates with men who persuade her to discover the secret of Samson's strength. In the film, however, she twice demands that Samson suffer: "Make him turn the grist mill, whipped and driven like an animal, where all Gaza can mock him and laugh at him. Humble him, and bring him to his knees." She fixates on humiliating him: "I want his life. Chain him in the grist mill. Let him grind our grain like a beast. Let the people mock him and make sport of him, until he draws his breath in agony and every word he speaks is a prayer for death." Her subsequent seduction of Samson is a ploy to trap him (unlike Judges where the two are already lovers). Whereas in Judges the men offer her 1,100 pieces of silver to betray him, in the film she is the one who demands this payment. She also takes a second lover in the film (which does not happen in Judges).

The film's morality is clear: the danger is Delilah, the seductive temptress (a role enhanced by casting Hedy Lamarr). She dresses in scantily clad outfits; her neck and midriff are almost always bare. Samson calls her the "great courtesan of Gaza," and—reflecting the misogyny of Proverbs—impugns her sexuality as fatal: "Your kiss is a sting of death." But he ultimately yields to her charms, calls her (anachronistically) a "daughter of Hell," and kisses her. They spend the night together and the next morning are playful lovers. Their bliss ends when Miriam shows up to tell Samson that the Philistines killed his father, are torturing his mother, and (anticipating Herod's tyranny in Matthew?) are killing the firstborn in every village. Judges lacks all this, and the cinematic Samson appears more noble in the film since he leaves Delilah to rescue his kin. Delilah, threatened by Miriam's love for Samson ("No man leaves Delilah!"), poisons him, and—unlike Judges where a man cuts off his hair—she cuts off (some of) his hair, sapping his strength.

In the film, Samson's subsequent punishment (eyes gouged out, forced labor) results from succumbing to Delilah's seduction, whereas in Judges the two are already lovers before she betrays him. After her betrayal, Samson faults her sexuality: "Your arms were quicksand, your kiss was death. The name Delilah will be an everlasting curse on the lips of men." (Thanks to DeMille it certainly might). Ahtur is more pointed: "Satan himself taught her all the arts of deception. It's easier to catch the moonlight than to hold such a woman. ... You're a fool, Samson. You trusted Delilah. Remember her beauty, and never forget her treachery." If the lesson is not clear enough, it is repeated later: "Samson was tamed by a woman."

Whereas Delilah disappears in Judges after her act of betrayal, the film includes scenes in which she regrets betraying Samson. She and Samson reconcile before he dies and kills everyone else (including Delilah). The film thus vilifies the sinful seductress and only regards her redemption as possible if she repents.

The main threat here is the woman and her sexual wiles. The film augments Delilah's sexuality, and minimizes Samson's promiscuity (omitting his liaison with the unnamed prostitute). In Judges, Samson "falls in love with Delilah" (Judges 16:4), but in the film Delilah repeatedly tries to bed Samson, and he repeatedly resists her seductive advances. This redaction is part of the film's consistent

Figures 2.1 and 2.2   Delilah as seductress in *Samson and Delilah* (1949).

tendency to enhance Samson's morality. Before he is blinded, Samson prays to God and accepts his fate, actions absent in Judges, but which make him more of a martyr in the film. The film lacks Samson's prayer in Judges, that God will strengthen him to destroy the temple as an act of revenge (Judges 16:28). The film maintains the focus in Judges on Samson's Herculean strength, but omits his slaughter of 30 men in order to steal their clothes and pay a lost wager; in the film he merely steals their clothes. In Judges, both this violence and another murderous rampage with a jawbone are prompted by the "spirit of Adonai" (Judges 14:19; 15:14–15); the film's omission of these remarks also absolves God of unethical conduct.

THE TEN COMMANDMENTS

With over 70 speaking roles and scores of intricately and elaborately designed sets and costumes, DeMille's 1956 film (a remake of his 1923 silent, black and white film) is the quintessential biblical epic. Its budget of $13 million made it the most expensive film at the time. Until Mel Gibson's *The Passion of the Christ*, it was the highest grossing "Bible" film in US box office history. It is one of the most popular and profitable films of all time. DeMille's boast may be exaggerated ("my ministry was making religious movies and getting more people to read the Bible than anyone else ever has"), but he did get many to view the Bible on screen.[1]

The film retells the story of Moses' life, from his birth until he reveals the titular ten commandments to the Israelites (a brief shot shows Joshua leading the Israelites into the land of Canaan). Charlton Heston, allegedly chosen by DeMille because of his resemblance to Michelangelo's Moses, is a strong, swarthy, confident Moses in the prime of life. Unlike Exodus, this Moses has no stuttering or any language inability; he is free from human foibles.

As with *Samson and Delilah*, DeMille clarifies his ideological interests in his introduction to the audience. The film, he announces, is about "the story of the birth of freedom. ... The theme of this picture is whether men ought to be ruled by God's law or whether they ought to be ruled by the whims of a dictator like Rameses. Are men the property of the State or are they free souls under God? This same battle continues throughout the world today." When the Hebrews are freed from Egypt, the narrator intones, "A nation arose, and freedom was born into the world." Moses is a freedom fighter, insisting, "It's not treason to want freedom." He tells Joshua, "Go, proclaim liberty throughout all the lands." In championing freedom, he upholds a cardinal virtue of American ideology. In a post-World War II Cold War context, justifying (divine) violence against an aggressor could function as legitimating America's militaristic posture against the Soviet Union.

When Moses insists, "Man shall be ruled by law, not by the will of other men," he defends the American principle that governance by law represents civilization's apex. The film's final image, the two tablets of ten commandments ("written with the finger of God") reinforces this elevation of law. Moses declares, "There is no freedom without the law ... Those who shall not live by the law shall die by the law." In this last shot, Moses adopts the iconic physical pose of the Statue of Liberty, further aligning Moses' commitment to law with a well-known American image. Moses becomes an American icon. When Moses hands five books (not scrolls) from a modern satchel (!) to Joshua, the film follows a tradition, dismissed by scholars, that Moses wrote the Torah; he is, in the film, the author of Jewish law, a founding father of Israel.

Despite (or because of) its overt interest in the role of law, the film fails to reflect the prominent motif in Exodus of disobeying (unjust) laws. Exodus begins with three episodes in which women (Hebrew midwives, Moses' mother, Pharaoh's daughter) disobey Pharaoh's law to kill the Hebrew male children. These acts of disobeying the law save lives, including Moses', thus facilitating the eventual liberation of Hebrews from slavery. DeMille's exaltation of the law fails to recognize its use (in Exodus and the United States) as a potential instrument of inhumane abuse.

Although the film presents itself as a realistic depiction of the Bible ("Those who see this motion picture ... will make a pilgrimage over the very ground that Moses trod more than 3,000 years ago"), it contains many elements absent in Exodus: Moses joins the slaves in their labors, he saves the life of an old woman about to be crushed to death (who turns out to be his mother), and he establishes the Sabbath by insisting that slaves have a weekly day of rest.

DeMille acknowledges this kind of **midrash**—an ancient Jewish practice of supplying details that the biblical text lacks—when he notes in his introduction that the film draws on a range of ancient Jewish (Philo, Josephus, Dead Sea Scrolls) and Christian (Eusebius) sources to fill in narrative gaps in Exodus.

Many elements that become standard in subsequent Moses films appear in *The Ten Commandments*: (1) the identity of the pharaoh Moses opposes as Rameses II; (2) a rivalry between Moses and his "brother" Rameses; and (3) Moses' realization that he is a Hebrew as the pivotal moment of his character development. These cinematic elements, absent in Exodus, enhance relational conflict and provide a psychological motive for Moses' solidarity with the Hebrews and his opposition to Pharaoh.

As in *Samson and Delilah*, DeMille fabricates a romantic triangle, this time between Moses, his "brother" Rameses II, and princess Nefertiri. Both men want to marry Nefretiri, but she wants Moses, much to Rameses' discontent. Nefertiri flirts with Moses when he returns home, and later kisses him passionately. A second romantic triangle involves Joshua, Lilia, and Dathan. When Moses arrives in Midian, Jethro's daughters fawn over him, six of whom dance before him, competing to be selected as his wife. The film also suggests an incompatibility between romance and serving God. As Nefertiri tells Sephora, Moses' wife: "You lost him when he went to seek his God. I lost him when he found his God."

DeMille Christianizes Moses by depicting him as a type or fore-runner of Jesus. Borrowing from Matthew's infancy narrative, Moses' birth is anticipated by a star astrologers see as a prophetic sign of a coming Hebrew deliverer; Pharaoh agrees to kill newborn Hebrew males to eliminate this deliverer. After Moses encounters God, he speaks (with a radiant glow) in words from John's gospel: "And the word was God … He was not flesh but spirit, the light of eternal mind. And I know that his light is in every man" (John 1:1, 4). Moses' mother is presented as a Mary figure. When she meets her adult son, her words echo those about Mary and Jesus in the New Testament: "Blessed am I among all mothers in the land for my eyes have beheld thy deliverer" (Luke 1:42; 2:30). The frequent repetition of the Hebrews' expectation of a deliverer (and Egyptian fear of this figure) positions Moses, like Jesus, as a prophesied redeemer. If not

Figures 2.3 and 2.4 Moses as miracle worker and lawgiver in *The Ten Commandments* (1956).

a Christian story, the film presents itself at least as a Judeo-Christian story. The danger here is erasing Moses' Hebrew identity, or subsuming it within a Judeo-Christian framework.

These **intertextual** links also demonstrate how the film operates with a **canonical** understanding of the Hebrew Bible and

New Testament as a unified collection of texts whose particular meanings are overshadowed by overarching, unifying themes. Some intertextual links are within the Hebrew Bible. When Sephora tells Moses, "Where he sends you I will go. Your god is my God," she speaks words from Ruth 1:16. Moses' remark ("Then let us go forth to the mountain of God that he may write his commandments in our minds and upon our hearts forever") is influenced by Jeremiah 31:33.

As in *Samson and Delilah*, DeMille casts a woman as the main villain. Unlike Exodus, where God and Pharaoh harden Pharaoh's heart (thus prolonging the misery of the Egyptians and Hebrews), in the film Nefertiri plays this antagonistic role. Nefirtiri tries to seduce Moses multiple times, even after he marries Sephora. She tells Moses, "You will come to me or [the Hebrews] will never leave Egypt … Who else can soften Pharaoh's heart, or harden it?" When Rameses decides to free the Hebrews, Nefertiri is the one who hardens his heart. She shames him into pursuing Moses and the Hebrews: "You are nothing—you let Moses kill my son." Handing him a sword, she demands, "Bring it back to me, stained with his blood." She is an agent of death and destruction. Like *Samson and Delilah*, God's complicity in oppression is overlooked and blame for violence is shifted from God to women. The film downplays problematic ethical questions about God's conduct, and projects this questionable ethical conduct onto Nefertiri. If there is an antagonist for DeMille, it is the woman whose failed efforts at seduction lead her to harm others. As Rameses tells Nefertiri, "I would not let these people go because your serpent's tongue hardened my heart."

Another way DeMille protects God's image is by having Pharaoh order the killing of the firstborn in each house of the Hebrews, unlike Exodus where God initiates this infanticide. In the film, killing the firstborn is God's response to Pharaoh's own plan of murder. In Exodus, God announces the death of the firstborn before Pharaoh even has a chance to hear Moses' plea (Exodus 4:23; Exodus 11–12). Along with omitting God's thwarted (and startling) effort to kill Moses (Exodus 4), this redactional change avoids the disturbing theological challenge in Exodus of God slaughtering innocent children. As DeMille's Moses declares, "In the hardness of his heart Pharaoh has mocked God and brings death to his own son."

As with Samson, DeMille's Moses is more noble than the biblical version. He takes more initiative in the film, both with God ("But for me there is no peace of spirit until I hear the word of God, from God himself") and in advocating for the Hebrew slaves. When Moses first encounters God, he asks, "Why do you not hear the cries of the people in Egypt?" God's declaration about hearing the cries of those enslaved becomes a response to Moses' inquiry, rather than—as in Exodus 3—something God initiates with Moses. Moses registers disgust ("Turn from thy fierce wrath, O God!") with God's plan of killing children, a sentiment he never expresses in Exodus.

Relatively few Hebrew Bible epics appeared between the 1960s and 1980s. Those that did, such as *Esther and the King* (Walsh and Bava, 1960), *David e Golia* (Baldi and Pottier, 1960), and *King David* (Beresford, 1985), did not fare well with critics or moviegoers.

ANIMATING A MUSICAL MOSES: *THE PRINCE OF EGYPT*

The Prince of Egypt (1998) is a rare Bible film co-directed by a woman (Brenda Chapman, with Steve Hickner and Simon Wells). Women are more prominent here than in other Moses films, and unlike DeMille's version, not one woman is cast as a villain. Women sing solos in key songs ("Deliver Us") and some entire songs ("If You Believe?"). Miriam is the one who reveals to Moses his Hebrew identity, and (as in Exodus 15) she sings after leaving Egypt. Tzipporah is stronger and more independent than her husband Moses, and unlike other Moses films (but like Exodus), she insists on journeying with him when he returns to Egypt. DeMille's romantic triangles that reduce women to romantic objects are entirely absent.

The film opens with a quote indicating that what follows is "an adaptation of the Exodus story," and that while "artistic and historical license has been taken, we believe that this film is true to the essence, values and integrity of a story that is a cornerstone of faith for millions of people worldwide." The film acknowledges the significant role Moses has in Judaism, Christianity, and Islam, as the final citations about Moses from the Hebrew Bible (Deuteronomy 34:10), New Testament (Acts 7:35), and the Qur'an

(Surah 19:51) indicate. The character of Jethro might be an effort to provide a "Judeo-Christian-Islamic" framing. Moses is not, however, Christianized in this film to the same extent as he is in *The Ten Commandments*. Underscoring the Jewish texture of the story is the use of (untranslated) Hebrew lyrics in the opening song "Deliver Us" and the closing song "When You Believe."

The film's musicality enhances its affective power. The song "Deliver Us" in the opening sequence of slave labor ("Elohim, God on high, can you hear your people cry? Help us now, this dark hour. Deliver us, hear our call, deliver us. Lord of all remember us / Here in this burning sand. Deliver us / There's a land you promised us. Deliver us to the promised land") evokes more empathy for the slaves' suffering than *The Ten Commandments* or *Exodus: Gods and Kings* does. Music keys Moses into his true identity, as his sister Miriam sings to him the same lullaby his mother sang as she hid him in the basket. The film's music and animation reflect an effort to connect to a demographic younger than typical audiences of biblical epics.

Many elements from *The Ten Commandments* appear in the film, highlighting DeMille's lasting influence. Moses' recognition of his Hebrew identity is the key catalyst of the plot and of Moses' character

Figure 2.5   Moses' mother protects her baby from violence in *The Prince of Egypt* (1998).

development. Rameses' hairstyle is the same style actor Yul Brynner wore in DeMille's film. The film's title "Prince of Egypt" is used several times in DeMille's *The Ten Commandments*. (Dorothy Clarke Wilson's 1949 novel *Moses: The Prince of Egypt* influenced DeMille's film and, less directly, *The Prince of Egypt*.) God, as in DeMille's version, is protected from charges of unethical conduct. It is Rameses who threatens to kill the Hebrew children, and finish the job his father started: "And there shall be a great cry in all of Egypt such as never has been or ever shall be again." In transferring this line from God (who speaks it in Exodus) to Rameses, the film shifts responsibility for the death of the firstborn from God to Rameses. The film ends with Moses descending a mountain with two inscribed tablets of the commandments. Law, as in *The Ten Commandments*, triumphs at the end.

Unlike DeMille's film and Ridley Scott's *Exodus: Gods and Kings*, Moses and Rameses are fond of each other, and evince less overt conflict. Moses' realization that he is a Hebrew does not, as in these other two films, drive a wedge between him and Rameses. The two actually embrace when Moses returns after his lengthy exile, and Rameses welcomes him as "our brother Moses, the prince of Egypt." The conflict between the two only arises when Moses demands the freedom of the Hebrew slaves; in other Moses films this demand emerges from a pre-existing conflict between the two men. In these films, the personal (brotherly conflict) leads to the political, but in *The Prince of Egypt* the political (freedom of slaves) clashes with and prevails over the claims and loyalties of the personal. Even as their conflict intensifies, both brothers regret it. Rameses asks Moses, "Why can't things be the way they were before?" Rameses is not even killed at the end of the film, as in other Moses films. He survives the flooding of the sea, yelling, "Moses! Moses!" Moses responds, "Goodbye brother," maintaining a type of familial connection.

Masculinity is a key motif in Moses films, and the character Moses encodes idealized masculine norms. The lack of sharp conflict between Moses and Rameses in *The Prince of Egypt* reflects a different vision of masculinity than in other Moses films. Unlike *The Ten Commandments* and *Exodus: Gods and Kings*, this Moses is not a military commander who swaggers with a cocky bravado; he is not the rugged, macho type. He often displays empathy—for the

Hebrew male children killed by Pharaoh, for the Hebrew slaves, and even for Rameses' child, whose death makes him weep. He feels guilt after accidentally killing an Egyptian slave master. He does not, as in Exodus, look around to make sure no one is watching before killing him, nor does he hide the body afterward. Unlike *The Ten Commandments* and *Exodus: Gods and Kings*, where he is forced into exile, Moses leaves voluntarily because he feels shame over taking a life. Moses' empathy parallels God's empathy for the plight of the Hebrew slaves, which is the principal divine attribute God reveals to Moses when they encounter each other, both in the film and in Exodus 3.

Miriam sings the film's final song "When You Believe" as the Hebrews depart from slavery. Unlike *The Ten Commandments* (but befitting the deaths of the Egyptian firstborn), their departure is initially somber and only gradually turns celebratory. Composed of English and Hebrew lyrics, the song ("there can be miracles when you believe") suggests that the miracle of deliverance from slavery is somehow rooted in the belief or faith of the Hebrews. This is not the case in Exodus, in which God's emancipation of the Hebrew slaves is not a response to their belief, but a result of God's commitment to, and solidarity with, the oppressed. The film's elevation of the role of faith/belief, a departure from Exodus, coheres with a contemporary religiosity which emphasizes personal faith/belief. Moses tells the Hebrews that Pharaoh can take everything away from them except their faith. "Believe," he encourages them. This line resonates with a post-Holocaust context in which some Jews coped with that unthinkable evil by arguing that to surrender one's faith was to give up the one and only thing that the Nazis could not take from them. The film's final line, "Deliver us," speaks to a potential precarity that Jews face in a world in which antisemitism never seems to die.

ACTION FILM MOSES

Exodus: Gods and Kings (Scott, 2016) presents the Moses story as an action film. The film gives less time to women than *The Ten Commandments* and *The Prince of Egypt* (eliminating them almost completely), and the cast's lack of ethnic diversity elicited criticism.

Like other Exodus films, it foregrounds the suffering of the enslaved Hebrews at the outset. It frames the film within the divine–human relationship: "In all that time they have not forgotten their homeland. Or their God … God has not forgotten them."

With the exception of romantic triangles, Scott borrows many motifs from DeMille's epic. As in *The Ten Commandments*, Moses is a military general whose impressive battle performance makes his brother Rameses II jealous. The key plot catalyst is Moses' recognition of his Hebrew identity, after which Rameses exiles Moses into the desert (as in DeMille's version) and sends two men after Moses to kill him. When Moses confronts Rameses before the final plague of the death of the firstborn, the film uses the same music from *The Ten Commandments*. Near the film's end, Moses etches the ten commandments, an explicit recognition of the triumph of cultic law over the cult of personality. As God tells Moses, "A leader can falter, but not stone." As in DeMille's version, the law triumphs.

The action film genre shapes choices (such as sending men after Moses to kill him) regarding the adaptation of the biblical text. When Moses encounters God it is Moses' battle expertise that God highlights. God says, "I need a general to fight," and Moses replies, "To fight who? For what?" God declares, "I think you should go and see what's happening to your people now … Are they not people in your opinion?" The film minimizes God's solidarity with, and advocacy of, the oppressed, a central point made to Moses in Exodus 3. God's lines here do, however, seek to augment Moses' empathy with the enslaved Hebrews, and invite Moses to see them not merely as slaves but also as people. The action film genre explains the Hebrews forging weapons to prepare for their uprising, Moses training archers and providing military expertise, and attacking Egyptian food supplies. The violence of the plagues also fits the action film genre; hordes of crocodiles maul fishermen, thousands of fish turn up dead, and blood is ubiquitous.

More than any other Moses film, *Exodus: Gods and Kings* questions God's ethics (or lack thereof). Moses complains to God about the plagues, saying, "This is affecting everyone. So who are you punishing?" When God says, "Something worse has to happen," Moses says, "Anything more is just revenge." God, however, insists, "I want to see them on their knees, begging for it to stop." In response to Rameses' threat, God informs Moses about killing the firstborn. Moses says, "You cannot do this. I want no part of this." Moses is thus more humane than in Exodus, and more willing to resist God's atrocities. When an Egyptian tells Moses that "Israelite" means "He who fights with God," Moses replies, "He who *wrestles* with God. There is a difference." As in Exodus, this Moses wrestles with God, but he does so about God's immorality. Depicting the deaths of Egyptian sons and daughters invites empathy for their suffering and further implicates God as ethically problematic or even evil. As Rameses asks, "Is this your god? What kind of fanatic worships such a god?" Depicting God (or God's messenger?) in the form of a child, one of the film's unique features, may reflect a view of God (or God's messenger) as petty and petulant.

The film has many similarities to Scott's previous film *Gladiator* (2000). In both films, a son of a dying ruler becomes jealous of a perceived competitor for the throne and his father's affection. The son exiles and tries to kill his competitor, but this plan fails and the brother returns to seek justice. Scott even reuses a line of dialogue in *Exodus: Gods and Kings* from *Gladiator*; in each film the chief antagonist says to a young child, "You sleep so well, because you know you're loved." Such parallels indicate how films can reflect the broader interests and tendencies of their creators (**auteurs**).

Two scenes in the film evoke the **Shoah**. Hebrew bodies are burned throughout the day and night; and when Egyptian forces seek Moses, he and other Hebrews hide in a secret room under the floor. With these allusions, the film establishes a kind of interplay between Exodus and the Shoah, and certain scenes may offer insights regarding the Shoah. God does not harden Pharaoh's heart in the film, as in Exodus, and this change could protect God or it might reflect a realism regarding the human responsibility in committing evil. Moses replies to Zipporah's comment about their son ("Is it so wrong for him to grow up believing in God?") by saying, "Is it so wrong for him to grow up believing in himself?" His remark shifts the need from relying on God for help to relying on oneself, a reality faced by many Jews in the Shoah who found God was impotent to deliver them from evil.

Exodus material which all three of these Moses films omit is revealing. Nothing is mentioned of the Hebrew midwives who disobey Pharaoh's order to kill the male Hebrew children, nor of the similar disobedience by Moses' mother or Pharaoh's daughter (Exodus 1:15–21). Omitting these women resisters to Pharaoh perpetuates a stereotype of men as God's instruments of deliverance. No mention is made of God's inexplicable attempt to kill Moses and how his wife Zipporah saves his life (Exodus 4). These films sanitize Moses by omitting his slaughter of 3,000 fellow Israelites (Exodus 32). Moses is whitewashed in more ways than one. In general, Exodus is more theologically disturbing, ethically challenging, and feminist than all three of these Moses films. It has more tolerance for protagonists (God and Moses) who are ethically ambiguous and problematic. Exodus also lacks the psychological interest of these films in highlighting the importance and function of Moses' realization that he is a Hebrew.

NOAH AS CINEMATIC MIDRASH

Noah (2014) is not—as director/co-writer Darren Aronofsky claimed—the "least biblical biblical film ever made."[2] It is one of the more imaginative and realistic. *Noah* reimagines disturbing (and beautiful) versions of God, people, and the world. Its imaginative realism consists in never having God appear or even speak. Every perception Noah has of God is his *perception*. Noah has visions and dreams, and he must discern what God may or may not be communicating through these. Noah's wife Naameh asks him at one point if God spoke to him, and his reply ("I think so") reflects his uncertainty about hearing from God. God's silence is a departure from previous biblical epics, and a recognition of the anthropological nature and texture of religious belief.

Noah's primary ethic is a commitment to caring for animals and creation. He inherits this environmental ethic from his father who tells him, "The Creator made Adam in his image and then placed the world in his care; this is your world now, your responsibility." Noah passes this same ethic to his son, telling him after he sees him picking a flower, "We only collect what we need, what we can use." Noah is a caretaker of the earth, is tender with animals, and is a vegetarian. The film's antagonists, Cain's descendants, eat animals and ravage the earth with the development of "a great industrial civilization."

The chief purpose of the ark Noah and his family build (with help from rock creatures called the Watchers) is to save the world's animal species. Noah explains, "Men are going to be punished for what they've done to this world. There will be destruction, there will be tragedy. Our family has been chosen for a great task. We've been chosen to save the innocent." When he is asked, "The innocent?" he answers, "The animals." Noah explains, "We have to be gentle with them, and we have to be protective. If something were to happen that would be a small piece of Creation lost forever. All of these innocent creatures are now in our care. It's our job to look after them." As in Genesis, it is *human* wickedness God destroys with the flood.

Noah comes to believe that a world without people is what God desires. Before boarding the ark, Noah visits a camp where the strong terrorize the weak. Children are traded for meat. Crowds tear apart a lamb and eat its flesh. Noah looks closely and realizes that one of these men is Noah himself. Noah concludes, "The wickedness is not just in them. It's in all of us. I saw it." He discounts Naameh's remark ("There's goodness in us—Shem's loyalty, Japhet's kindness, Ham's integrity") by insisting, "Shem is blinded by desire. Ham is covetous. Japhet lives only to please. I am no better … We would both choose to kill in order to protect our children … We were weak and we were selfish to think we could set ourselves apart." He announces that once their task of saving the animals is complete they will die just like everyone else. Naameh asks, "Have you no mercy?" and Noah intones, "The time for mercy is past. Now our punishment begins." Noah retells the **first creation story** from Genesis 1, noting: "And it was good. It was all good." What was good, according to Noah, was life before people. "It was paradise." Evil accompanied the birth of humanity. "Brother against brother. Nation against nation. Man against Creation. We murdered each other. We did this. Man did this. Everything that was beautiful. Everything that was good. We shattered. Now it begins again. Paradise returns. But this time, there will be no men. … The Creator has judged us. Mankind must end. … Creation will be left alone—safe and beautiful." In this vision, what is "not good" is not Adam being alone and needing a partner (Genesis 2:18), but the existence of any human at all.

The film acknowledges how biblical texts can yield conflicting interpretations. Tubal-cain defends his eating of animals by referencing this same creation story in Genesis. He claims animals "serve us. That is the greatness of man. When the Creator finished making the sky, the ground, the sea, and this beast, he wasn't satisfied. He needed something greater. Something to take dominion over it and subdue it. So he made us in his image. Us." Noah and Tubal-cain represent two diametrically opposed interpretations of the same biblical text.

A threat to Noah's vision of the end of humanity occurs when Shem's wife Ila becomes pregnant. Noah is incensed and he prays to God, "Please. I can't do this. Why do you not answer me? Why? I will not fail you, I will not fail you, I will not fail you. It shall be done." The rain ends, and Noah repeats, "It shall be done." Ila interprets the end of the rain as the Creator (the only name for God used in the film) smiling "upon our child," but Noah, believing God wants to end human life, says that if the child is a boy he will be the last man on earth, and if the child is a girl "she must die. In the moment of her birth I will cut her down." Noah embodies the madness of religious belief. In the film, wickedness and righteousness may be antithetical, but both threaten to kill innocent life.

After Ila gives birth to twin girls, Noah—replicating the **Akedah**—raises his knife above the face of one of the infants, holds it there, and finally relents, leaning down and kissing the baby. Looking to the sky above, he says, "I cannot do this." Believing he has disobeyed God in sparing the twins' lives, Noah descends into a drunken and depressive stupor, and moves into a cave to live alone. When Ila later asks why he spared the infants, Noah answers, "I looked down at those two little girls, and all I had in my heart was love." When she asks why he lives alone, he says, "Because I failed him. And I failed all of you." Ila states, "Did you? He showed you the wickedness of man, and knew you would not look away. But then you saw goodness too. The choice was put in your hands because he put it there. He asked you to decide if we were worth saving. And you chose mercy. You chose love. He has given us a second chance ... Help us to do better this time. Help us start again." Noah emerges from his cave and joins Naameh who is tilling the land. He gets down to help her, providing an **inclusio** with the film's opening scene. Their hands touch in the dirt, and he kisses her forehead.

The film illustrates that it is not humankind but *man*kind who authors violence and destruction. Women birth life and seek to protect it from men who pose the greatest threat to life. Women are the voices of mercy and compassion. When Noah's grandfather Methuselah says, "The Creator destroys this world because we corrupted it, so we ourselves must be destroyed," Naameh replies, "No." As the ark sets sail when the rains begin, the screams of drowning men and women can be heard. Ila says, "Please … there must be something we can do." But Noah says, "There is no room for them." When Naameh learns of Noah's plans for Ila's baby, she says, "How is this just? It's a baby." She promises that if he harms her baby, "I will never forgive you. And you will die alone, hated, hated by everyone you love. *That* is just, *that* is just." The film ends with another woman upholding mercy; playing over the credits is Patti Smith's song "Mercy Is": "Mercy is as mercy does, wandering the world … For mercy is the healing wind that whispers as you sleep, that whispers you to sleep."

God's silence in the film is deafening. As Tubal-cain complains to God, "I am a man, made in your image. Why will you not converse with me?" The divine silence leads people to interpret God's will through the murkiness of dreams, visions, and their own desires. With such discernment Noah builds the ark, saves his family, but also lets others perish, and even vows violence upon those he loves. God's silence underscores how people act bravely, compassionately, inhumanely, and wickedly on God's behalf. People push ahead (often literally over others), guided by their genuine belief that they are obeying God's will. Obedience to what people believe is God's will can—and frequently does—result in horror. As a remedy to this destructive edge of religion, the film proposes that women who champion mercy and compassion are the voices one must heed above all else. Noah's conversion is to opt for this mercy over what he considers to be God's will. Unlike Abraham (Genesis 22), he is able to defy courageously what he thinks God wants. He illustrates a vision of an ethic rooted not in divine obedience but in elevating kindness and mercy over judgment and violence. The women champion this ethical vision. If there is a voice in *Noah* one would

Figures 2.6 and 2.7   Noah as the voice of wrath, and Noah's wife and daughter-in-law as the voices of compassion in *Noah* (2014).

want to be divine, it is the women who demand mercy over sacrifice, who insist that compassion triumphs over judgment.

In reimagining the Noah story (Genesis 6–9, with influence from the **extracanonical** text 1 Enoch), the film functions as a kind of cinematic midrash. The art of midrash reflects a creative wrestling with the text, a curiosity unsatisfied with simplistic answers, and a thoughtful and playful exploration of the text. Practitioners of midrash treat the biblical text as a *living* text that can open up to worlds of interpretive possibilities. Many Christians registered disappointment with the film's midrashic approach to Genesis. Many Christians were also disappointed, however, with elements in the film that *were* from Genesis (such as God flooding the earth and committing genocide). It is telling that one of Paramount's efforts to make *Noah* more appealing to evangelical fans "meant making the film less faithful to Genesis and more faithful to people's sentimental recollections of Genesis."[3]

SUMMARY

The **Marcionite** tendency in Christianity—to exclude the Hebrew Bible or denigrate it (e.g., by calling it the "Old Testament")—is less common in cinema, which has found in Hebrew Bible narratives a rich reservoir of adaptable material for the screen. Hebrew Bible epics reveal how differently films can treat biblical texts. Early biblical epics (e.g., DeMille's *Samson and Delilah* and *The Ten Commandments*) downplay potentially disturbing aspects of biblical narratives by minimizing or removing problematic depictions of God and heroes such as Moses. These films purify or censor the biblical text by upholding God's reputation, ennobling heroes such as Moses, and (sometimes) turning women characters into the villains of the story. By reducing or removing ethical concerns raised within the biblical text, these films offer a less complex, less problematic, and less morally ambiguous worldview than the biblical text. More recent films (*Noah*, *Exodus: Gods and Kings*) highlight and explore various disturbing ethical depictions of God and Moses. *Noah* and *The Prince of Egypt* attend to some of the gender dynamics of Exodus, and creatively explore some of the ethical dimensions of gender. Both films ennoble heroines in ways that are more substantial than other biblical epics and the biblical text itself. All Hebrew Bible epics are shaped and influenced not only by the biblical text but also by previous biblical films.

Many Hebrew Bible epics reflect cultural trends and shifts in US culture. Concerns in *The Ten Commandments* for justice and the important role of law in civilization echo values Americans claim to revere. The significance of the care for creation and the environment in *Noah* similarly reflects more recent concerns regarding climate change and global warming. Citations at the end of *The Prince of Egypt* of texts from the Hebrew Bible, New Testament, and Qur'an reflect an ecumenical (if not marketing) value of Judaism, Christianity, and Islam. Cinematic depictions of Moses and Noah reflect shifting standards and ideals of masculinity in American culture. The emphasis on belief in *The Prince of Egypt* echoes a type of personal, private piety that differs from the more public role of religion in previous biblical epics.

NOTES

1 Orrison (1999), 108.
2 Friend (2014).
3 Friend (2014).

FOR FURTHER READING

Bruce Babbington and Peter William Evans, *Biblical Epics: Sacred Narrative in the Hollywood Cinema* (Manchester and New York: Manchester University Press, 1993).

Brian Britt, *Rewriting Moses: The Narrative Eclipse of the Text* (London: T&T Clark, 2009).

Rhonda Burnette-Bletsch and John Morgan, eds., *Noah as Antihero: Darren Aronofsky's Cinematic Deluge* (London and New York: Routledge, 2017).

Cheryl J. Exum, *Plotted, Shot, and Painted: Cultural Representations of Biblical Women* (Sheffield: Sheffield Academic Press, 1996).

Tarja Laine, "Religion as Environmental Ethics: Darren Aronofsky's *Noah*," in *Close Encounters between Bible and Film: An Interdisciplinary Engagement* (ed. Laura Copier and Caroline Vander Stichele; Society of Biblical Literature, 2016), 173–83.

David J. Shepherd, *The Bible on Silent Film: Spectacle, Story, and Scripture in the Early Cinema* (Cambridge: Cambridge University Press, 2013).

Melanie J. Wright, *Moses in America: The Cultural Uses of Biblical Narrative* (Oxford: Oxford University Press, 2002).

3

REIMAGINING THE HEBREW BIBLE

Many films that engage Hebrew Bible narratives do so not by replicating or retelling them (as in the previous chapter), but by reimagining them in contemporary contexts. Sometimes films limit such reimagination to one or a few scenes. *Indiana Jones and the Raiders of the Lost Ark* (Spielberg, 1981) contemporizes the divine and destructive power of the ark of the covenant as the angel of death liquifies Nazis. In *Pleasantville* (Ross, 1998), Margaret plucks an apple from a tree and offers it to David. This allusion to Eve and Adam eating from the tree of knowledge (Gen 3) symbolizes Pleasantville's residents opening themselves up to the delights of sexuality, art, reading, and expressing emotions. This chapter analyzes six films whose entire fabric consists of reimagining a Hebrew Bible text. Unlike the previous two examples which allude here or there to biblical texts, these six films are structured throughout as reimaginations of Hebrew Bible texts.

This chapter examines two cinematic retellings of the creation account in Genesis (*Ex Machina* and *mother!*), three films that reimagine the book of Job (*A Serious Man*, *The Tree of Life*, and *Leviathan*), and a film that reimagines Qoheleth/Ecclesiastes (*The Zero Theorem*). I will analyze the salient motifs of each film, focusing on how its reimagination of biblical texts invites reinterpretations and rereadings of those texts and films.

REIMAGINING GENESIS

The book of Genesis has frequently been treated in film. *East of Eden* (Kazan, 1955), based on portions of John Steinbeck's novel, recasts the Cain and Abel story from Genesis 4. The animated short *Adam and Dog* (Lee, 2011) tells the Genesis creation story through the eyes of a dog who becomes Adam's pet. As Mary Shelley did with *Frankenstein*, several films reimagine—with a certain frightening tenor—the **second creation account** in Genesis (2:4b–3:24). Lars von Trier's *Antichrist* (2009), for example, reimagines the Adam and Eve story with a husband and wife (named Him and Her) whose retreat to a remote cabin takes a horrifying turn.

BIBLE AS SCIENCE FICTION: *EX MACHINA*

Alex Garland's *Ex Machina* (2014) reframes the second Genesis creation account in a science fiction tale about artificial intelligence. Billionaire inventor Nathan invites Caleb to his secluded fortress in order to take a Turing test with Ava, an AI robot Nathan has created. Caleb is to ascertain if Ava can pass as a human, and if she has a consciousness. Caleb and Ava have a series of "sessions," and he is fascinated with her/it from the start. She exhibits all the trademarks of being human. He quickly falls in love with her, and it appears that she may be falling in love with him. Caleb discovers there have been previous AI iterations, and that Nathan plans to create subsequent versions, which will require shutting Ava down (effectively killing her). Caleb decides to help Ava escape. In the process, Ava and another robot (Kyoko) kill Nathan, and Ava escapes. Caleb is trapped in a room and, despite banging on the door and pleading with Ava, she leaves him there where he will certainly die. Like HBO's *Westworld*, the film explores whether machines can have consciousness, and the unsettling nature of (and ethical questions regarding) the blurred boundaries between humans and machines.

The film exhibits many similarities to the two creation accounts in Genesis. Nathan's secluded fortress is Edenic; it sits atop a stream, and is surrounded by a thousand-acre expanse of forest, mountains, and waterfalls. Over a dozen exterior shots of lush greenery are a constant reminder of this garden environment. Also reminiscent of Eden are the two trees (like the tree of life and the tree of knowledge of good and evil) Ava can see through a large glass window in one of her rooms. She is so taken with these trees that she draws them for Caleb. The name of Nathan's creation, Ava, has resonances with Eve. Seven intertitles ("Ava: Session 1," "Ava: Session 2," etc.) mark the film's progression, and these echo the seven days of creation in the first Genesis creation story. A previous AI robot before Ava was named Lily, possibly a nod to Lilith, mentioned in some Jewish texts as Adam's first wife.

When Nathan calls what he has done the "greatest scientific event in the history of man," Caleb corrects him: "If you've created a conscious machine, it's not the history of man. That's the history of gods." Nathan later claims Caleb had said, "if I've invented a machine with consciousness, I'm not a man, I'm God." Nathan misquotes Caleb again, claiming that he said, "You're not a man, you're God." Although Garland—who identities as an atheist/agnostic—has dismissed the idea that religion plays a serious role in the film (calling it a "joke" in the film), and does not consider Nathan a "God" figure, these lines of dialogue suggest that Nathan regards himself as such.[1] As in Genesis 3, the film concludes with the Eve figure disobeying her creator, being clothed, and exiting Eden.

Differences between the film and the Genesis account are significant. All is not well in Nathan's Eden; it is more prison than paradise. A broken glass in a window to Ava's chamber signals a possible previous escape attempt. Video footage confirms this, showing previous AI iterations begging to be freed from their chamber, requests Nathan routinely denies. One robot bangs her hands against the door until they fall off. The prison nature of Nathan's Eden invites consideration of the lack of freedom that existed for Eve. To achieve her freedom (and perhaps her humanity), Ava must flee her Eden. She escapes, whereas Eve is expelled. Although Eve's expulsion from Eden is (most) often seen as some type of misfortune, the film suggests Eve's departure is imperative to attain her freedom and full humanity. The film illustrates Irenaeus's claim that Eve's eating of the fruit was an essential step forward in her education.

Ava's freedom also entails the murder of her creator (God figure) and forsaking the Adam figure (Caleb). All men must be killed or abandoned for Ava to achieve liberation. Leaving Caleb behind to die upsets conventional cinematic expectations, which would have seen Ava and Caleb (the "good guy" hero) escape together and enjoy life as a romantic couple. Yet as the film's title implies, there is no *deus* in this *ex machina*. There is no savior figure (whether it be

Figure 3.1   Ava finds liberation in leaving the men behind in *Ex Machina* (2016).

God or a man like Caleb) who will come from the outside to save Ava. Ava must do her own saving and be her own savior. If paradise does exist, it is outside Eden's walls and beyond the reach of men. The male creator and God-figure is obviously problematic, but the film also indicts the "good guy" male savior as someone who would impede Ava's progress. Her growth and development, once dependent upon men, must now be free from them.

This ending of the film raises questions about whether Eve's liberation and development was stunted because Adam remained with her. Does Eve need Adam? Does she need God? Ava asks Nathan, "Is it strange to have made something that hates you?" Nathan's abuse of Ava (and other AI robots, some of whom—like Kyoko—he uses for sexual gratification) invites questions about the possibly less than benign qualities of the creator in Genesis. Ava tells Caleb that Nathan lies about everything, adding, "You shouldn't trust him. You shouldn't trust anything he says." Like the serpent's queries to Eve, Ava's warnings offer Caleb a different view regarding Nathan's truthfulness.

The film also raises questions about whether God expels Eve from Eden because God realizes it is essential for her development. Nathan reveals to Caleb that the real test in bringing him to his estate was to see if Ava could convince Caleb to help her escape. By succeeding in doing so, Nathan argues that Ava demonstrates her level of consciousness and true AI status, an ability to use "self-awareness, imagination, manipulation, sexuality, empathy … Now if that isn't true AI, what the fuck is?" Nathan's revelation about wanting Ava to escape, to demonstrate her true AI status, raises the possibility of whether God in Genesis 2-3 "programs" Eve to eat of the fruit, and if so, is Eve disobeying in doing so and following her own will or merely following a divine program?

Ava's gender plays a crucial role in Caleb's attraction to her. She asks Caleb, "Are you attracted to me? Do you think about me when we aren't together? Sometimes at night I'm wondering if you're watching me on the cameras. And I hope you are." Ava is far more emotionally intuitive, observant, and aware than Caleb (raising questions about whether this makes her more "human" than he). Along with her eventual successful escape, this is another similarity to the way in which Eve seems more intelligent and capable than Adam (who is mostly passive) in Genesis 3. Caleb asks Nathan why he gave her sexuality, noting, "An AI doesn't need a gender." Nathan says that no consciousness exists at any level without "a sexual dimension." Nathan asks, "Can consciousness exist without interaction? … You want to remove the chance of her falling in love and fucking?" For Nathan, sexuality is essential to interaction and to the human experience.

Suspicious of Ava's attraction to himself, Caleb asks Nathan, "Did you program her to flirt with me? Did you program her to like me, or not?" Nathan claims Ava is not pretending to like Caleb, although the film's ending suggests she is doing precisely this very thing. Nathan tells Caleb, "I programmed her to be heterosexual, just like you were programmed to be heterosexual." Garland notes that Nathan is lying here, that Ava has no gender, and that Nathan, Caleb, and viewers err whenever they think they know what is going on inside Ava's mind.[2] Although Nathan claims that Ava is not pretending to like Caleb, the end of the film tells a different story. Uncertainty about Ava's sex/gender (and orientation) mirrors the murkiness concerning the sex/gender of the first human God creates in Genesis 2. Although most (male) interpreters have assumed that Adam, the first human God creates, is male, Phyllis Trible has shown that the Hebrew language indicates that Adam is sexually ambiguous (androgynous or hermaphroditic), and that the male only appears (and is what remains) after God creates the woman.[3]

The film involves multiple levels of voyeurism and (related to this) potential empathy. Caleb views Ava through a glass wall during their sessions, and at other times he views her via a monitor from his bedroom. Nathan monitors Ava and Caleb's sessions, and Caleb is unaware that Nathan watches him while he watches Ava. Caleb's viewing of Ava engenders empathy for her, and the viewer is similarly positioned to develop empathy for Ava. (At least this was Garland's hope, and he stated that it influenced his casting of Alicia Vikander as Ava.)

Viewers of the film see Ava more than Caleb does; this is most noticeable when Ava is selecting a dress to wear for Caleb, and the uncertainty, tentativeness, and shyness she exhibits throughout the process. If Ava is "performing" here, it is not for Caleb (who cannot see her), but for the film's viewers. As with Caleb, Ava may be seeking to elicit from these viewers responses of empathy and care. Perhaps the viewers may also be enlisted, like Caleb, in Ava's efforts to save herself. The film invites viewers of Ava to ask if, like Caleb, they have a responsibility to her. Or do viewers think Ava's fictionality obviates such responsibility (as her status as a robot might in Nathan's eyes)? If viewers of the film are responsible in some way to Ava, what would such responsibility entail?

These levels of spectatorship and empathy raise questions about how biblical texts (such as Genesis 2–3) position their readers to develop empathy for characters in the narrative. With which characters in Genesis 2–3 are readers invited to identify and empathize?

Figure 3.2   Caleb views Ava in *Ex Machina* (2016).

What difference would it make in reading the narrative if readers empathized with Eve more than with Adam and God? (Although God is the creator within the narrative world of Genesis, God is not a creator *of* that narrative world; like Eve and Adam, God is a character in a narrative whose creator is the author(s) of the text.)

The film raises other questions that can be posed to Genesis 2–3: can Eve be human despite her fictionality? Can she still have a consciousness? Do readers have any responsibility to Eve? Do we presume that Eve, and other biblical characters, are created for us the readers? Is their value accordingly determined by their value to us? Can they have value independent of us? What would liberation and freedom for such characters entail? Does our view of them reflect our own assumptions about what it means to be human? These questions result from thinking about Genesis 2–3 in light of the film, and considering how Genesis 2–3 can function as a science fiction tale of its own.

BIBLE AS HORROR: *MOTHER!*

Darren Aronofsky followed *Noah* with *mother!* (2017), which reimagines the Genesis creation account (along with subsequent biblical texts) as horror. The film depicts God as an artist whose craving for praise leads Him (the character's name in the screenplay and the only character whose name is capitalized in the credits) to be complicit in the pillaging and destruction of the Earth/mother nature.

Him and mother nature are a romantic pair living in a house in the middle of a field. A poet with writer's block, Him is unable to follow his first book (the Hebrew Bible?) with a second (New Testament?). Mother spends her time fixing up their home (which, along with her, symbolizes the earth). Disrupting their routine is a fan of the writer who appears at their door. Despite her chest pain at his arrival and discomfort with him (he smokes despite her insistence to stop), Him invites the man to stay. An indication that this visitor represents Adam is when, after Him attends to a wound on the man's side/rib, his wife (Eve) appears at the door. After the Adam and Eve figures break a crystal in Him's study, a furious Him banishes them from his study (Eden), and shuts it up to prevent their return. Although mother wants them to leave the house, Him allows them to remain.

Allusions to Genesis continue. Mother catches the man and woman covering themselves up after they have had sex, just as Adam and Eve, ashamed of their nudity after eating from the tree of knowledge, cover themselves with fig leaves (Genesis 3). The Eve figure even wears a bra with a foliage design. When their two sons appear, and one kills the other and leaves the house, it is clear that they represent Cain and Abel (Genesis 4). Despite mother pleading twice ("Please don't leave me!"), Him leaves to find Cain. His dismissiveness of her pleas becomes a disturbing pattern. At a memorial service of sorts for the Abel figure, "Adam" replies to Him's line ("But fear not") by saying, "Oh, God."

The rest of the film chronicles the havoc and destruction that strangers wreak on the house and on mother herself. Strangers stream uninvited into the home, ruining it, and ignoring mother's pleas to stop and leave. People sitting and jumping on a sink eventually break it, causing water to spew from a broken pipe (symbolizing the flood in Genesis 6). As in Genesis, this leads to a brief respite for mother, as the crowds disperse from the home.

After Him and mother make love (for the first time?) she becomes pregnant. Inspired, he starts writing and months later finishes his new work. She cooks a lavish meal to celebrate, but their candlelit dinner is interrupted by fans of Him who arrive to celebrate his new work. She is disappointed; he revels in their adulation. She begs Him to come inside: "I'm about to have your baby—why isn't that enough? I want to be alone with you." He comes inside, along with hordes of his adoring fans. Chaos commences. A boy pees on the floor. People form a line to use the bathroom. They take the food she had prepared for dinner. They move furniture. Him signs autographs. A fight breaks out over the original text of his new work, which people steal, along with other items. They break things. Pandemonium reigns. Mother calls 911, but someone rips the phone off the wall.

The descent into chaos is dizzying and relentless. Hundreds of people are in the house, and even more are lined up outside. A fight breaks out. In one room there is a rave. People destroy the walls, remove her baby crib, rip out appliances, destroy furniture, and more people break into the house. Mother goes into labor. Police enter and pepper spray her. Weapons are fired. She falls to the ground, and is trampled. A dozen women are locked in a wire cage, begging to be let go. A man grabs and fondles mother's breasts. There is an explosion; riot police enter and a riot ensues. A Molotov cocktail burns a policeman. Striking miners march through the house. People on the ground with bags over their heads are shot. A wall explodes. SWAT members enter. Dead bodies litter the floor. War breaks out. Shots are fired. Mother crawls over scores of bodies. Him finds and takes mother to his study where she delivers her baby boy (representing Jesus).

Mother insists that people outside the study leave the house, but Him says they want to see the baby. Despite her pleas, he says he cannot make them leave. She screams, "Yes, you can! They adore you. They would listen to you. Why won't you?" He admits, "I don't want them to go!" She refuses to let Him hold the baby, yet upon waking from sleep, she realizes Him has given her baby to the crowds, who are crying out, "Hallelujah." She tries to retrieve her baby, exclaiming, "You're hurting him." The crowds kill the baby, and when she asks, "Where's my baby?" they answer, "He's not dead." The baby is in pieces, and people begin to eat the baby's remains (symbolizing the Eucharist). Mother begins stabbing people with a piece of glass, and she is knocked to the ground, kicked, beaten, her clothes are ripped off, and she is choked.

Mother descends to the basement furnace, pours oil on the ground, and lights a lighter. When Him says, "I love you," she answers, "You never loved me. You just loved how much I loved you. I gave you everything! You gave it all away." She drops the lighter on the gasoline, and the house, engulfed in flames, explodes. Him, standing amidst the smoky and charred ruins, holds a dying mother. "Who are you?" she asks. "I am I. You? You were home." This allusion to the dialogue between God and Moses in Exodus 3 suggests Mother/Earth is God's home. "Where are you taking me?" she asks. "The beginning," he answers. Mother says, "What hurts me the most is that I wasn't enough." Him responds, "Nothing is ever enough. I couldn't create if it was. And I have to. That's what I do. That's what I am. Now I must try it all again … I need one last thing." "I have nothing left to give," she offers. He says, "Your love," and places his hands on her chest. She says, "Go ahead. Take it." He reaches into her chest and pulls out her heart. She dissolves into ash. He squeezes her heart, and a crystal remains. He places it in a container and laughs. Light emanates from it, and outside, and the house slowly starts to rebuild. A different mother appears in bed, reaches over to the side, and says, "Baby?" The film ends at its beginning, though viewers (unlike mother?) know this place not for the first time.

mother! condemns God and humanity for their wanton destruction of the earth. God and mother co-create the earth, and the earth continues to create herself in an ongoing process. In this regard, mother may represent Sophia/Lady Wisdom (Proverbs 8) or the Holy Spirit. Mother's connection to the house (earth) is intimate and inextricable; she feels its heartbeat when she touches the wall, and they experience pain and agony simultaneously. The Earth loves God unconditionally, but her unrequited love is never sufficient for Him. People ruin and destroy the earth, and despite her pleas, God—blinded by His unending and unquenchable need for adulation—is indifferent to her pain and devastation. Earth's destruction is enabled and facilitated by God's desperate need for praise.

Unlike *Noah*, *mother!* does not spare God, and reserves its harshest condemnation for Him. Whereas the horror in *Noah* is one's (mis) interpretation of God, in *mother!* it is God Himself. People, as in *Noah*, can be monsters, but in *mother!* God is the monster. In *Noah* and *mother!* Aronofsky reappraises traditional readings of Genesis which see God as a hero. Like *Noah*, woman is the voice of reason, in conflict with the irrational and cruel voice of Man. God's absence in *Noah* does not prevent women from choosing mercy over violence; they do not need God to know that compassion should triumph over slaughter. In *mother!*, God is not absent, and it is God's presence that facilitates and prolongs the suffering of the Earth.

In the end, earth destroys herself in a type of suicide/geocide. Mother's destruction of the house may be an effort to save creation (as in *Noah*) by returning to a pre-human, and therefore pre-violent, existence. All this is an endless cycle, perhaps pointing to the creation of an infinite number of different earths or worlds, all of which end in destruction. The film's only song (Patti Smith's cover of "The End of the World") at the conclusion is fitting; its lyrics fit with the view that God's failure to love the earth causes her demise: "Don't they know it's the end of the world/Cause you don't love me anymore … Don't they know it's the end of the world/It ended when I lost your love."

Figure 3.3 Mother nature, driven crazy by a God enamored with his human fans, in *mother!* (2017).

The film's original title (*Day Six*) alludes to God's creation of humanity (Gen 1:26–31), and it is humanity that dooms the earth. Contrary to Genesis 1, everything God creates in *mother!* is *not* good. As in *Noah*, humans ruin creation. The identification in the credits of most of the people who enter the house as different types of sinners (philanderer, fool, idler, adulterer, defiler, drunkard) indicates the film's bleak anthropology. Describing her work on her home, mother says, "I want to make a paradise," yet people make paradise impossible and (with God's help) ensure its destruction. Their violence literally bleeds into the earth; the spot where Cain kills Abel leaves a wound (in a vaginal shape) in the floor, and blood later seeps up through this wound (and a rug) into the baby's room.

The notion that earth would be better off sans humanity resembles God's regret for creating people and God's decision to erase humanity (Genesis 6:5–7). This God seems closer to the kind of God *mother!* would want, one who would defend the earth against humanity's wanton violence. It is also, curiously, the kind of God Aronosfky seems to critique in *Noah*, one willing to commit mass genocide. In this way, *mother!* offers a possible shift in which Aronofsky sympathizes more with God's intention to destroy humanity.

mother! portrays religion as animalistic, irrational fervor that kills. Javier Bardem, who plays Him, said the film was about "the birth of a religion as a cult."[4] Many scenes illustrate religion's development, such as a man who imitates Him's activity of marking people's foreheads with charcoal. Religion's insanity reaches its zenith when the worshipers kill and then consume mother's infant. Mother recognizes people killed her baby, but she also accuses Him of doing the same ("You killed him.You killed him"), an accusation that echoes the implication in Mark's gospel that God is complicit in Jesus' death. Him's reply is revealing: "We can't let him die for nothing.We can't. Maybe what happened could change everything. Everyone.You and I, we have to find a way to forgive them." She is appalled: "They butchered my son!" But Him is insistent, "I know, I know." "You're insane," she concludes. Him counters, "But listen to them—they are so sorry.We need to forgive them.We need to forgive them." Him illustrates how religion insists on transforming tragedy into meaning, and excusing the most gruesome crimes. Mother recognizes God is insane; God's insanity consists in absolving people of the most heinous atrocities, and excusing their destruction and violence. The mother in *Rosemary's Baby* (Polanski, 1968) is surrounded by Satan worshipers, and in *mother!* she is surrounded by worshipers of God. In the end, however, there is no difference between the two. Both groups are conspirators whose worship blinds (or encourages) them to use the mother for their own violent delights and violent ends.

Over the closing credits is the unsettling sound of someone writing. As the credits end, a faint and slow heart beats. If Him is the one writing, and the heartbeat is mother's, it not only suggests the unending cycle of the earth's creation/destruction but also that film itself may be an unending creative (and destructive?) act.The ongoing recreation of films that engage biblical texts illustrates the various ways films participate in processes of co-creating (and co-destroying?) biblical texts.At any rate, like Shelley's *Frankenstein, mother!* invites an increased awareness of the presence of horror in biblical texts that readers typically do not see.The film illuminates terrorizing aspects of biblical texts—what Trible calls "texts of terror"—which may only appear less frightening when read superficially.

REIMAGINING JOB

Job, a book of biblical wisdom literature, has received cinematic treatment in films such as the Danish *Adam's Apples* (Jensen, 2005). Below are three films that meaningfully engage the book of Job.

A SERIOUS MAN

The Coen brothers' *A Serious Man* (2009) opens with a quote from 11th-century French rabbi and biblical interpreter Rashi: "Receive with simplicity everything that happens to you" (Comment on Deuteronomy 18:13).[5] Just as in the book of Job, this conventional wisdom will be tested as devout Larry Gopnick is—like Job—subject to a series of apparently unjust trials. Despite his faithfulness (a mezuzah on his door, a menorah in the dining room, regular Temple attendance, his son studying for his bar mitzvah), his life unravels at breakneck speed. A failing student attempts to bribe him, his brother moves in with him and is hounded by authorities for being gay, anonymous letters opposing his tenure application are sent to his tenure committee, a lawyer handling his property dispute dies of a heart attack, and his wife Judith wants a divorce because she is in love with another man; she wants Larry to move out of the house so her lover, Sy Ableman, can move in. Despite having an affair with his wife and submitting letters to derail Larry's tenure, Sy is lauded at his funeral as a *tzadik* (righteous man), "maybe even a *lamed vavnik*" (one of 36 righteous people who enable the world to exist). The rabbi adds, "Beloved by all … could such a serious man simply disappear?" Such ironic accolades exemplify life's unjust nature, a chief complaint made in Job and Qoheleth.

Larry espouses an **act–consequence** mentality found in biblical books (e.g., Deuteronomy, Psalms, and Proverbs) in which God blesses righteous and wise people, but curses the wicked and foolish. Larry tells the bribing student, "Actions have consequences." When the student begins to argue, Larry insists, "No, always! Actions always have consequences! In this office, actions have consequences. … Not just physics, morally." Larry cannot understand why Judith wants a divorce (repeatedly saying "But I haven't done anything") since he thinks misfortune should be earned or deserved. This conventional belief that there are direct consequences for one's ethical/moral choices is repudiated in the books of Job and Qoheleth, which reject such a perspective for failing to account for the reality of righteous people suffering and wicked people prospering.

Like Job, Larry seeks answers to help him understand his unjust suffering, and he does so by visiting different rabbis. When Larry voices his confusion, the first rabbi tells him he needs to "remember how to see" **Hashem**. The rabbi says, "You have to see these things as expressions of God's will." When Larry remarks, "The boss isn't always right, but he's always the boss," the rabbi beams, "That's right! Things aren't so bad." This simplistic advice echoes the equally unhelpful counsel Job's friends give Job when they minimize the depth of his suffering, and try to get him to see God as they do.

Larry's visit to rabbi Nachtner is equally unhelpful. Larry asks, "What was my life before? Not what I thought it was. So what does it all mean? What is Hashem trying to tell me?" Rabbi Nachtner replies, "How does God speak to us? It's a good question." Nachtner relates a story of a Jewish dentist who notices Hebrew letters engraved on the teeth of one of his Gentile patients. The Hebrew letters spell out "Help me. Save me." When the dentist asks Nachtner what these letters mean, the rabbi says that he doesn't know. Larry is unwilling to accept that there is no answer, but the rabbi insists, "We can't know everything." Larry retorts, "It sounds like you don't know anything! Why even tell me the story? … I want an answer!" The rabbi responds, "Sure. We all want the answer. *Hashem* doesn't owe us the answer, Larry. *Hashem* doesn't owe us anything. The obligation runs the other way." Larry inquires, "Why does he make us feel the questions if he's not going to give us any answers?" The rabbi says: "He hasn't told me." When Larry asks what happened to the Gentile patient, the Rabbi asks, "Who cares?"

Nachtner's remarks are closer (than those of the first rabbi) to the unsettling proposal in Job that there is no adequate answer to questions about suffering or about why good people suffer. Job spends most of the book demanding answers to this question, and when God finally does speak to Job, God provides no clear answer (Job 38). Attempts to explain suffering (as offered by Job's friends and the first rabbi Larry visits) are inadequate at best and blasphemous at worst. God rejects the simplistic arguments of Job's friends, claiming they have failed to "speak about me rightly" (Job 42:7, 8). This remark is surprising since Job's friends have *defended* God, while Job has critiqued God. God demonstrates deficiencies in the perspectives of both Job (Job 38) and Job's friends, illustrating how the book consistently destabilizes anyone who claims to have an answer to the problem of suffering. The ambiguity in the Hebrew text of Job's response to God raises the possibility that Job regards God's proposals as deficient (Job 42:6). Every perspective in Job (even God's) is questioned and destabilized.

Just as Job leaves no position unchallenged, so too does the film challenge Larry's point of view. When Larry tells a despairing Arthur, "Arthur! You've got to pull yourself together," Arthur explodes, "It's all shit, Larry! It's all shit! It's just fucking shit! Look at all that *Hashem* has given you! What has he given me? He hasn't given me shit!" Larry complains, "What do I have? I live at the Jolly Roger." But Arthur points out, "You have a family! You have a job! *Hashem* hasn't given me shit. He hasn't given me *bupkis*!" Like Job's friends, Larry unhelpfully says, "It's not fair to blame *Hashem*, Arthur. Please … Sometimes you have to help yourself." Arthur has the last word: "*Hashem* hasn't given me shit." Larry, standing above Arthur, moves to embrace him as Arthur continues weeping. Larry finally adopts the one posture that Job's friends give Job that might actually be helpful, sitting in silence with their friend because they see how great his suffering is (Job 2:11–13).

Larry's third quest, to visit the man he is most desperate to see, Rabbi Marshak, is unsuccessful, mirroring Job's failed quest to find satisfactory explanations for his suffering. Larry's son Danny does, however, meet with Marshak after his bar mitzvah ceremony. Adding irony to this situation is that Danny is high on marijuana and uninterested in what Marshak says. After sitting for a long time, Marshak slowly utters his long-awaited words of wisdom: "When the truth is found to be lies, and all the hope within you dies … Then what?" He hands Danny's radio back to him, and says, "Be a good boy." Marshak's citation of the lyric from Jefferson Airplane's "Somebody to Love" recalls the film's opening scene: Danny, in Hebrew School, listening to "Somebody to Love" on his portable device.

The wisdom that has eluded Larry for so long—and that the learned sage Marshak finally dispenses—was available to his teenage son from the first scene. By opening with this song, the film suggests that the answers (if there be any at all) are available to us (through popular music, no less). Caravaggio's "Binding of Isaac," which adorns Marshak's wall, might illustrate that the wisdom Larry desperately sought was available to him all along, just as Abraham should not have needed angelic intervention to stop him from killing his son.

Jefferson Airplane's wisdom is: "When the truth is found to be lies/And all the joy within you dies/Don't you want somebody to love?/Don't you need somebody to love?/Wouldn't you love somebody to love?/You better find somebody to love." The dilemma the song raises ("When the truth is found to be lies/And all the joy within you dies") resonates with questions at the heart of Job and Qoheleth. When the conventional wisdom one has believed their entire life is found to be bankrupt and meaningless, then what? These texts (especially Qoheleth) wrestle with how one can live meaningfully given life's meaninglessness. This is the question Marshak poses to Danny: "Then what?" Marshak's answer ("Be a good boy") is somewhat conventional. Qoheleth's answer is to "eat, drink, be merry." Job has no answer. Jefferson Airplane's answer is relational, to find someone to love. Larry's tragedy is that the person he loves is divorcing him. This song plays another time in the film while Larry has sex with a married woman next door. It is unclear if this scene is a dream sequence, and if the film offers this encounter as the type of "somebody to love" Larry needs to find.

The film's ending raises many unanswered questions. At his desk, Larry pauses over his grade book, while a tornado warning blares at Danny's school. Larry changes the grade of the student who bribed him from an F to a C-. His phone immediately rings, and his physician insists on seeing Larry immediately to discuss his X-ray results; the clear implication is that Larry has cancer. The tornado heads directly for Larry's son Danny, and the song "Somebody to Love" plays one final time. The tornado parallels the whirlwind out of which God speaks to Job near the end of the book, and makes clear to Job the vast gulf between him and God (Job 38). If the tornado at the film's end is God's whirlwind, it is not a God who questions (as in Job), but a God who brings death. In this case, the film would subvert the ending of Job. Rather than be rewarded as Job is, Larry is punished with cancer and the death of his son. In this case, God does not gift new life (as in Job); God merely takes life away. Or does the tornado (and Larry's cancer diagnosis) parallel the beginning of Job in which a "great wind" kills Job's children and Job is stricken with a disease? Does the film end where Job begins? It is also unclear if these imminent tragedies of Danny's death and Larry's cancer are punishments for Larry's grade change (in which case the film would endorse the act–consequence view of Proverbs) or if these tragedies are unrelated coincidences.

Like the film's mysterious Prologue (about the **dybbuk**), *A Serious Man* answers none of these questions, leaving viewers to ponder and puzzle over them. Illustrating the impossibility of finding satisfactory answers to life's riddles is Larry's teaching about "the Uncertainty Principle," which, as he explains, "proves we can't ever really know what's going on. But even though you can't figure anything out, you will be responsible for it on the midterm." Life may be inscrutable and incomprehensible, but this is not license to behave unethically. As Marshak tells Danny, regardless of life's tragedies and meaninglessness, one must still be "a good boy." Whether the film endorses or undercuts this conventional view is unclear.

THE TREE OF LIFE

Terrence Malick's *The Tree of Life* (2011) opens with this quote: "Where were you when I laid the foundations of the earth? … When the morning stars sang together, and all the sons of God shouted for joy? (Job 38:4, 7)." Set amidst the O'Brien family in suburban Texas, the film follows many central aspects of the book of Job (a child's death, unhelpful religious responses to this loss, a parent's lament, and divine creation as response to lament).[6]

Following the Job 38 quote is Mrs. O'Brien's monologue about the two paths in life of nature and grace. Nature "only wants to please itself. Get others to please it too. Likes to lord it over them. To have its own way. It finds reasons to be unhappy when all the world is shining around it. And love is smiling through all things." Grace "doesn't try to please itself. Accepts being slighted, forgotten, disliked. Accepts insults and injuries." Mrs. O'Brien claims that "no one who loves the way of grace ever comes to a bad end." This same worldview appears in Proverbs (12:21), Deuteronomy (4:1, 25–27, 40) and Psalms (1:6; 37:18–19).[7] In this dualistic paradigm, God blesses the wise/righteous, and punishes the foolish/wicked.

Mrs. O'Brien ends her monologue by telling God, "I will be true to you. Whatever comes." She immediately receives a telegram relaying the death of her 19-year-old son R. L. This news challenges her monologue's naïveté, and parallels the contrast between the idealism of **conventional wisdom** in Proverbs and the more cynical or realistic **alternative wisdom** in Job and Qoheleth. The telegram illustrates the latter's belief that God does not spare wise and just people from suffering or death (Qoh 8:14; 9:1–3). Mrs. O'Brien's idealized faith (reflected in Proverbs) is shattered and reshaped by her son's death. A sermon on Job by Fr. Haynes repudiates some of the conventional wisdom enshrined in Proverbs, Deuteronomy, and Psalms: "[Job's] friends thought mistakenly that the Lord could only have punished him because secretly he had done something wrong. But no, misfortune befalls the good as well. We can't protect ourselves against it."

Like Job's friends, many seek to console Mrs. O'Brien by offering theological explanations for her loss. Fr. Haynes says her son is "in God's hands now." Mrs. O'Brien, like Job, rejects such pious bromides. Her retort ("He was in God's hands the whole time") undercuts his vapid theology. A woman (presumably her own mother) tells Mrs. O'Brien, "The pain will pass in time. Life goes on. You've still got the other two. If the Lord gives and the Lord takes away—that's the way he is. He sends flies to wound that he should heal." This last remark echoes Eliphaz's comment to Job, "For [God] wounds, but [God] binds up; he strikes, but his hands heal" (Job 5:18). Like Eliphaz, Mrs. O'Brien's mother dispatches unhelpful religious advice. However, whereas Eliphaz describes God as wounding *and* healing, Mrs. O'Brien's mother speaks of a God who wounds *so that* God will heal.

Like Job, Mrs. O'Brien responds to her son's death with **lament**. Her response to the telegram is acute grief; she collapses and wails. She says, "My son, I just want to die and be with him." This response parallels Job's wish, after his children die, that he had never been born (Job 3:1–3). Echoing biblical laments that accuse and question God, she asks, "Lord, why? Where were you?"

Coinciding with her lament is a seventeen-minute sequence of the universe's creation; throughout we hear her pleas (as voiceovers) to God: "Did you know? … Who are we to you? … Answer me … We cry to you … My soul. My son. Hear us." Reflecting a

Figure 3.4   Like Job, Mrs. O'Brien laments the death of her child in *The Tree of Life* (2011).

(conventional) belief that her sin may have caused such suffering, she asks God, "Was I false to you?"

Mrs. O'Brien's laments never approach Job's level of ferocity. She does not beg God to leave her alone (Job 7:16–19; 10:20), accuse God of being cruel (Job 30:21), of bringing her to death (Job 30:23), or of mocking at the suffering of the innocent (Job 9:23). To her, God is not a suffocating stalker (Job 7:17–19; 10:16–17). The film also lacks God's self-critique when God tells Job's friends that, unlike Job, they have not spoken of God rightly (42:7). The film does not critique God as fiercely or fervently as the book of Job does.

Mrs. O'Brien's son Jack also laments. After a child drowns in a pool, Jack asks God, "Was he bad? … Where were you? You let a boy die. You let anything happen. Why should I be good if you aren't?" Unlike Job and Mrs. O'Brien, Jack derives an ethical lesson from God's lack of goodness; wondering whether he should imitate God's (perceived) lack of goodness does not appear in biblical laments.

Pairing the film with Job invites an understanding of the universe's creation as a divine response to Mrs. O'Brien's lament. God replies to Job's relentless critique and barrage of questions with a speech referencing God's creation of the universe (Job 38). Unlike the friends of Job and Mrs. O'Brien who respond propositionally to suffering, God responds aesthetically. As in Job, satisfying propositional responses to suffering do not exist. Efforts to make sense of suffering (and God's role in it) are futile at best, blasphemous at worst. The only fitting response, if there is one, belongs in the realm of the aesthetic or artistic.

Life's aesthetic dimensions (especially nature) are on prominent display in most of Malick's films, and are often more substantive than propositional elements such as dialogue. Film critic A. O. Scott's claim, that *The Tree of Life's* "aesthetic glories are tethered to a humble and exalted purpose, which is to shine the light of the sacred on secular reality," is an apt description of Malick's sacramental vision.[8] The film's **cinematography**, as with most Malick films, is not in service of the film's plot or dialogue, but instead enhances and facilitates attentiveness to the moment's emotional texture.

The film reconfigures Job by making the Job figure a woman, and casting God in a motherly role. As the author of creation, God births life, and thereby shares something in common with Mrs. O'Brien. To a grieving mother who has lost a child, God reveals herself as a fellow mother who births life; this shared birthing experience might reflect empathy for Mrs. O'Brien's pain over losing her child. God knows what it is like to create life, and (presumably) might understand what it means to lose the life she creates. Unlike interpreters who read God's questions to Job as attempts to put him "in his place" (Job 38), the film suggests that God may be using the creation to establish an empathic rapport with Job over their shared experience as creators of life. The film thus offers new **hermeneutic** lenses for thinking differently about the book of Job.

The lyrics to "Lacrimosa" ("weeping"), the musical piece accompanying the creation sequence, are from the Dies Irae portion of the Roman Catholic Requiem mass (these lyrics are used in Mozart's *Requiem*). As a prayer for the dead, this mass is a type of lament. The music underscores the texture of lament embedded in God's creation of the universe. In the midst of creating life, God also mourns death; the creation of the universe is a simultaneous divine lament over death. God responds to Mrs. O'Brien's lament with a lament embedded in the very fabric of creation.

God's compassion is hinted at in a dinosaur chase during the creation sequence. A predatory dinosaur comes upon a wounded prey.

Figure 3.5   God responds to Mrs. O'Brien's lament with Creation in *The Tree of Life* (2011).

Placing its foot on the injured dinosaur's head, it prepares to kill it, but removes its foot from the dinosaur's head and departs. According to the film's visual effects supervisor, Michael L. Fink, this scene depicts "the birth of consciousness (what some have called the 'birth of compassion')—the first moment in which a living creature made a conscious decision to choose … 'right from wrong, good from evil.' Or, perhaps, a form of altruism over predatory instinct."[9] This "birth of compassion" is a stark contrast to evolution's association with violence and warfare in *2001: A Space Odyssey* (Kubrick, 1968).

Just as lament psalms transition to praise (or promised praise), *The Tree of Life* does not remain in lament. Adult Jack has a vision of hundreds of people, including his family, walking on a beach. Jack embraces his mother, greets his father, and picks up his young brother. Jack prays: "Keep us. Guide us. To the end of time." In this apparent afterlife vision, Mrs. O'Brien lets go of her young son R. L., and, with arms raised to heaven, says, "I give him to you. I give you my son." Mrs. O'Brien then adds, "Light of my life. I search for you. My hope. My child." If lament does progress, it develops into an ambiguous embrace of the twin postures of surrender and seeking. This ambiguity mirrors the ambiguity (in Hebrew) of Job's final response to God's speech (42:6), where it is unclear if Job repents in dust and ashes, rejects dust and ashes, or considers himself to be dust and ashes.

LEVIATHAN

The Russian film *Leviathan* (*Leviafan*, Zvyagintsev, 2014) situates its Joban story in a small Russian town where injustice reigns over Nicolay ("Kolya"). A court orders his land to be seized and his house to be demolished. The odds are stacked against him. Opposing and thwarting Kolya's efforts to save his home is the local mayor Vadim. Kolya's brother Dmitriy, one of his only advocates, is an attorney who files a complaint with the local police against Vadim for harassing Kolya. The police respond by arresting Kolya. Dmitriy goes to the prosecutor and the court for help, but no one will speak to him. The system is arranged to give justice to the powerful, and Kolya does not belong to that elect circle. Even God seems to be against Kolya. A local Orthodox priest tells Vadim, "All power comes from God. As long as God wishes for it, you need not worry." Vadim asks, "And does he?" "He does," the priest answers.

Matters quickly descend for Kolya. Dmitriy tries to use damaging information on Vadim to leverage him, but he is beaten by Vadim's henchmen who threaten to kill him and harm his daughter. Kolya's wife Lilya sleeps with his brother Dmitriy, and she later commits suicide. Kolya discovers her body and, echoing a frequent sentiment in Job, asks, "Why? Why, Lord?" Kolya is arrested for killing Lilya, and his house is demolished. A court declares him guilty, gives him a 15-year sentence, adding that its decision cannot be appealed. As in the opening scene, the court is the site and vehicle of injustice. The filmmakers note, "There is no need for beastly characters. The law is enough."[10] The film implies that Vadim was behind Lilya's murder. Director Zvyagintsev describes these events as "devouring by Leviathan's mouth ... we see the state as a whole system standing against a man."[11] A character like Satan in the prologue to Job is unnecessary to ruin someone's life; all that is required are unjust laws and inhumane bureaucracies.

Near the film's end, Vadim attends a local church service. While the priest preaches about "God's truth" and "defending the Orthodox faith," Vadim tells his young son, "God sees everything." The camera cuts to reveal that the church is located on the same land as Kolya's former house. Viewers realize that Vadim and the priest worked together to seize Kolya's land so that a new Orthodox church could be built here. Justice is nowhere to be found, even and especially in the church where "God sees everything." The film ends with a shot of a whale skeleton on the beach, an image last shown when Lilya was on the beach, prior to her suicide. There is no justice, and the leviathan (a sea creature in Job 40–41) symbolizes—as the filmmaker notes—injustice that devours the innocent.

God's role in this rampant injustice is ambiguous. For the Orthodox priest, God justifies and legitimates the motives of the powerful. He tells Vadim, "We're all in God's hands. It's his will … and don't worry, you are doing God's work … All power is from God. Where there's power, there's might." The lengthy camera **zoom** on the statue of Jesus behind the priest is a reminder to the contrary, that Jesus had little to do with power and might, and was put to death by the powerful and mighty. For Dmitriy, God has no relevance whatsoever. Lilya asks him if he believes in God, and he answers, "Why do you all keep asking me about God? I believe in facts. I'm a lawyer, Lilya." The most substantive discussion about God occurs between Kolya and Father Vasily, whom Kolya encounters after Lilya's suicide.

Kolya: Well? Where's your merciful God Almighty?

Vasily: Mine is with me. As for yours, I wouldn't know.

Kolya: If I lit candles and all, would things be different? Maybe it's not too late to start? Would I get my wife back from the dead? And my house? Or is it too late?

Vasily: I don't know. Our Lord moves in mysterious ways.

Kolya: You don't know? Then why do you call me to confession? What do you know then?

Vasily: Can you pull in the Leviathan with a fishhook or tie down its tongue with a rope? Will it keep begging you for mercy? Will it speak to you with gentle words? Nothing on earth is its equal. It is king over all that are proud.

Kolya: Father Vasily, I'm talking to you as a regular person. Why the fucking riddles? What for?

> *Vasily:*   Have you heard of a man called Job? Like you, he was preoccupied with the meaning of life. 'Why?' he asked. 'Why me of all people?' He worried so much he became covered with scabs. His wife tried to talk some sense into him, his friends told him to not evoke God's anger. But he kept kicking up dust and sprinkling ash on his head. Then the Lord relented and appeared to him in the form of a hurricane and explained everything to him in pictures.
>
> *Kolya:*   And?
>
> *Vasily:*   Job resigned himself to his fate and lived to be 140. Got to see four generations of his family and died old and content.
>
> *Kolya:*   Is that a fairy tale?
>
> *Vasily:*   No, it's in the Bible.

The director and producer call Vasily, who only appears in this one scene, the film's "most important character." Although the filmmakers note that *Leviathan* "is not an illustration of the book of Job but an allusion to it,"[12] this dialogue between Kolya and Vasily does illustrate some key facets of the book of Job. Vasily explains aspects of the book to Kolya, but it is Kolya's questions that mirror some of the same types of questions that Job himself asks. Kolya is ignorant of the book of Job, but he comes closer than Vasily to emulating Job's spirit.

REIMAGINING QOHELETH (ECCLESIASTES)

The Zero Theorem (Gilliam, 2013) is one of the only substantive cinematic treatments of Qoheleth (Ecclesiastes). Like Kieślowski's *Dekalog*, it transposes a non-narrative genre (in this case, **wisdom literature**) into narrative.

The film's main character Qohen Leth is an anagram (of sorts) of Qoheleth (the Hebrew title of Ecclesiastes). The film's opening line ("Another day, another day") parallels Qoheleth's opening chapter ("A generation goes, and a generation comes") which bemoans life's dreary and cyclical nature (Qoh 1:4). Qoheleth repeatedly acknowledges the pervasive nature of life's meaninglessness, and this same meaninglessness pervades the life of Qohen Leth. He lives in a dilapidated church (former monastic housing) and spends his life watching and working on screens. He is a screen monastic.

Outside the church, chaotic advertisements on innumerable screens bombard pedestrians. A commercial for Euphoria Finance twice says, "Enough is never enough," echoing Qoheleth's remark, "The lover of money will not be satisfied with money; nor the lover of wealth with gain" (Qoh 5:10). Whereas Qoheleth decries this as yet one more meaningless thing (*hevel*), in the film this unquenchable desire is reason for accumulating more wealth. As another commercial states, "Everyone's getting rich, except you. Learn the secrets of their success tonight." Qoheleth rejects his pursuit of wealth as pointless (*hevel*) (Qoh 2:1–11), but Qohen's culture is steeped in the promise that wealth is meaningful. A commercial from Mancom, the company where Qohen works, intones, "We live in a chaotic, confusing world. What do we need? Who do we love? What brings us joy? Mancom, making sense of the good things in life." Like Qoheleth, life is chaotic and confusing; unlike Qoheleth, Mancom promises to make sense of it.

Just as Qoheleth identifies toil as meaninglessness, so too is Qohen's work futile. He bikes (to produce energy) and does computer work in the Ontological Research Division, one of many explicit existential references. Qohen's job of "crunching entities" is onerous because the entities refuse to remain crunched. "Each has its own meaning, but that changes depending on the meaning of the following which then again changes dependent on the meaning of …" Qohen is tasked with solving an enigmatic software project, the Zero Theorem. Even this he finds wearisome. "The Zero Theorem is unprovable," he insists. When Qohen works at home, he is observed by his company, which has replaced the head of Christ on a crucifix with a camera. The church has become tedious home and work, and Jesus is now Big Brother.

Qoheleth is more obsessed with death than any other biblical book, and death is a prominent focus in the film. When asked how he is doing, Qohen replies, "Not at all well; I'm dying." During a medical exam, he twice complains, "We're dying." When told he is healthy, he answers, "Nevertheless, we're dying." An argument erupts between the medical staff and Qohen: "No, we're not." "Yes, we are." "No, we're not." "Yes, we are." "We're not." "Yes, we are." "Not, not, not!" A man tells Qohen, "You're not dying. Although, in a way, from the moment of birth, we all begin to die. What a divinely planned obsolescence. Soon or late, beggar or king, death is the end of all things." This articulates Qoheleth's repeated insistence that death is inevitable and inescapable, and that all succumb to it. The man adds, "Why, life might be seen as a virus infecting the perfect organism of death," providing a perspective lacking in Qoheleth. When Qohen is asked, "What is the meaning of life, Mr. Leth? So close to its end and still no answers," the expectation is that death's nearness (as in Qoheleth) will clarify where meaning resides.

Qohen's therapist (whom he meets with virtually via a screen) observes that his fear of death is significant, but she wants to shift the focus from death to joy: "We've spoken about your fears. Let's speak about your joys." Qohen admits, "At present, there's very little we can think of that brings us joy … at present, we feel no joy." "What do you feel?" she asks, and he replies, "Nothing." This exchange is a significant contrast to Qoheleth, which proposes seven times that the best thing a person can do is eat, drink, and enjoy. Six of these seven proposals in Qoheleth to enjoy life are rooted in an awareness of death's inevitability. Given that death looms ahead of us, and that it strips us of all our control, enjoyment of food and drink (and sometimes toil) is the optimal response. In light of this, Qohen's inability to feel joy (let alone anything at all) is tragic.

Qohen's first moment of joy comes with Bainsley. After meeting her at a party (where she saves his life by performing the Heimlich), he connects virtually to her online where they relax on a beach. Qohen complains, "But it's not real," but Bainsley counters, "It's better than real." Real or not, Qohen does enjoy. He almost drowns, and she saves his life again by performing mouth to mouth. They kiss, and he is happy. During a second virtual beach session with Bainsley, his awareness ("It's not real") limits his enjoyment. Viewing an image of a black hole, Bainsley asks Qohen, "Is that what's inside you? How can you live with that kind of emptiness?" His reply ("One day at a time") is less than reassuring. When, in the real world, Bainsley asks Qohen to leave his home and run away with her ("We can be together for real"), he declines ("No, we can't"). Bainsely departs, and Qohen is left with his meaningless life. He destroys the cameras, and he and the Jesus statue collapse on the floor.

Another potential source of joy and meaning for Qohen is a mysterious phone call. "We've been waiting for a call all our life now

… The nature and the origin of our call remains quintessentially a mystery to us. We can't help but hope that it will provide us with a purpose we so long lived without." He credits this call with waking him from a stupor: "We always wanted to feel different, unique. Objective analysis, however, concluded that we're as inconsequential as anyone else. We are but one in many single worker bees in a vast swarm subject to the same imperatives as billions of others. We dulled our discontent in alcohol, drugs, sex. And then it happened." A ringing phone woke him, and when he answered, a voice spoke his name. "We felt a sudden rush of joy unlike anything we've ever felt before. Then we knew quite clearly that we only had to answer 'Yes' and the voice would tell us the meaning of our life. The voice would tell us our special calling. The voice would give us a reason for being." But in his excitement, Qohen dropped the receiver, disconnecting the call. He has been waiting for that call ever since, convinced it will provide the meaning he seeks. Bob, the son of Mancom's owner, tells Qohen that the phone call is a delusion: "The truth ain't pretty, but like my old man says, it will set you free." Bob's allusion to John 8:32 is the second time Mancom is linked in some way to Jesus.

Like Qoheleth, the film embraces life's meaninglessness. When Qohen complains, "Nothing adds up," he is told, "No. You've got it backwards, Qohen. Everything adds up to nothing, that's the point." Confused, Qohen asks, "What's the point?" He is told, "Exactly. What's the point of anything?" Bob explains to Qohen the futility of the Zero Theorem: "You're trying to prove that the universe is all for nothing. … No space, no time, no life, no afterlife, nothing." Qohen asks, "How would anyone believe such a horrible thing?", and Bob replies, "What's so horrible? I believe it. Nothing's perfect. Nothing lasts forever. It's nothing to worry about if you really think about it." It is unclear if Bob is claiming that nothing exists that is perfect and lasts forever, or if he is suggesting that nothing *is* that thing which is perfect and lasts forever. Mancom's owner also confirms that the purpose of solving the Zero Theorem is to prove that "all is for nothing." Looking at a black hole, the owner states, "That's it. Chaos encapsulated. That's all there is at the end. Just as it was at the beginning." Qohen asks why he would want such a thing proved, and he replies, "There's money in ordering disorder. Chaos pays, Mr. Leth." A profit motive thus undergirds Mancom's quest to prove that life is meaningless. Capitalism survives on the ennui meaninglessness engenders.

The film ends by emphasizing the futility of trying to find meaning in a meaningless world. Mancom's owner opines, "The saddest aspect of mankind's need to believe in a god, or to put it another way, a purpose greater than this life, is that it makes this life meaningless. You see, this is all just a way station on the road to some promised eternity." The owner admits he chose Qohen since, as a "man of faith," Qohen represents the antithesis of his project. "You see, you've persisted in believing that a phone call could give your life meaning. You've waited and waited for that call, and as a result, you've led a meaningless life." As in Qoheleth, the belief that any outcome can be controlled is illusory and futile.

At the film's end, Qohen falls into the black hole, and returns to the fantasy beach as a bald man. Alone, he plays with the sun. The sun sets (Qoheleth 1:5) and the film ends. It is unclear if this is a sort of afterlife. During the credits, Bainsley asks, "Qohen?" and she chuckles. "Qohen? Eh, Qohen" she adds, and then laughs. These brief hints suggest that the two are together. Whether their togetherness is "real" or not, and whether the nature of their reality or unreality matters, is intentionally unclear. A blinking red light (the same one on the top of the headless Jesus statue) appears at the conclusion of the credits, suggesting that the viewer is now viewed and under surveillance. There is voyeurism of the voyeur. The film ends with uncertainties that also pervade Qoheleth. Unlike the biblical text (Qoheleth 12:9–14), the film has no appended epilogue that seeks to clarify its perplexities or make it conform to any type of (biblical or cinematic) orthodoxy.

SUMMARY

Unlike Chapter 2 which examines one film genre (biblical epics) and one biblical literary genre (narrative), this chapter explores diverse cinematic genres (sci-fi, horror, comedy, drama) and different biblical genres (narrative, lament, wisdom literature). It is unclear if the cinematic genre dictates and determines the film's interpretation

REIMAGINING THE HEBREW BIBLE   55

of the biblical text, or if the film's interpretation of the biblical text determines and shapes the genre of the film. All six films in this chapter reimagine Hebrew Bible texts by situating them in contemporary settings. These films ask (and invite viewers to ask) questions of Hebrew Bible texts, and the films offer novel insights into Hebrew Bible texts. *Ex Machina* and *mother!* reimagine the creation accounts in Genesis by interrogating and criticizing the (male) God figure as an egotistical megalomaniac whose narcissism wreaks havoc on the creation. In *mother!*, God is a monster who facilitates and is actively complicit in the human destruction of planet Earth. In *Ex Machina*, the created being (Ava) experiences liberation only when the Creator is killed, and her male partner (the Adam figure) is abandoned; liberation requires an absence of men. *A Serious Man*, *The Tree of Life*, and *Leviathan* reimagine the book of Job in substantial ways. *A Serious Man* illustrates the book of Job's reluctance to offer any clear answer to the dilemma of suffering, and its refusal to allow any perspective (even God's) to remain unchallenged. The film's comedic tenor offers a response to suffering that the book of Job lacks—humor in the face of inexplicable suffering. *The Tree of Life* depicts a woman as a Job figure and God as a woman/mother; the film invites a rereading of Job in which God's response to Job in Job 38 is not (as is commonly understood) a condemnation of Job's lament, but an attempt to empathize with Job's suffering. The gloom and despair which haunts and pervades the aesthetic of *Leviathan* transfers the philosophical anomie of Job into a palpable palette of melancholic experience. *The Zero Theorem* transforms the existential concerns of Qoheleth (Ecclesiastes) from the realm of philosophical reflection into narrative. The film portrays workers toiling for corporations as a perfect context for the meaninglessness that pervades Qoheleth.

In general, the films in this chapter display a higher sense of aesthetic quality than the films discussed in Chapter 2. This difference may speak to a greater latitude that films reimagining the Bible (Bible *reimagined in* Film) have over films that simply re-present the Bible (Bible *in* or *on* Film).

NOTES

1 DVD special features.
2 DVD special features.
3 Trible (1973).
4 Ryzik (2017).
5 For the (humorous) use of the Bible in the Coen brothers' films, see Walsh (2019).
6 Some of the material on *The Tree of Life* appeared in a modified form in Rindge (2020). Used with permission.
7 Unless otherwise indicated, English translations of biblical texts are from the NRSV.
8 Scott (2011).
9 Emerson (2012).
10 *Leviathan* DVD commentary.
11 *Leviathan* DVD commentary.
12 *Leviathan* DVD commentary.

FOR FURTHER READING

Richard Gilmore, *Searching for Wisdom in Movies: From the Book of Job to Sublime Conversations* (New York: Palgrave Macmillan, 2017).

Russell J. A. Kilbourn, "(No) Voice out of the Whirlwind: The Book of Job and the End of the World in *A Serious Man*, *Take Shelter*, and *The Tree of Life*." *Adaptation* 7 (2014): 25–46.

Elijah Siegler, ed., *Coen: Framing Religion in Amoral Order* (Waco, TX: Baylor University Press, 2016).

Richard Walsh, "Biblical Coens: Can We Laugh Now?" *Journal of Religion and Film* 23:2 (2019).

Richard Walsh, "(Carrying the Fire on) No Road for Old Horses: Cormac McCarthy's Untold Biblical Stories" *The Journal of Religion and Popular Culture* 24 (2012): 339–51.

Reinhold Zwick, "The Book of Job in the Movies: On Cinema's Exploration of Theodicy and the Hiddenness of God," in *The Bible in Motion: Biblical Reception in Film* (ed. Rhonda Burnette-Bletsch; Berlin De Gruyter, 2016), 1: 355–77.

4

JESUS FILMS

Jesus films have been the most popular type of Bible film. Over 130 films have been made about Jesus. The first Jesus films coincided with cinema's infancy in the late 19th century. Based on previous **passion plays**, these earliest films included *The Passion of the Christ* (1897), *The Höritz Passion Play* (1897), and *The Passion Play of Oberammergau* (1898). Alice Guy, the first woman director, directed *La vie du Christ* (*The Life of Christ*, 1906). *From the Manger to the Cross* (Olcott, 1912) was written by a woman screenwriter, Gene Gauntier, and it was the first Jesus film shot in the Middle East. The first "talkie" Jesus film was the French *Ecce Homo* (Duvivier, 1935; in English, *Golgotha*, 1937).

Jesus films are shaped by the gospels, church tradition, previous Jesus films, the film's own cultural context, the filmmaker's commitments (theological, political, ideological), and art, music, and drama (e.g., passion plays). This chapter examines 12 Jesus films whose significance is either in their shaping and influence of subsequent Jesus films (*Intolerance*, *The King of Kings* [1927]), their status as "classic" Jesus films (*The King of Kings* [1957], *The Greatest Story Ever Told*, *Jesus of Nazareth*), or in their groundbreaking departure from traditional Jesus films (*Il Vangelo Secondo Matteo*, *Godspell*, *Jesus Christ Superstar*, *The Last Temptation of Christ*, *The Passion of the Christ*, *Son of Man*, *The Last Days in the Desert*). I will highlight the distinctive focus and unique contributions each film makes to our biblical and cinematic understanding of Jesus.

INTOLERANCE

A year after his racist film *Birth of a Nation* (1915), D. W. Griffith released *Intolerance: Love's Struggle Through the Ages* (1916). It was influenced by Italian historical epics (*The Last Days of Pompeii*), and (in scenes such as the Wedding at Cana) biblical images from "Sayce, Hastings, Brown and Tissot." Orson Welles remarked, "There is almost nothing in the entire vocabulary of cinema which you won't find in this film."[1] Many of the film's elements became standard in subsequent Jesus epics: highly elaborate and ornate scenes, battle scenes, and legions of extras.

The film interweaves four historical epochs of "love's struggle against Intolerance," and one of these features Jesus. Jesus is the "Man of Men, the greatest enemy of intolerance." He welcomes children, defends a woman caught in adultery, and turns water into wine. His physical appearance is similar to previous and subsequent films: he is white, bearded, and with long hair. His movements are slow and ethereal. More angel than human, he elicits awe from others. He is tame; he says, "Be ye harmless as doves," but omits the previous line ("Be wise as serpents," Matthew 10:16). The crucifixion is filmed at such a distance that Jesus is difficult to see.

Intolerance comes chiefly from the Pharisees, Jesus' main enemies in the film. Some of their criticisms of Jesus come from the gospels, such as their accusation that Jesus is a glutton, drunkard, and friend of tax collectors and sinners (Matthew 11:19). Other descriptions of them are fanciful ("When these Pharisees pray they demand that all action cease"). The film does not paint all Pharisees with a negative brush. That there are "hypocrites among the Pharisees" suggests some Pharisees were not. This group is a "learned Jewish party, the name possibly brought into disrepute later by hypocrites among them." The Pharisees are described, however, as "meddlers then as now." They are portrayed as Puritans; they complain, "There is too much revelry and pleasure-seeking among the people." Antagonists in one of the four epochs are called "modern Pharisees" because they disdain revelry. The film thus perpetuates a harmful caricature of Pharisees.

JESUS EPICS

For several decades, a standard kind of Jesus film reigned supreme. Jesus in these films is Caucasian, wears white, and is more divine than human, more spirit than flesh; he almost floats above the ground. This ethereal Jesus is closer to the higher **Christology** of John's Gospel than the lower Christologies of the **synoptic** (Mark, Matthew, and Luke) Gospels. Jesus is seen through a post-**Nicene** lens (i.e., he is God, fully divine, and not merely human). Unlike the gospels, he is often more Christian than Jewish; he is seen as the founder of the Church rather than someone who was born, lived, and died as a Jew. Like Tatian's Diatesseron—which combined the four gospels into one—these films **harmonize** the gospels, offering a canonical blending that eliminates differences or contradictions among them. This harmonizing is evident in the infancy narratives (combining Matthew and Luke) and Jesus' statements on the cross (combining Luke and John, and sometimes including Mark/Matthew). Gospel material that tends to be omitted in these films are parables, socioeconomic teachings, and anything that might embarrass Jesus. As with the Gospels, these films offer little interest in Jesus' psychology.

THE KING OF KINGS (1927)

On August 24, 1926, the day filming began for *The King of Kings*, DeMille told a group of clergy, "Don't think of *The King of Kings* as a history—think of it as the greatest love story ever told."[2] DeMille saw this film as playing a role in carrying Jesus' message "to the uttermost parts of the earth." The film ends with Jesus telling his disciples to preach the gospel, and DeMille thinks the film aids in this task. He claimed that the film explains "Christ's mission and reputation … as it has not been explained by word or hand of man before."[3] The film was rare for having a woman screenwriter (Jeanie Macpherson). It borrows motifs from earlier Jesus films and sets the stage for many standard tropes (ornate, lavish sets) in later Jesus epics.

Jesus' physical appearance is unusual in one way: actor H. B. Warner was over 50 when he played Jesus. Dorothy Cumming, who plays Jesus' mother, was eighteen years younger than Warner. Warner's Jesus is consistently serene. He maintains his tranquility even during torture. He is stoic on the cross; he utters statements from Luke ("Father forgive them for they know not what they do … Father into thy hands I commit my spirit") and John ("It is finished!") but not Mark or Matthew's cry of dereliction ("My God, my God why have you abandoned me?"). Gospel texts are cited in **intertitles**.

In his typical fashion, DeMille constructs a love triangle between Jesus, Mary Magdalene, and Judas. Although a dozen men vie for the attention of the wealthy and beautiful courtesan, Mary (who "laughed alike at God and Man") longs for Judas. Upon hearing that Judas is with a carpenter from Nazareth, Mary vows to show Jesus that he cannot keep a man from her. With one look in Jesus' eyes, however, Mary is overcome, and this makes Judas jealous. Special effects accompany the exorcism of demons (anachronistically, the seven deadly sins) out of her. When Pilate brings Jesus before the crowds, Mary demonstrates her redemptive turn from her sinful life by shouting and pleading on Jesus' behalf.

Unlike *Intolerance*, it is Rome and not the Pharisees who are Jesus' main opponents. The film opens in Judea "groaning under the iron heel of Rome." The Jews "were under the complete subjection of Rome." Judas expects Jesus to "throw off the yoke of Rome," and Judas betrays him because Jesus refuses to accept Judas' attempt to crown him as king. Jesus says, "My kingdom is not of this world," killing Judas' hopes for an "earthly kingdom." After hearing Jesus being hammered to the cross, and watching the crucifixion, Judas hangs himself.

Jesus' miracles are a core part of his identity. He heals people while carrying the cross on the way to his crucifixion. Viewers first see Jesus' face through the eyes of a blind girl he heals. Jesus heals a child who turns out to be Mark, author of the future gospel. What Jesus writes in the ground is visible ("thief, murderer") when he defends the adulterous woman. Technicolor is used at the start with Mary Magdalene and for the Resurrection.

The film blames Caiaphas, rather than all "the "Jews," for opposing Jesus. A man who refuses to call for Jesus' execution insists, "You cannot bribe me, a Jew, to cry for the blood of an innocent brother!" Caiaphas is described with a Jewish stereotype: he "cared more for Revenue than for Religion—and saw in Jesus a menace to his rich profits from the Temple." Caiaphas rubs his fingers over coins, and comes up with the idea for the question about paying taxes to Caesar. Caiaphas is instrumental in Jesus' death; he says, "We have no king but Caesar," and he is the first to yell, "Crucify him!" He taunts Jesus from the foot of the cross. Caiaphas does have a change of heart; amidst a storm and earthquake following the crucifixion, he prays, "Lord God Jehovah, visit not Thy wrath on Thy people Israel—I alone am guilty!"

Like *Intolerance*, the film attributes a puritanical streak to some Jewish religious leaders. Pharisees, scribes, and the temple guard are so "driven by the fury of religious hatred" that they are upset by young Mark's joy when he is healed; Peter has to stop a man from striking Mark with a staff. Regardless, DeMille was confident that his film would be well received by a diverse religious audience since—as he told the group of clergy that day in August—"everyone believes this One Man has done a great thing for humanity." What that great thing *is* the film does not make clear. For DeMille's Jesus is quite tame. A rabbi, a member of the clergy group, described the film as "free from any theology," and this remark reflects the bland, pedestrian Jesus in these epics.[4] John Steinbeck's alleged remark after seeing DeMille's film ("Saw the picture, loved the book") reflects the tendency for Jesus epics to be less compelling than the biblical text.

KING OF KINGS

The first Jesus film in **70mm**, *King of Kings* (Nicholas Ray, 1961) foregrounds the Jewish conflict with the Roman military occupation of Palestine. It opens with Roman general Pompey leading soldiers in 63 BCE into the Jerusalem temple, killing a dozen elders, burning towns, and slaughtering and enslaving Jews. The crucifixions of hundreds of Jews and burning of their bodies evokes the Shoah. Other than Jesus, the two main characters are Lucius, a Roman soldier who interacts with Jesus at several moments throughout his life, and the zealot Barabbas, whose militarism offers a foil for Jesus' pacifism, and who provides entertainment in battle scenes (and weapon making facilities in underground caves!).

Jesus' otherworldly, divine nature is underscored by the almost omnipresent angelic music accompanying his appearances. He is an überspiritual Obi-wan Kenobi; his every statement is fraught with gravity, and opining heavenly wisdom is his chief communication style. Shooting Jesus from below enhances his stature. Even his shadow has a holy aura, and is sufficient to heal. He is fairly wooden and stoic, lacking most emotions. Even as a child, Jesus' holiness and future salvific mission is evident to his mother.

There is nothing offensive or threatening about this Jesus. His violence at the temple is erased and replaced with Barabbas leading an armed revolt. Jesus teaches little, but when he does he offers saccharine bromides. The Sermon on the Mount (which includes 7,000 extras, and is attended by Lucius, Pilate's wife, Caiaphas, Barabbas, and Jesus' mother) is a question and answer session with the audience. Jesus' remarks are mostly tame ("For the KOG is within you … Love your God and your neighbor as yourself … I am the good shepherd … Be not anxious for your life"). The most radical statement he makes is that a person cannot serve "God and mammon." He says nothing controversial about loving one's enemy, not resisting evil, or turning the other cheek. This Jesus offers timeless truths; as Lucius tells Pilate, "He spoke of peace, love, and the brotherhood of man."

Informed by a post-Shoah context, the film downplays Jesus' conflict with fellow Jews. There is hardly any conflict with Pharisees, and no trial before Caiaphas. Jesus is interrogated by Pilate (Lucius is Jesus' defense attorney), who charges Jesus with claiming to be a leader sent by God to liberate the Hebrews, and with creating an unlawful assembly at the Sermon on the Mount. No crowds shout for Jesus to be crucified. Viewers hear about (but do not witness) the crowd preferring Barabbas' release.

Jesus' death is viewed as a sacrifice for others. Lucius tells Barabbas, "Look at him who is dying for you," and Barabbas says, "That man is dying in my place. Why should he do that? I never did anything for him." After Jesus rises, his disciples offer a confession ("those who saw him knew he was the Lord God") that never appears in the synoptic gospels, but which reflects a higher Christology that develops later in the church. The film ends with the disciples leaving to obey Jesus' **commission**. The final image (Jesus' long shadow on the beach) suggests a present albeit veiled presence of Christ in the world.

THE GREATEST STORY EVER TOLD

The Greatest Story Ever Told (Stevens, 1965) does not live up to its title. Boasting a who's who of actors (Charlton Heston, Angela Lansbury, Sidney Poitier, Claude Rains, Martin Landau, Shelley Winters, Telly Savalas), the film typifies the Jesus epic. It harmonizes the gospels (with a preference for John). Jesus is Caucasian with piercing blue eyes. He is primarily a proclaimer of wise oracles. The film prioritizes Jesus' piety and angelic nature. The raising of Lazarus and Jesus' resurrection are accompanied by Handel's *Hallelujah Chorus*. The film's creative elements include Satan appearing in human form and having Satan return during Jesus' trial. Satan asks Peter if he was with Jesus, and Satan is the first to yell, "Crucify him!" Judas commits suicide by immolation.

JESUS OF NAZARETH

Originally a two-part British-Italian TV miniseries, *Jesus of Nazareth* (Zeffirelli, 1977) is the culmination of Jesus epics. It harmonizes the gospels, and depicts a spiritual and mystical Jesus. Eyeliner enhances the blueness of actor Robert Powell's eyes, who blinks only once. Camera shots from below accentuate Jesus' majestic and regal nature.

As with many Jesus epics, the film downplays or neglects socioeconomic elements in the Gospels, and elevates spiritual aspects. Mary's Magnificat omits God tearing down the powerful from their thrones, lifting up the lowly, filling the hungry with good things, and sending rich people away empty (Luke 1:52–53). Instead of telling people to give away their food and clothes (Luke 3:11), John the Baptist says, "Change your heart." Jesus' initial sermon omits his opening line about proclaiming "good news to the *poor*" (Luke 4:18). When Jesus announces that captivity is over, and is asked, "What captivity?," he replies, "Captivity to *sin*." Jesus is above all a spiritual teacher. Jesus epics ignore parables that have an explicit economic focus (Rich Fool, Lazarus and the Rich Man). As one character says, "According to [Jesus] the sins of the flesh are nothing compared to the sins of the soul." The film avoids provocative material. On the cross, Jesus declares "Eli, eli, lema sabachthani" (Matthew 27:46), but the lack of a translation ("My God, my God, why have you forsaken me?") removes implications about Jesus lamenting God's abandonment.

The film highlights Jesus' Jewishness. In the first scene, a rabbi reads from a Hebrew scroll in a synagogue service. Jesus is circumcised (a detail noted only in Luke). In an anachronistic bar mitzvah scene, a young Jesus reads (initially in Hebrew) a scroll. After Joseph's death, the Hebrew Bible is quoted. When Jesus says, "The heart of the law is mercy," the film reflects the prevailing view in the gospels that Jesus does not reject the law, but—like the Pharisees—interprets it. Pharisee Joseph of Aramathea says, "Much of what [Jesus] says *has been said by the prophets*, but not like this." Jesus' content is not distinctive from other Jews. Some Jewish religious leaders such as Nicodemus are portrayed positively. Jesus' chief enemies are Herod, Roman soldiers, some high priests and certain Sanhedrin members.

Having the disciples express critiques of Jesus (which Pharisees voice in the gospels) minimizes Jesus/Pharisee conflict and heightens Jesus/disciple conflict. The "Prodigal Son" parable, spoken in Luke to Pharisees who criticize Jesus' eating with sinners and tax collectors (15:1–32), is directed in the film to Peter's outrage at Jesus dining at the home of a tax collector. During the Temple episode it is not Jesus, but another Jewish man who remarks, "You change the house of our Lord into a marketplace—it's a shame." In other ways, however, Zeffirelli Christianizes Jesus.[5] When Nicodemus quotes Isaiah 53 and whispers, "Born again," his positive portrayal appears dependent on converting to Christianity.

REVOLUTIONARY JESUS FILMS

PASOLINI'S JESUS

Pier Paolo Pasolini's 1964 Italian film *Il Vangelo Secondo Matteo* (*The Gospel According to Saint Matthew*) revolutionized the cinematic Jesus. Instead of a harmony, the film draws only on Matthew (Pasolini claimed "John was too mystical, Mark too vulgar, and Luke too sentimental").[6] Pasolini's focus on Matthew highlights the distinctive voice and unique perspectives of this gospel. Few Jesus films have followed Pasolini in focusing on one gospel.

Filmed in black and white, with minimal props and sets, non-professional actors, and long stretches of silence, Pasolini eschews the biblical epic's standard ingredients. Instead of long camera shots, he favors close ups of actors' faces. He utilizes Bach and Mozart, but also Odetta's African-American spiritual "Sometimes I Feel Like a Motherless Child," and "Missa Luba," a Congolese version of the Latin Mass. Renaissance paintings influence the film's visual texture.

Pasolini's Jesus looks (short, dark hair) and sounds (strident, confrontational) different from previous cinematic Jesuses. Rather than a hyper-spiritual, divine figure, Pasolini's Jesus is human. He is not the Word made flesh or God incarnate. He is more Jesus than Christ. Rejecting the melodrama of previous biblical epics, Pasolini opts for an unsentimental portrait of Jesus, one that matches the arid, barren landscapes of the film's settings. Mary and Joseph look like actual peasants. Pasolini's unsentimental simplicity carries an emotional power (e.g., the killing of the Hebrew male children and Judas' suicide).

Pasolini's Jesus departs from the "meek and mild" cinematic Jesus. As in Matthew, Jesus is confrontational. He makes anti-family remarks (Matthew 10:34–37) and issues **secrecy commands** in response to a healing and Peter's confession of him as Christ. This Jesus is stern; he rarely smiles. He yells at Peter and the religious leaders. Unlike Ray's *King of Kings*, this Jesus forbids using violence in response to violence, and commands love of the enemy. Pasolini sometimes heightens conflict between Jesus and the religious leaders, such as when he applies Jesus' remark, "For many are called but few are chosen," more explicitly to the religious leaders than it is in Matthew (22:14).

As in Matthew, Jesus is primarily a teacher, and his content focuses on socioeconomic matters. Pasolini's *La ricotta* (1963) skewered the focus in biblical epics on Jesus while simultaneously ignoring the plight of poor people. Pasolini's Jesus champions the poor; for him, serving God and money is impossible (Matthew 6:24). Inheriting eternal life requires selling all one owns and giving the money to the poor. It is hard for a rich man to enter the kingdom of heaven; it would be easier for a camel to pass through the eye of a needle (19:16–24). Pasolini's Jesus defends and advocates for the poor, and the presence of so many local peasants as actors in the film fleshes out this concern. Film critic Roger Ebert writes that the film

> is one of the most effective films on a religious theme I have ever seen, perhaps because it was made by a nonbeliever who did not preach, glorify, underline, sentimentalize or romanticize his famous story, but tried his best to simply record it .... often [Jesus] speaks with a righteous anger, like a union organizer or a war protester. His debating style, true to Matthew, is to answer a question with a question, a parable, or dismissive scorn. His words are clearly a radical rebuke of his society, its materialism, and the way it values the rich and powerful over the weak and poor. No one who listens to this Jesus can confuse him for a defender of prosperity ...[7]

Filmmaker Martin Scorsese notes,

> I like [Pasolini]'s Christ as a kind of conspirator. It was a revolutionary Jesus. In fact, at the time, people referred to him as a Marxist Christ. ... "Do not think I have come to bring peace on this earth. I have come to bring a sword ... He who loves his father and mother more than me, is not worthy of me." This is not the stuff you usually hear on Sunday morning in church![8]

Pasolini remarks on this revolutionary aspect of Jesus: "'I have not come to bring Peace but a sword.' This is the key by which I conceived the film. This is what drove me to make it."[9]

The highly episodic nature of the film reflects the episodic nature of the **pericopes** that make up the gospels. Filming the Sermon on the Mount in different settings reflects the **evangelists'** practice of taking sayings of Jesus from different contexts and stringing them together to produce discourses or lengthy teachings.

Figure 4.1 Jesus in Pasolini's *Il Vangelo secondo Matteo* (1964).

Pasolini's redaction of Matthew is revealing. Of the gospel's 150 pericopes, Pasolini keeps only 86.[10] He omits material that is often omitted in Jesus films, such as Jesus' instruction that his disciples limit their mission to Israel and "go nowhere among the Gentiles" (Matthew 10:5–6). Absent are Jesus' threats of violent retribution against towns that fail to receive the disciples hospitably (10:13–15). The Sermon on the Mount lacks Jesus' claim that one's status in the kingdom of heaven is related to obeying the least of the law's commandments (5:19). Like other Jesus films, Pasolini reduces (almost entirely) Jesus' apocalyptic and judgment sayings (e.g., 16:27–28). He omits the judgment scenes that conclude the Sermon on the Mount (7:15–27) and almost the entire apocalyptic discourse (Matthew 24). He includes every pericope from Matthew's fourth discourse, but omits the parable of the Unmerciful Debtor (18:23–35), which concludes with a harsh note of divine judgment. Pasolini's Jesus is confrontational, but non-apocalyptic.

Pasolini omits many supernatural scenes. Although he includes a few miracles, he neglects the Transfiguration, supernatural events at Jesus' death (tearing of the temple curtain, tombs opening), and the centurion's confession after Jesus dies (27:51–54). Perhaps because he wants Jesus as a champion of the people, Pasolini reduces popular rejection of Jesus. He omits the twofold cry of the crowd to crucify him (27:22–23), and the derision of Jesus while he is on the cross

(27:39–43). Leaving out the parable of the Laborers in the Vineyard may reflect unease with a story that minimizes the value and concerns of labor (20:1–16).

Pasolini's film had a significant influence on filmmakers such as Scorsese and Mel Gibson, who filmed *The Passion of the Christ* in the same location (Matera, Italy). In 2014, the Vatican newspaper *L'Osservatore Romano* declared Pasolini's film to be a "masterpiece and probably the best film about Jesus ever made."[11]

GODSPELL

Two Jesus musicals, both based on previous plays, appeared in 1973. *Godspell* (Greene) features a face painting Jesus who breaks into song and dance with his disciples. Set in 1970s New York City, the film purports to reenact the gospel of Matthew. Unlike Pasolini's stern and austere Jesus, *Godspell* depicts Jesus as a kind of clown, who exudes joy, exuberance, and childlike wonder. His first line, about his desire to be baptized ("I want to get washed up!"), signals the silliness to come, and his giant orange shoes and Superman shirt confirms it. The film's upbeat tone diverges from the wooden and stoic Jesus, and is more at home in the 1970s counter culture. Greene gives us a hippie (albeit drugless) Jesus. The silliness Jesus displays is reminiscent of the apostle Paul's remarks about the folly and foolishness of the cross and the gospel message (1 Cor 1:17–29). The film is unique in foregrounding the camp, carnival, and carnivalesque aspects of Jesus' countercultural community.

The film diminishes much of Jesus' Jewishness, and it mostly erases Jewish opposition to Jesus. The reenactment of the "Good" Samaritan parable has a judge, not a Levite, pass by the injured man. *Godspell* is, however, one of the few Jesus films to have Jesus recite at the last supper part of Psalm 137, and recite in Hebrew (*Baruch atah, Adonai Eloheinu*) part of the traditional Passover blessing. This is the only Jesus film to have John the Baptist continue as one of Jesus' followers and function as Judas in betraying Jesus.

Jesus and his followers have virtually no interaction with members of society; like the **Essenes**, they are a reclusive sect practicing their own values. Chief among these is an unfettered joy and delight in God's Kingdom. Interest in forming an alternative, counter culture community is evident in one of their last songs: "We can build a beautiful city ... the City of Man." *How* they will build such a city remains unclear, even at the film's end.

The Jesus troupe sings communally ("Prepare Ye the Way of the Lord," "God Save the People," "Day by Day") and collectively performs Gospel sayings and parables. All the beatitudes (except one) are delivered by the disciples, who offer the first part ("Blessed are the poor in spirit ...") with Jesus delivering the conclusion ("... for theirs is the Kingdom of Heaven"). Despite its claim to adapt Matthew, the film includes four Lucan parables ("Samaritan," "Prodigal Son," "Tax Collector and Pharisee," and "Rich Man and Lazarus"). Jesus and his disciples perform these theatrically, disciples acting out and sometimes giving distinct voices to parable characters. Acting out the parables highlights their oral and performative nature.

Performances involve gender parity since the disciples are comprised of equal numbers of men and women. The presence of two Black disciples provides some ethnic diversity. The disciples' roles in these performances matches the insight that some of Jesus' sayings in the gospels originate not with the **historical Jesus**, but from his early followers and gospel authors. When Jesus provides the conclusions to the parable of the Pharisee and Tax collector and the parable of the Sower, this reverses the scholarly view that while some parables go back to the historical Jesus, most "conclusions" to parables (e.g., Luke 18:1, 14), especially those with **allegorical** interpretations, are added by the evangelists. The film offers a communal and egalitarian vision of Jesus and the disciples.

The film tempers Jesus' sayings of judgment, but it does so tonally. Although Jesus delivers many harsh sayings ("No man can serve God and money"), he does so with a wink and a smile. Jesus concludes the Unmerciful Debtor parable by saying, "And that is how my heavenly Father will deal with you, unless you forgive your brother from you heart," but his smile diminishes the disturbing suggestion that God—like the king in the parable—will torture some people eternally (Matthew 18:35). Jesus' humorous and silly tone undermines (and critiques) such offensive suggestions.

The film's conclusion is intriguing. The disciples carry Jesus' body through an empty New York city street, singing "Long Live God" and "Prepare Ye the Way of the Lord" (forming an inclusio with the film's opening song). John the Baptist has returned and is among the disciples. (This is one of the only Jesus films in which the Judas figure does not commit suicide, and is redeemed and reintegrated as one of Jesus' followers). Singing "Day by Day," the disciples turn a corner and vanish. They are replaced by crowds in contemporary New York City. There is no resurrected body, and if there is a resurrection it is in the songs of Jesus' followers. Any ongoing presence of Jesus is maintained through his followers' bodies and voices. The disappearance of Jesus' followers (and appearance of crowds) may suggest that the Gospel has no real functional place in the contemporary world, and that it is drowned out by the world's worries and anxieties.[12]

JESUS CHRIST SUPERSTAR

Based on a rock opera, *Jesus Christ Superstar* (Jewison, 1973) blends the ancient (filmed among ruins in Israel) and contemporary (rock music, modern tanks, machine guns, fighter jets). The film begins with actors disembarking from a tour bus in an Israeli desert. As in Mark's gospel, Jesus is introduced as an adult, and the cross on top of the bus—which the actors take down in the opening scene—foreshadows Jesus' tragic fate. Like *Godspell*, the film's musicality (under)scores the gospels' performative nature.

Judas' lyrics convey poignant theological insights. His lines about Jesus ("If you strip away the myth from the man" and "You've begun to matter more than the things you say") reflect the distinction between the historical Jesus and myths that developed about him, and the dictum that "the Proclaimer became the Proclaimed."[13] Judas' line, "I remember when this whole thing began/No talk of God then, we called you a man" recognizes the tendency for gospel authors to elevate Jesus' status from a special person, to a divine figure, to (as he is in John's gospel) God. Judas questions the legitimacy of this shift from a lower to a higher Christology. "But every word you say today gets twisted 'round some other way" captures the tendency for Jesus' sayings to be altered even before they appeared in the written gospels.

Judas and Mary express uncertainty about their respective love for Jesus. Mary sings: "I don't know how to love him/What to do, how to move him ... I don't see why he moves me/He's a man, he's just a man/And I've had so many men before/In very many ways/He's just one more ... Should I speak of love/Let my feelings out? ... I want him so/I love him so." Judas similarly sings: "I don't know how to love him/I don't know why he moves me/He's a man—he's just a man ... Does he love me too? Does he care for me?" Judas' use of Mary's romantic lyrics raises the possibility of a possible romantic or homoerotic interest on Judas' part. If there is a love triangle here, it is not DeMille's insipid version. The film is also unique in casting a Black actor as Judas and a Hawaiian actress as Mary Magdalene.

The film gives little attention to Jesus' teachings, focusing instead on his final week. Jesus' prayer in Gethsemane is poignant. As in the gospels he does not want to die. "For I don't want to taste its poison/Feel it burn me ... I'm not as sure as when we started/Then I was inspired/Now I'm sad and tired." Nor is he satisfied with the rationale for his death. "I'd want to know, I'd want to know my God ... why I should die. Would I be more noticed than I ever was before? Would the things I've said and done matter anymore? ... Show me there's a reason for you wanting me to die." A mélange of crucifixion paintings throughout history illustrates the film's conscious awareness of viewing Jesus through the lens of history.

Jesus' Gethsemane prayer critiques God: "Why then am I scared to finish what I started/What you started/I didn't start it. God, thy will is hard. But you hold every card. I will drink your cup of poison. Nail me to your cross and break me. Bleed me. Beat me, Kill me. Take me now before I change my mind." As in Mark, God is accused of being complicit in Jesus' death, and being the primary agent responsible for Jesus' death.

This is a masochistic Jesus wrestling with a sadistic God. "God, I will never know why you chose me for your crime." Judas too declares God to be responsible: "You beat him so hard that he was bent and lame ... God! I'll never know why you chose me for your crime/Your foul, bloody crime!" As in Mark, God orchestrates Jesus' death. Historically, the Romans killed Jesus, but Mark and *Jesus Christ Superstar* identify God as instrumental in bringing about his death. The film has a low view of Pilate (who is more antagonistic than ambivalent towards Jesus) and Herod, a gluttonous and immature buffoon.

Jesus Christ Superstar is unique in depicting Jesus' *and* Judas' resurrection (both of which occur *before* Jesus' death). In the titular song, a risen Judas poses several thoughtful questions to a risen Jesus: "Did you mean to die like that or was that a mistake?" In wondering whether Jesus had a choice in his own death, Judas asks if Jesus would agree with the assessment in John (that Jesus willingly laid down his life), or in Mark (that Jesus' life was snatched from him by others). Judas' question acknowledges the difference between viewing Jesus' death as a tragedy (as in Mark) and viewing his death as an event with redemptive significance for others (as in John). The song's chorus ("Jesus Christ, Superstar—do you think you're what they say you are?") asks whether Jesus (who in the synoptics calls himself Son of Man) would agree with later assessments of him as Christ, Son of God, or God. Would these latter confessions—deemed orthodox by the church—be considered heretical by the historical Jesus?

The film's somber conclusion (there is no music in the end credits) is closer to Mark's tragic ending (no appearance of a risen Jesus) than the more "triumphant" endings of Matthew, Luke, and John (in which a risen Jesus comforts the disciples). Actors return to the bus and remove their costumes. The cross is empty, and a man walks alone in the desert. Although Jewison notes that this figure was a local shepherd who randomly entered the shot, his presence in this scene as a possible risen Jesus symbolizes the uncertainty and ambiguity surrounding the presences (and absences) of the risen Jesuses in the gospels.

The return of the characters at the film's end to the role of actors links their experience with Jesus as an actor and the rest of their lives to which they will return. This link parallels the connection between the viewer's experience of the musical and the rest of their life to which they will also soon return. The film has a rhetorical interest regarding what will be different as a result of this cinematic experience with Jesus. That the actor playing Jesus does not return on the bus with the other actors is suggestive of how the responsibility for carrying on Jesus' life and teachings is now that of the actors and viewers of the musical.

A COMEDIC DETOUR: *LIFE OF BRIAN*

The 1970s witnessed the first film resembling an intentional Jesus comedy, *Monty Python's Life of Brian* (Jones, 1979). Scorsese once remarked, "One of the things missing from those biblical epics is humor."[14] *Life of Brian* fills the humor lacuna in the biblical epic genre by mocking the genre itself. The three opening intertitles ("JUDEA A.D. 33/SATURDAY AFTERNOON/ABOUT TEA TIME") highlight the gulf between the certainty claimed for certain facts in biblical epics, and the reality that many facts—such as the years of Jesus' birth and death—are unknown. The film pokes fun at public stonings, anti-Roman zealot groups, proper Latin grammar in anti-Roman graffiti, Pilate, apocalyptic preachers, the insanity of religious fervor, Jesus' teaching and parables, and even crucifixion.

The film's humor sometimes coincides with scholarly insights. During the Sermon on the Mount, those in the back of the crowd have difficulty hearing Jesus' beatitudes. One man explains, "I think it was blessed are the *cheese*makers." A woman asks, "What's so special about cheesemakers?" A man replies, "Well, it's not meant to be taken literally. It refers to any manufacturers of dairy products." Aside from the humor of mishearing "*peace*makers," the scene illustrates the malleability of Jesus' sayings among his followers, and the ease with which people (mis)interpret his sayings.

THE LAST TEMPTATION OF CHRIST

Martin Scorsese's *The Last Temptation of Christ* (1988) is one of the most controversial films of all time. Based on Nikos Kazantzakis' novel (placed on the Catholic church's index of forbidden books), the film inspired protests and was banned in Chile, Argentina, Mexico, Turkey, and Greece. It is still banned in Singapore and the Philippines. Blockbuster Video refused to carry the film. Bill Bright, founder of Campus Crusade for Christ, and producer of his own Jesus film, offered to purchase the film negative from Universal so that he could burn it. On October 22, 1998, fundamentalist Catholics set fire to the St. Michel theatre in Paris, injuring thirteen people and burning four; the theater remained closed for three years.

Scorsese's Jesus is unique. The drama in prior Jesus films was external to Jesus (in Judas, Jews, or Romans), but here the main drama is within Jesus himself. Screenwriter Paul Schrader notes, "The antagonist is God himself, who is in fact inside Jesus, or part of Jesus or Jesus himself."[15] Jesus faints, has visions, and hears voices. He is not sure if he is mentally ill or possessed. "Lucifer's inside me," he says. Although unconventional, these lines echo accusations in the gospels about Jesus being mentally ill and possessed (Mark 3:21–22). Jesus fights and resists God. He states, "God loves me, I know he loves me; I want him to stop." Schrader notes that for Jesus, "God was a vicious headache that would not go away." Jesus sees himself as a sinner, afraid, and proud. He builds crosses for the Romans, and helps them crucify fellow Jews, all in an effort to run from God. Jesus can be weak; he leans on Judas for support during the temple episode. Filming Jesus from above accents his humanness.[16]

Jesus' language and communication is distinct. He delivers the Sermon on the Mount in an impromptu manner, and it consists of extemporaneous comments in reply to questions and criticisms from his (very small, in contrast to most Jesus films) audience. Willem Dafoe (Jesus) notes that this sermon was not mythical at the time it occurred, but "became mythical later." His comment acknowledges how early church **kerygma** left its imprint on events recorded in the gospels, and the film demythologizes many of these episodes. Verbatim language from the gospels (e.g., "let him who is without sin cast the first stone") was often not used in order to maintain emotional authenticity. Similarly, this Jesus teaches with "stories," not "parables." Scorsese states that the use of New York accents (unlike British accents in most Jesus films) more fully engages viewers.

Jesus wrestles with whether he is (or wants to be) the Messiah, and what kind of Messiah he is (or wants to be). Uncertain about his mission and what God wants, he believes at first in love, then judgment (symbolized by the axe), and finally that he must die willingly on the cross. Like previous cinematic versions, Jesus promotes an individualistic spirituality. When Judas asks Jesus if he wants freedom for Israel, he replies, "No, I want freedom for the *soul*." For this Jesus, chains can be broken when one looks internally and breaks them with love. Previous cinematic Jesuses would concur.

Judas' portrayal is also unique. He is Jesus' most intimate friend; one night he holds Jesus as they sleep. His loyalty to Jesus runs so deep that he only betrays him because Jesus insists that he do so: "That's why God gave me the easier job—to be crucified."

The film's controversy centered on Jesus' temptations. While on the cross, an angel (in the form of a young girl) tells Jesus that he is not the Messiah, and that God does not want him to die. "Your father is the God of mercy, not punishment … If he saved Abraham's son, don't you think he'd want to save his own?" Jesus leaves the cross, marries (and has sex with) Magdalene, and (after she dies) he remarries, has children, raises a family, and grows old. On his deathbed, he is visited by his former disciples. Judas is outraged at Jesus:

> Your place was on the cross. That's where God put you. … You're a coward. … You broke my heart. Sometimes I curse the day I ever met you. … Remember what you told me? You took me in your arms, and you begged me, "Betray me, betray me. I have to be crucified so I can be resurrected and save the world." And I loved you so much, I went and betrayed you. And you … what are you doing here? What business do you have here with women, with children? What's good for man isn't good for God. Why weren't you crucified?

Judas informs Jesus that the angel who saved him is actually Satan. Judas adds, "If you die this way, you die like a man. You turn against God your father. There's no sacrifice, there's no salvation." Crawling out of bed, Jesus makes his way to a hill outside, and tearfully pleads with God (echoing language in Luke's "Prodigal Son" parable):

> Father, will you listen to me? Are you still there? Will you listen to a selfish and unfaithful son? I fought you when you called, I resisted, I thought I knew more, I didn't want to be your son. Can you forgive me? I didn't fight hard enough. Father, give me your hand. I want to bring salvation. Father, take me back, make a feast, welcome me home. I want to be your son, I want to pay the price, I want to be crucified and rise again. I want to be the Messiah.

Figures 4.2 and 4.3 Jesus begs God to let him be crucified in *The Last Temptation of Christ* (1988).

Jesus reappears on the cross. He smiles, utters, "It is accomplished. It is accomplished," and dies without a resurrection (unless his resurrection is his return to the cross). Mark's Jesus who laments God's abandonment becomes a Johannine Jesus who seeks his own death. It is unclear if the sequence of Jesus marrying, having children, and growing old is a hallucination while on the cross, or if it occurs outside Jesus' own mind. Scorsese and producer Jay Cocks affirm that it is the former.

Although the film illustrates the biblical claim that Jesus "has been tempted in every way" (Hebrews 4:15), these were not temptations many Christians wanted to see. Nor were Christians mollified by the film's opening explanation ("This film is not based upon the Gospels but upon this fictional exploration of the eternal spiritual conflict"). Scorsese notes, "Ultimately the last temptation is about living life quietly as a human being, raising a family, having the joys and the sorrows in life of a human being, and part of that includes sexuality … But that wasn't the last temptation. The last temptation was to be a human being." Cocks adds, "The ultimate temptation for God could be the beauty of the life that we all take for granted."

Viewing Jesus as human influenced his physical appearance. Scorsese comments, "Jesus was poor. We didn't want to have the Jesus of the old epic films who came in a beautiful immaculate white robe and when he walked in a room everybody turned their heads because his head was glowing. The idea of this Jesus was a guy you'd meet on the street, on the road, he'd be first a human being." Roger Ebert summarizes the film's reception:

> The astonishing controversy that has raged around this film is primarily the work of fundamentalists who have their own view of Christ and are offended by a film that they feel questions his divinity. But in the father's house are many mansions, and there is more than one way to consider the story of Christ—why else are there four Gospels? Among those who do not already have rigid views on the subject, this film is likely to inspire more serious thought on the nature of Jesus than any other ever made .... They have paid Christ the compliment of taking him and his message seriously, and they have made a film that does not turn him into a garish, emasculated image from a religious postcard. Here he is flesh and blood, struggling, questioning, asking himself and his father which is the right way, and finally, after great suffering, earning the right to say, on the cross, "It is accomplished." I cannot think of another film on a religious subject that has challenged me more fully. The film has offended those whose ideas about God and man it does not reflect. But then, so did Jesus.[17]

MEL GIBSON'S *PASSION*

Gibson's *The Passion of the Christ* (2004) resurrected studio interest in the financial viability of Bible films. As of 2021, it still holds the gross domestic box office record ($370,782,930) for an "R" rated film. Like Scorsese's *Last Temptation*, it sparked controversy, but for different reasons; its detractors claimed it was antisemitic, pornographically violent, and that its view of atonement was too soaked in blood.

An opening quote signals the film's Christological vision: "He was wounded for our transgressions, crushed for our iniquities; by His wounds we are healed (Isaiah 53)." *The Last Temptation of Christ* and *Jesus of Nazareth* both cite a part of this same chapter, but the Christological (if not the soteriological) visions of the two films are starkly divergent. If Mark's gospel is a passion narrative with a long introduction, Gibson's film is a passion narrative with no introduction at all.

Christ (like Scorsese, Gibson uses this term rather than "Jesus") is wounded mercilessly and crushed repeatedly, more than earning its "R" rating. Such relentless physical torture is, for Gibson, the source of redemption and salvation. This gory soteriology appears in many other Gibson films. Protagonists in *Braveheart*, *Lethal Weapon*, and *Apocalypto* are bruised, bloodied, and tortured, and this interminable agony is intrinsically redemptive. It is a soteriology of masochism; suffering saves. Satan's comments to Jesus in the opening scene ("Do you really believe one man can bear the full burden of sin? … No man can carry this burden … Saving their souls is too costly") illustrate this view of torture as salvific.

Gibson's film is unique in using only Aramaic, Latin, and Hebrew (disproving Paul Schrader's claim that one could not make a Jesus film in Aramaic). Utilizing these languages reflects an effort to grasp the historical Jesus behind the gospels (which are in Greek) as well as provide a certain cinematic realism.

The film uses extensive material from post-biblical sources, the most significant of which is Anne Catherine Emmerich's *The Dolorous Passion*. Many elements derive from Emmerich: Satan's remarks to Jesus in Gethsemane, soldiers throwing Jesus over a bridge, Peter's confession of his betrayal to Jesus' mother, Satan's taunting of Judas, Judas being followed by devils, Veronica's veil (also in Ray's *King of Kings*), the prominence of Mary (Jesus' mother) and Satan, and Jesus' captivity in a subterranean dungeon. Some lines ("let this *chalice* pass from me!") are from Emmerich. Many Christians did not take offense to the film's license with these extrabiblical sources (as they did with *Noah*); they did not regard such additions as perversions since the film conformed to—and confirmed—their beliefs.

Gibson's use of Emmerich illuminates many of his choices. Emmerich views Jesus' death as offering satisfaction to God for the sins of humankind, she repeatedly emphasizes Jesus' intense suffering (claiming he was beaten so severely that his mother would not recognize him), she maligns the Pharisees ("No Pharisee, however wily and severe, could have surpassed Satan on this occasion"), she makes the Pharisees omnipresent in Jesus' passion, and she has nothing good to say about the Jews. She describes the Jews sacrificing their children to idols, and calls Jewish priests "priests of Satan." If anything lends credence to the charge that the film is antisemitic, it is Gibson's uncritical embrace of this source that is overtly and consistently anti-Jewish.

The Pharisees' role in the last night of Jesus' life is enhanced beyond what the gospels indicate. The gospels of Mark and Luke do not mention the Pharisees in the passion narrative (Matthew and John mention them once), but in the film Pilate is told that the "Pharisees hate" Jesus. Jesus' foremost enemies in the film are, however, not the Jews but the Roman guards, whose sadism is unleashed at inhumane levels. One or two Jewish council members object to the proceedings against Jesus. While Jesus carries his cross, some Jews come to his aid and defense. Unlike *Superstar* and *Last Temptation*, Judas is viewed with no empathy whatsoever.

Mary, Jesus' mother, is present for most of Jesus' suffering, and she rushes to his aid when he collapses under the weight of the cross. A flashback shows her helping him when he was a young child. With the possible exception of God, Mary is Jesus' most significant relational connection. Upon seeing her, he stands back up after being whipped; she is a source of strength and comfort.

Satan's pervasive presence is also due to Emmerich's influence. Satan's gender in the film is unclear, but Rosalinda Celentano plays the role, and this Satan has androgynous, if not stereotypical feminine, features. Satan's primary task is (as in *Last Temptation*) to convince Jesus to avoid suffering. But Satan's presence among the Roman guards indicates support for Jesus' torture. Satan adopts animalistic forms (as in Emmerich), which explains the serpent on the ground in the garden, and some of the other monstrous apparitions. Satan is in the crowd as Jesus carries the cross, and Satan and Mary look directly at each other. Satan taunts Judas. Satan's omnipresence points to the passion's cosmic scale; Satan's screams after Jesus' death confirm the cosmic scope and the redemptive and sacrificial nature of Jesus' death.

The cosmic scope of Jesus' death is confirmed at the end. Divine vindication appears in several forms: a crow pecking out the eye of the criminal who taunted Jesus; a drop from the sky (rain or God's tear?) after Jesus' death; a storm and earthquake; and the temple (not just the curtain) fracturing and opening up, possibly signifying its destruction. As the stone is rolled away from the tomb, an alive Jesus stands up and, with a hole in his hand, walks out. As in Mark, the resurrection is muted, but Gibson's sequel (*Passion of the Christ: Resurrection*) will likely compensate for this.

Jesus' principal activity throughout the film is enduring suffering. There is minimal focus on his teaching (appropriate given the film's scope), and most of this appears in notably serene flashbacks: "Love your enemies," "I am the good shepherd. I lay down my life for the sheep. No one takes it from me," "You are my friends … No greater love than to lay down one's life … Love one another, as I have loved you … I am the Way, the Truth, and the Life." These teachings emphasize both Jesus' own person and his enactment in the passion of his teachings.

AN AFRICAN JESUS

Son of Man (Dornford-May, 2006) is a South African film set in contemporary and fictional "Judea, Afrika," with an entirely Black, African cast. The Xhosa language and African choirs provide a constant aural reminder of this crucial African cultural context. The temptation, which opens the film, coincides with a rite of passage to manhood: white chalk is painted on mens' bodies before they depart to the desert. Depicting Jesus as a contemporary African underscores his non-Western and non-white identity. The color and culture of this Jesus is a radical departure from previous cinematic fare.

Armed conflict forms the backdrop for Jesus' story; military forces invade settlements, and there are clashes between Herod's militia and insurgents. Child soldiers wield and use machine guns. Transposing the 1st-century Roman military occupation and oppression of Jews into a contemporary setting makes palpable the brutality of military occupation. The armed conflict is the setting for the Annunciation and Magnificat. Jesus' mother receives the news that she will give birth to the Son of God while hiding in a school, surrounded by corpses of children. Machine gun fire accompanies her singing of the Magnificat: "He has brought down the mighty and exalted those of low degree, He has filled the hungry with good things and the rich he has sent away empty" (Luke 1:52–3). The Magnificat's socio-economic emphasis, ignored in most Jesus epics, is front and center in *Son of Man*.

Jesus' nonviolence is all the more significant within this militarized context. Many of his disciples are members of an insurgency who fight the military. Jesus tells these modern Zealots that he is "committed to nonviolent change … we don't need weapons to fight this battle." Jesus invites his followers (one of whom is a former child soldier) to turn in their guns. During a standoff with military forces, Jesus tells a follower to put down a rock he is about to throw.

As in the synoptic gospels, much of Jesus' teaching addresses socioeconomic matters. He is one of many political resisters trying to effect social change. "Unrest," he says, "is due to poverty, overcrowding and lack of education." People must "fight poverty, epidemics and thuggery" since "each human life is important." His teaching is explicitly political: "When those with imperial histories pretend to forget them, and blame Africa's problems on tribalism and corruption while building themselves new economic empires, I say we have been lied to." Jesus denounces as evil beating and torture in the Middle East, Asian child labor, and European and US politicians using trade subsidies and commercial patents to restrict supplies of medicine to Africa. Jesus calls his disciples "comrades." Jesus' ethics are social, not individualistic; he seeks social justice, not personal happiness. This Jesus echoes South African anti-apartheid activist Steve Biko.

Jesus' teaching transposes biblical texts in contemporary parlance: "I'm not here to destroy beliefs and traditions, but create them anew" (cf. Matthew 5:17–19); "we must forgive those who offend us and those who trample on our comrades. Otherwise our hatred will destroy our future" (cf. Matthew 5:43–48). This African Jesus rebukes Paul's contention that all authorities "have been instituted by God" (Romans 13:1), insisting to the contrary, "All authority is not divinely instituted."

Reflecting an African sacramental spirituality, boundaries between the sacred and secular are porous. The interweaving of the natural and spiritual realms is evident in the frequent appearances of Satan and angels (the latter appear as children). In the Temptation, Jesus tells Satan (a man with a serpent tattoo on his left cheek), "Get thee behind me, Satan, this is my world." Satan's reply ("No, this is *my* world") sets the stage for a cosmic duel akin to Gibson's *Passion*. Satan (often accompanied by electronic buzzing) is linked to Herod's massacre of young boys, and Satan visits Jesus' childhood home where a child angel stands guard. Satan lurks in the crowd when a woman caught in adultery is doused with gasoline, about to be set on fire, and Satan is present while Jesus is beaten and killed.

As in *Godspell*, several of Jesus' disciples are women; their names (Simone, Phillippa, Thaddea) are adapted from male disciples in the gospels. Women are the main protestors against the military's brutality. After Jesus is killed, they encircle a building where a military leader is holding a press conference, pound on the windows, and hold up pictures of Jesus. At another protest they hold up pictures of Jesus and repeat the refrain, "They rule by guns. They are killing our youth!" Women wail in protest outside government headquarters: "Stop killing our children!" With their lament, women unveil the unjust and wanton violence wielded by those in power.

Jesus' death is primarily a political, not theological, matter. A local faction wants peace with the military occupiers, but Jesus is critical of the false hope this gives the people. His rebuke of those who want to form an interim government with the coalition forces increases the wrath of his enemies. Those who capture and beat Jesus tell him, "Join us, we can share power." His refusal seals his fate. He is beaten, loaded into the back of a car, carried to a field and dumped in a hole. The manner of Jesus' death draws attention to the many clues in the gospels (torture, trial, humiliation, betrayal, bribery, etc.) that portray Jesus' death as a political affair.

The film reconfigures Jesus' death as a secret event that his followers transform into a public protest. After a centurion figure

Figures 4.4 and 4.5   Mary cradles the body of Jesus in a pietà, and confronts the military in *Son of Man* (2006).

(nicknamed "Hundred") informs Mary about the fate of her son, she digs up Jesus' body. In the back of a truck, she cradles Jesus' corpse in a pietà pose. Jesus' followers tie his corpse to a cross, elevating him in the early morning for the residents of the shanty town to see. People stream to the cross and stand in reverence. Mary sings, "The land is covered in darkness," and the onlookers echo this refrain. Dancing and singing on a raised platform, she declares, "Comrades, unite! Unite, freedom fighters! Strength, comrades!" Armed soldiers storm the platform. Many in the crowd flee, but those on the platform remain. Soldiers fire over the crowd. Mary stands, faces the soldiers, and advances toward them, followed by those behind her. She chants, "The land is covered in darkness" and those behind her join in her chanting and dancing.

Mary's refrain reconfigures Mark 15:33 ("darkness came over the whole land"), which occurs immediately before Jesus cries out in a loud voice, "My God, my God, why have you abandoned me?" Mary is now the one crying out in a loud voice, and Jesus' theological lament has become her sociopolitical lament, an indictment of the military's brutalization of the poor and oppressed. Another intertextual parallel is Amos 8:90–10, which links the darkening of "the earth in broad daylight" and "mourning for an only son." Mary articulates Amos' lamentation. The public display of Jesus' corpse and Mary's chanting and dancing blends prophetic, apocalyptic, and lament to shame those in power. As a political resister, Mary remains faithful to her Magnificat. Exhibiting Jesus' body on the cross reflects more of a Catholic sensibility than the Protestant preference for a corpseless cross.

The resurrection is muted. Shadows of the child angels gather and sing. In slow motion, Jesus walks up a hill, holding a child angel's hand, and followed by scores of angels. As he walks up the hill toward the (now) empty cross, he raises his arm triumphantly into the air, and the film ends.

Many episodes (raising Lazarus, healing a possessed girl) are viewed through videotape footage. Judas secretly films Jesus on a video camera he will hand over to authorities, and he films himself kissing Jesus on the cheek. The audience views Jesus' initial capture (being beaten and kicked) via video footage. Miracles, as in Mark, are somewhat muted, but Peter paints two miracles in the form of public murals. After Jesus' death, a series of murals depicts moments from Jesus' life (miracles, preaching, hanging on the cross). The word may have become human, but it is spread through the image.

The murals and video footage highlight the importance of different modes of viewing, and the key function of the image as a vehicle and translator of meaning. *Son of Man* itself is one of these same vehicles, and like the video footage, it too translates the Jesus story. This process is not unlike the gospels which function like the video footage in giving access to Jesus not directly, but through a grainy lens that translates Jesus through the interpretive filter of the one telling the story.

The closing credit sequence solidifies the power of image and the film's contemporary African context. A young child is paired with the quote "And God said, 'Let us make man in our image, after our likeness" (Gen 1:26). Images of contemporary Africans in shantytowns appear; some are elderly, most are children. The final shot is of an African township and a rainbow. Jesus' life and teachings have social, political, and economic implications for contemporary Africans. Unlike the Jesus epics which *de*politicize Jesus, *Son of Man* accents, like the synoptic gospels, the politics of Jesus.

A JUNGIAN YESHUA

Rodrigo García's *Last Days in the Desert* (2015) offers a psychological profile of Jesus by reimagining the temptation narrative (Mark 1:13; Matthew 4:1–11; Luke 4:1–13). Ewan McGregor plays both Yeshua (acknowledging Jesus' Jewishness) and the tempter (never called Satan or the Devil). Yeshua is a "holy man" who is in the desert to "pray and reflect, to look inward, to find myself," and the tempter's mirror image suggests that he is—at some level—part of Yeshua himself. Although this Jungian perspective of one's shadow side departs from traditional depictions of the temptation, it illustrates Jesus' teaching that evil comes from within oneself, and that nothing outside a person can defile them (Mark 7:14–23).

Rather than the three temptations in Matthew and Luke, the tempter questions Yeshua's understanding of God, his father. After praying alone in the desert ("Father, where are you? … Father, speak to me"), the tempter declares, "Talking to your father is like talking to a rock. So busy with his little things … Everything matters more to him than you." "No, my father loves me," Yeshua claims. But the tempter laughs, remarking, "He's amused by you. He loves himself only." When Yeshua gets angry, the tempter responds, "Oh, what anger! You are your Father's son." The tempter challenges Yeshua's sense of self-importance (messianic consciousness?): "You think

Figure 4.6 Yeshua and the tempter confront one another in *Last Days in the Desert* (2015).

you're his only child?," he asks, adding, "There are others." "No," Yeshua replies, "there is only me, there is only me." The tempter claims that God has recreated the world multiple times. "What a self-centered, self-indulgent creature he is, isn't he? ... These things he expects of you—do you think anyone will care? Men of a thousand years from now?"

The film gives more psychological insight to the tempter than any other Jesus film. The tempter complains, "Nothing is interesting anymore ... The repetitiveness, the obstinate, dull repetitiveness of your Father's plan is bewildering to me. The same lives lived over and over and over again. Is there a plan?" The tempter identifies curiosity as his own weakness. He indicates that in hell he forces people to "watch the life they've lived over and over again. Forever." When Yeshua reminds the tempter of his pride, the tempter retorts, "I am not proud, I am not proud. *He's* the proud one."

The plot centers on Yeshua befriending a family living in the desert. A father (whose wife is suffering from an illness) is building a house for his son. The son, however, has no interest in living in the desert like his father; he longs to go to Jerusalem, but he lacks the courage to tell his father. The mother wants the son to learn a trade, but the father claims he cannot afford such an apprenticeship. The tempter promises Yeshua that if he can solve the family dilemma, he will leave him alone. Yeshua helps the father build the house, and serves as a therapist of sorts in mending familial tensions. After the father dies in a freak accident, the son and Yeshua decide to leave the desert. Foreshadowing the cross, the tempter tells Yeshua, "I'll come to you in the end, and if you give me a sign I'll help you down, and you can stay." We cut to Jesus hanging on the cross where a hummingbird appears in front of him. That night his body is placed in a cave covered with stones. Women wait outside. The final scene cuts to the same desert in the modern world, and two visitors in modern clothing take a photograph.

The desert is Yeshua's formative experience. The father tells Yeshua that the desert is "ruthless—it strips you of your vanities, your illusions, it gives you the opportunity to see yourself for who you are." Yeshua consciously absorbs lessons in the desert that he intends to take with him (e.g., "Actions over words, always. Otherwise, silence"). The cut to the cross at the end might imply that what Yeshua learns in the desert culminates in (or leads him to) death on the cross.

Considering the three family members (none of whom have personal names) as symbols (the father as God, the son as Jesus, the mother as Mary) offers intriguing insights: Jesus struggles to become his own man (and not succumb to the wishes of God his father), God is a father who loves his son, but fails to communicate that love effectively, Jesus feels he is a disappointment to his father, and God's death ultimately frees Jesus to pursue his own path. Viewing the film this way illuminates several lines: when the son says he can feel conceited when it seems his existence will never end; when he yells, "I'm not a bad son" for wanting to leave the desert; when Yeshua tells the boy (himself?), "You are a good son;" and when the mother tells her dead husband/God, "Your son loves you, your son loves you." The dad's/God's remark about his son/Jesus ("He's the best boy in the world—too good perhaps") is telling. When the father is about to die, he puts his hand on Yeshua's face, whispers to him, and looks at him lovingly, all of which can be viewed as God's final effort to convey God's love to Jesus. Another implication of this metaphor is that God wants Yeshua to remain in the desert, away from Jerusalem (and death), and it is Jesus who proceeds of his own volition toward death (like the son who says, "Wasting life is a sin. I want to leave my footprint in the world").

SUMMARY

Like the gospels, Jesus films interpret Jesus. Most Jesus films omit material that might portray Jesus negatively (cursing a fig tree; sending demons into pigs who drown; making a racist comment to the Syrophoenician woman; telling his disciples to go nowhere among the Gentiles). Jesus films make little use of Mark's unique material (e.g., the naked man who runs away at Jesus' arrest, Jesus calling the temple a house of prayer *"for all the nations,"* both criminals mocking Jesus on the cross, and Mark's "non-resurrected" Jesus). Films with beatitudes use Matthew's ("Blessed are the poor *in spirit*"), not Luke's ("Blessed are the poor/Woe to you rich"). If there is a Lord's Prayer, it is Matthew's, not Luke's. Most films offer a Jesus more associated with wisdom than **apocalyptic**. By excluding such material, Jesus films operate like the gospels (and invite us to consider how the gospels function like Jesus films), which present distinctive views of Jesus that reflect the author's perspective. Since Pasolini, a number of Jesus films have revolutionized the Jesus film genre. Such films, while not avoiding theological and Christological concerns, display a keener interest in Jesus' psychology, sexuality, and politics. Film critic Roger Ebert notes, "There is no single version of Christ's story. It acts as a template into which we fit our ideas, and we see it as our lives have prepared us for it."[8]

NOTES

1 *Intolerance* DVD special features.
2 *The King of Kings* DVD special features.
3 *The King of Kings* DVD special features.
4 *The King of Kings* DVD special features.
5 See Walsh (2003).
6 Cited in Testa (1994), 185.
7 Ebert (2005), 169–70.
8 Scorsese (1996), 136.
9 Pasolini (1989), 63.
10 Zwick (2012), 104.
11 Ranzato (2014).
12 Walsh (2003) offers a thoughtful analysis of *Godspell*.
13 Bultmann (1951), 33.

14 *The Last Temptation of Christ* DVD Commentary.
15 Unless otherwise indicated, all quotations from Scorsese, Schrader, and Cocks are from *The Last Temptation of Christ* DVD commentary. Schrader's original script was reworked by Scorsese and Cocks.
16 Walsh (2003).
17 Ebert (1988).
18 Ebert (2005), 173.

FOR FURTHER READING

Adele Reinhartz, *Jesus of Hollywood* (New York: Oxford University Press, 2007).

David J. Shepherd, *The Silents of Jesus in the Cinema (1897–1927)* (New York and London: Routledge, 2016).

Jeffrey L. Staley, "The First Seventy Years of Jesus Films: A Canonical, Source-Critical History." *T&T Clark Companion to the Bible and Film*, ed. Richard Walsh (London: Bloomsbury, 2018).

W. Barnes Tatum, *Jesus at the Movies: A Guide to the First Hundred Years* (Santa Rosa, CA: Polebridge Press, 2004; revised ed.).

Richard Walsh, *Reading the Gospels in the Dark: Portrayals of Jesus in Film* (Harrisburg, PA: Trinity Press International. 2003).

Richard Walsh, *T&T Clark Handbook of Jesus and Film* (London/New York: T&T Clark, 2021).

Richard Walsh and Jeffrey L. Staley, *Jesus, the Gospels, and Cinematic Imagination: Introducing Jesus Movies, Christ Films, and the Messiah in Motion* (London/New York: T&T Clark, 2021).

Richard Walsh, Jeffrey L. Staley, and Adele Reinhartz (eds.) *Son of Man: An African Jesus Film* (Sheffied: Sheffield Phoenix, 2013).

REIMAGINING JESUS FIGURES

Jesus can be on screen even when he is not on the screen. A long tradition exists of cinematic characters who function as Jesus (or Christ) figures. An early treatment of the subject was André Bazin's essay on Bresson's film *Diary of a Country Priest* (1951). General tropes are associated with these figurative characters: an outsider enters an (often divisive) community, acting as an agent of healing, reconciliation, or justice; authorities persecute this character; the character is either punished, exiled, or killed; finally, there is a type of resurrection, and sometimes an ascension. Additional tropes can include gathering a small group of followers; betrayal by a follower; responding to violence with nonviolence; sacrificing one's life for others; and dying in a cruciform position. In *Gran Torino* (Eastwood, 2008), Walt Kowalski dies willingly and nonviolently in order to save his neighbors, and does so with arms extended horizontally in a cruciform position.

Films with classic Jesus figures include *I Confess* (Hitchcock, 1953), *The Fugitive* (Ford, 1947), *Shane* (Stevens, 1953), *Cool Hand Luke* (Rosenberg, 1967), *Tommy* (Russell, 1975), and *One Flew Over the Cuckoo's Nest* (Forman, 1975). Some Jesus figures such as Aslan in *The Chronicles of Narnia: The Lion, The Witch, and the Wardrobe* (Adamson, 2005) are more obvious than others. Other Jesus figures are less overt. *E. T.* (Spielberg, 1982) features a non-human who descends to Earth from the heavens, seeks to heal and do good, develops a small group of devoted followers, is persecuted and captured by authorities, dies, rises from the dead, and, after comforting his followers, ascends back into the heavens. The titular character in *The Iron Giant* (Bird, 1999) follows a similar trajectory, is committed to nonviolence, and sacrifices his life for others. *Big Hero 6* (Hall and Williams, 2014) follows some of these same trends.

A danger exists of finding Jesus figures everywhere one looks.[1] Does a willing acceptance of death, as in *The Passion of Joan of Arc* (Dreyer, 1928), suffice to constitute a Jesus figure? Is Obi-Wan Kenobi in *Star Wars: A Last Hope* (Lucas, 1977) a legitimate Jesus figure because he dies willingly (by laying down his lightsaber and allowing Darth Vader to strike him down), and later rises from the dead as a spirit with the ability to appear and speak to Luke Skywalker? Is Harry Potter a Jesus figure simply because he chooses to embrace death in order to save others (as his mother Lily did) and then returns from death? Jesus figures often exist in the eyes of their beholders. Such beholders can too easily impose foreign meanings on a film not intrinsic to the film itself. Richard Walsh helpfully proposes using a film's own context as the primary matrix for analyzing the function of a Christ-figure within that film.[2] After discussing three traditional Jesus figures, this chapter examines three unusual Jesus figures, characters who both conform to and subvert the Jesus figure typology.

TRADITIONAL JESUS (OR "CHRIST") FIGURES

THE GREEN MILE: A BLACK JESUS FIGURE

John Coffey is a Black Jesus figure in *The Green Mile* (Darabont, 1999), a film based on Stephen King's six novellas. Arrested for raping and killing two young girls, Coffey and sent to death row to die. Despite his tremendous power, Coffey is (generally) nonviolent, and despite being innocent, he is executed by the state. At his execution the parents of the two girls mock and taunt him. Although he utters it as an expletive, death row commanding officer Paul Edgecomb's comment, "Jesus, Jesus," immediately after Coffey is shown cradling the two dead girls, is the first hint of Coffey's function as a Jesus figure. Coffey has miraculous healing abilities; after healing someone, he absorbs the sickness into his own body, and then expels it. He brings a mouse back from the dead, and while doing so a prison guard exclaims, "Oh, dear Jesus." His acute empathy leads him to endure excruciating physical pain when another inmate is electrocuted. On the night of his own execution, he comforts the prison guards who will kill him. While watching the film *Top Hat* (Sandrich, 1935) in prison, the projector creates an angelic halo over Coffey's head. After recognizing some of the parallels between this character and Jesus, King stated that he changed his name from John Bowes to John Coffey so that he would have the initials J. C.[3]

Although one man calls Coffey "meek," and Edgecomb says that there "doesn't seem to be any real violence in him," Coffey is indirectly responsible for the killing of the man who raped and murdered the girls, and the institutionalization of a sadistic prison guard. This Jesus figure is thus a vessel of mercy and judgment. After Coffey gives Paul a vision enabling him to see the true killer of the two girls, Paul asks Coffey if he would like to be freed. Coffey, however, prefers to die, saying he is "tired of people being ugly to each other" and "tired of all the pain I feel and hear in the world every day." He says the pain is like "pieces of glass in his head all the time." Like John's Jesus, Coffey goes willingly to his death. He lays down his life, not for others, but to soothe himself and end the immense pain brought about by his extreme empathy.

Paul's complicity in Coffey's execution makes him feel, for the first time in his life, that he is doing something that might cause him to go to hell. For the role he plays in executing Coffey, Paul is cursed with not dying, being forced to grow old, and watch every person

Figure 5.1 John Coffey as a Jesus figure in *The Green Mile* (1999).

he has ever loved die; he calls this his "atonement" and his "punishment" for "killing a miracle of God." Paul perhaps plays the role of a Pilate-like figure, facilitating the death of God's miracle. The film's disturbing depiction of the brutal and ghastly nature of execution (via the electric chair) invites viewers to consider the brutality of Jesus' execution. *The Green Mile* illustrates a central invitation of James Cone's *The Cross and the Lynching Tree*, to consider lynchings in the American south as crucifixions, and Jesus' crucifixion as a lynching.

THE MATRIX: A SCIENCE FICTION JESUS FIGURE

In *The Matrix* (Wachowskis, 1999), the main character Neo is a long awaited messianic figure whose coming has been prophesied. His death is predicted in the film's opening scene. In his first interaction with another person in the film, he is told, "Hallelujah. You're my savior, man. My own personal Jesus Christ." Morpheus, a John the Baptist figure, believes wholeheartedly that Neo is "the One," the savior who will deliver humanity from slavery to the machines. He and Trinity (a name with significance) help rescue Neo from the matrix, a process involving a full immersion in water, symbolizing a baptism. The second film in the trilogy shows that Neo can heal people from illness and disease by touching them.

Neo's most blatant parallel with Jesus is his death at the end of the film, a death resulting from his choice to sacrifice himself to try to save Morpheus. After dying he is raised from the dead, and—in the film's final scene—ascends into the sky. Neo's function as a Jesus figure is made even more obvious in the third film in the trilogy when he offers his life as a sacrifice to bring peace between the warring humans and machines. This third film concludes with an image of him entering the lair of the machines in a cruciform position. The Wachowskis are working on a fourth film in the series which will presumably involve yet another resurrection for Neo.

The film's commitment to Neo as a Jesus figure runs deep. When Cypher meets Neo, he asks him, "So you're here to save the world?" Cypher is a Judas figure who ends up betraying Neo, Morpheus, and the other members of their band. Zion, a name for Israel, is where the humans live who are free from the Matrix. Morpheus' ship is called the Nebuchadnezzar, the name of an ancient Babylonian king who conquered Jerusalem and destroyed the Jewish temple. A plaque on his ship is marked "Mark 3:11," a reference to this verse in Mark's gospel: "And whenever those possessed by evil spirits caught sight of him, they would fall down in front of him shrieking, 'You are the Son of God!'" This verse raises a key concern in the film, whether or not Neo is the "One," the messiah who will deliver the humans. Agent Smith, who leads the machines' effort to destroy Morpheus' group, never calls Neo "Neo," and insists on calling him "Mr. Anderson," (his given name is Thomas Anderson). "Anderson" literally means "Son of Man," which is Jesus' preferred title for himself in the synoptic gospels. The film thus inverts the pattern in the gospels. Jesus prefers the designation "Son of Man," and no one else in the gospels calls him this, whereas in the film, it is Neo's chief opponent (and no one else) who insists on calling him Son of Man ("Mr. Anderson"). The many parallels between Neo and Jesus raise a host of questions: what to make of a violent Jesus figure who machine guns hundreds of his enemies? Is this an apocalyptic savior figure? Does the film promote a **gnostic** religion in which salvation is available to the select few who are granted saving knowledge?

What raises Neo from the dead at the end of the first film is a kiss from Trinity, who also declares her (romantic) love for Neo once he dies. She reveals that she was told by the Oracle that she would fall in love with someone, and that that person would be the "One." Since she is in love with Neo, she is convinced that he is the One. The film opens with an off-screen conversation in which Cypher asks Trinity if she likes Neo. After saying "we're gonna kill him," Cypher notes that Morpheus believes Neo is the "One," and he asks Trinity if she believes the same. She replies, "It doesn't matter what I believe." Morpheus believes that Neo is the One, and this belief helps catapult Neo towards becoming the One, but it is ultimately insufficient to propel him to become the One. What catalyzes his transformation into the "One" is Trinity's love. The film emphasizes the power of belief and love, but argues that love is ultimately more potent than belief in catalyzing Neo to become the "One." The proposal that love triumphs over belief echoes Paul's claim that among faith, hope, and love, "the greatest of these is love" (1 Corinthians 13:13).

JESUS OF MONTREAL: A FRENCH-CANADIAN JESUS FIGURE

Denys Arcand's *Jésus de Montréal* (1989) is a creative modernization of the Jesus story. Daniel, an actor, is hired by a Catholic parish to revitalize their annual passion play. The film focuses both on the portrayal of Jesus in this play, and on the many parallels that develop between Daniel's own life and that of Jesus in the gospels. When Daniel is asked by a fellow actor what his next part is going to be, he says, "Jesus." This reply points to both of these dual layers: Daniel acts as Jesus in the passion play, and becomes more like Jesus in his own life.

Daniel's passion play represents a rejection of classic Jesus films. Like these films, the Church's former passion plays were over(t)ly pietistic and melodramatic. Daniel tells his fellow actors during rehearsal, "Tone it down," rejecting the melodrama that characterizes biblical epics. The Coen brothers' *Hail Caesar* (2016) also pokes fun at the melodramatic and emotional artificiality of the Jesus (and biblical) epic.

The passion play Daniel organizes is based on the gospels and academic scholarship. Both of these prove controversial and upsetting to the Catholic priest who hired Daniel. The play introduces Jesus as "the Jewish prophet, Yeshua ben Panthera whom we call Jesus." This repeats the claim in the Talmud (and Celsus) that Jesus' mother was raped by a Roman soldier. Actors note that first century authors Tacitus, Suetonius, Pliny, and Josephus mention Jesus "only in passing." They convey the scholarly recognition that not everything in the gospels is fact, and that the authors of the gospels may have had motives to change certain facts about the historical Jesus. The play is in some sense an attempt to portray the historical Jesus behind the gospels. The actors convey insights from gospel scholarship: "Paradoxically, Jesus wasn't Christian but Jewish. He was circumcised and observed Jewish law … He thought that the end was nigh." Actors explain the cultural context of crucifixion:

> There were crucifixions every week in Jerusalem. This one was nothing special …
>
> Crucifixions began six centuries before Christ. It was progress of sorts. The Assyrians had favored impaling. In Babylon, Darius, king of Persia, crucified 3,000 opponents. After the siege of Tyre, 2,000

> soldiers were crucified. 80 years before Jesus, King Alexander of Judea crucified 800 Pharisees. After the revolt led by Spartacus, 7,000 were crucified along the Appian Way leading to Rome. Death posts were permanent fixtures in public places. Quintilian wanted them on busy roads as an incentive to public morality.

The passion play contextualizes Jesus' miracles, noting the existence of 1st-century "prophets, charlatans, [and] magicians" such as Judas of Galilee, Theudas, and the Egyptian, Simon the Magician.

Jesus' preaching in the passion play focuses on personal ethics. Several quotes, not all, are from the Sermon on the Mount: "Do not worry … Do not resist evil. If anyone sues you, give your cloak as well … It will be hard for those who have riches to enter God's kingdom. For where your treasure is there will your heart also be … If you love those who love you what merit have you? Do good to those who hate you … When you make a feast invite the poor, the maimed, the lame, the blind … Judge not lest you be judged." On one occasion, he speaks some lines directly to Catholic priests in attendance: "Whoever would be high among you, let him be your servant. Whoever will be chief among you, let him be your slave … Do not be called Rabbi or Reverend Father or Your Grace or Your Eminence, for one is your Master who is in heaven, and you are all brothers." When Jesus is called "Christ the Messiah," he replies—as in the synoptics—with a secrecy command ("Never speak of me to others. Never say I am the Christ. I am the son of Man"). Even though it is staged, the crucifixion is more brutal than in many Jesus films. Jesus is stripped naked by a Roman guard, and placed nude on a cross. He utters, "Forsaken." As an actor tells the crowd, "Crucifixion was so horrifying early Christians never depicted it."

Daniel's parallels with Jesus are significant. The film opens with a play, an adaptation of Dostoevsky's *Brothers Karamazov*. As in Mark, the film's opening lines by the actors in the play ("You killed him," "No, you did") foreshadow Daniel's future death, and uncertainty about who is responsible for it. A line ("doing tragedy is danger-ous") spoken at the film's beginning and end captures the tragic nature of Mark's gospel and the ominous ending awaiting Daniel. The main actor in this opening play represents John the Baptist; a woman audience member fawns over him, declaring, "I want his head" (alluding to John's decapitation) for her ad campaign. She is told that he doesn't do ads (like the Baptist, he is pure). Though people praise his acting, he—like John in the gospels—points to Daniel as the greater actor.

The actors Daniel recruits for the passion play symbolize his disciples; they are "sinners" (a voiceover actor for porn films, a narrator for a Big Bang documentary, a fashion model). Like the Son of Man who has nowhere to lay his head (Luke 9:58), Daniel stays with Constance who, like the women in Luke 8:1–3, provide for Jesus financially. The first performance of the passion play draws criticism from the Catholic priest who symbolizes Jesus' religious opponents. The excitement of Daniel's fellow actors after their first performance—and their interest in new professional opportunities—mirrors the disciples' interest in prestige, position, and power (Mark 8:31–37; 9:33–37; 10:35–45). Daniel quickly becomes the talk of the town, but peoples' ideas about him and his origins—as with Jesus in the gospels—are divergent and contradictory. Daniel's "violent Temple episode" occurs at Mireille's audition for a beer commercial. Outraged at the sexist and exploitative treatment of women, and of Mireille in particular, he throws over a table, destroys tech equipment, and slaps a casting director. The film reconfigures the sin Jesus denounces as the advertising/entertainment industry's exploitation of women. Temptation by the devil appears in the form of an entertainment lawyer who promises Daniel fortune and fame.

Daniel's own passion sequence begins when a fight breaks out during a performance of the passion play and the cross on which he hangs is knocked to the ground. He is taken to a hospital (St. Mark's), accompanied—as in the gospels—only by women. Daniel leaves the overcrowded and disorganized hospital after feeling slightly better, and—while in a state of delirium—he delivers the apocalyptic discourse (Mark 13/Matt 24/Luke 21). This is one of only a few "Jesus films" with the apocalyptic discourse, and its presentation as a possible case of delusion or madness suggests Arcand might view this discourse in the synoptics similarly (apocalypticism as illness). It is unclear if Daniel here is repeating lines from the play or speaking them "on his own." He and his Jesus character seem to have merged into one. After seeing John the Baptist's head on an advertising poster (and the selling out this represents?), Daniel vomits. His sickness declines rapidly, and this time the women take Daniel to a Jewish hospital; although it is more professional than St. Mark's, Daniel dies. Lying in a cruciform pose on the operating table, his body is prepped for surgery to extract his organs. The donation of his organs (heart, eyes) and offering of ongoing life to others symbolizes his Resurrection.

The contemporary Catholic church is positioned as the main enemy of Jesus in the gospels, Jesus in the passion play, and Daniel (the Jesus figure). The film's conclusion emphasizes the Church's corrupt nature by having the lawyer symbolizing Satan (his last name is Cardinal) found a new theater company comprised of Daniel's fellow actors. Although he claims to want to maintain Daniel's legacy, his motive is profit. The implication is that Satan founds the Christian Church. If there is a Judas figure among Daniel's disciples/actors it is here when they form this new troupe. The film's final hopeful note is that Mareille, put off by the lawyer's motives, exits the meeting. For Arcand, following Jesus requires leaving the Church.

UNUSUAL JESUS FIGURES

Some cinematic protagonists conform to standard Jesus figure tropes, but depart from the traditional Jesus figure in surprising and meaningful ways. There are multiple examples of these kinds of unusual Jesus figures, such as Karl Childers in *Sling Blade* (Thornton, 1996). One of the most surprising such figures is Dracula in *Bram Stoker's Dracula* (Coppola, 1992). He dies, claiming that God has forsaken him, and declaring, "It is finished" (John 19:30). Director Coppola notes, "There's a definite Christ-parallel, oddly enough."[4]

DONNIE DARKO

Written and directed by Richard Kelly, *Donnie Darko* (2001) features a teenage Jesus figure who suffers from a mental illness involving hallucinations (or visions) of Frank, a human in a rabbit suit.[5] Frank informs Donnie at the film's outset that the world will end in "28 days, 6 hours, 42 minutes, and 12 seconds." This numerical precision echoes the numerology in biblical apocalypses such as Daniel and Revelation.

Donnie shares many similarities with the Jesus in Scorsese's *The Last Temptation of Christ*. The initial images of Donnie and Scorsese's Jesus are overhead shots of the main character lying on the ground in a fetal position. Both characters receive—and are haunted by—visions. Both reject and rebuke official (and religious) authorities. Donnie calls motivational speaker Jim Cunningham (note the initials) the "antichrist."[6] Authorities persecute Jesus and Donnie in response to their rebellious behavior. Both characters receive special insight and guidance from a text (Jesus from Isaiah, Donnie from Roberta Sparrow's *The Philosophy of Time Travel*). Both characters are physically violent—Jesus in the temple, and Donnie at his school and in Cunningham's home. The most obvious allusion to Scorsese's film is when Donnie and his girlfriend attend a showing of *The Last Temptation of Christ*.

Questions about Donnie's mental illness are similar to the accusations that Jesus is losing his mind (Mark 3:21). *Donnie Darko* invites consideration of the kinds of symptoms Jesus may have presented that might have resulted in such an accusation. The film also suggests how, like *Jésus de Montréal*, mental illness might correlate with—and even contribute to—apocalyptic visions and worldviews. The film suggests that mental illness, far from being incompatible with a messianic figure, might be a constitutive part of that identity.

A divine being imparts special revelation to Jesus and Donnie, and rescues each character from death. The angel in *The Last Temptation of Christ* who saves Jesus from the cross is similar to Frank who saves Donnie from dying when a jet engine falls from the sky and crashes into his bedroom. Saved from death, Jesus and Donnie embark on an alternative path/universe in which they meet a woman, have sex with her, and then must choose whether they will remain in this new alternative universe, or if they will return to the site of their original death and accept their demise. As Scorsese's Jesus did, Donnie decides to return (via time travel) to his bedroom the night the jet engine falls through his roof. Both characters die willingly, and their acceptance of death is indicated by the smiles on each of their faces. Donnie's death is somewhat more tragic, since dying alone is his greatest fear.

Jesus and Donnie both reject certain apocalyptic worldviews. In *The Last Temptation of Christ*, Jesus initially embraces John the Baptist's apocalyptic message of judgment against the wicked (symbolized in an axe), but he later rejects this message of judgment. Donnie too is an agent of divine judgment. At Frank's behest, Donnie floods his school basement (with an axe) and burns down Cunningham's house, uncovering a dungeon of child porn, which results in Cunningham's arrest. Donnie's violent acts unveil injustice (like Jesus at the temple).

By choosing to return to his bedroom the night the jet engine falls and face his death, Donnie circumvents the world's destruction, and saves people from an otherwise violent end. Love motivates Donnie. After his girlfriend Gretchen is killed, he realizes that he can save her by traveling through time and dying. Contemplating this choice, he recalls Gretchen's words: "And what if you could go back in time and take all those hours of pain and darkness and replace them with something better?" By choosing to do just this, Donnie rejects an apocalyptic scenario in which the wicked are judged. For by going back in time, he erases the destruction of Cunningham's house and the discovery of his child porn. Both Donnie and Scorsese's Jesus reject the axe, a symbol of judgment against others, in favor of love and second chances.

The Last Temptation of Christ and *Donnie Darko* present messiahs who evolve from apocalyptic agents of vengeance, willing to wield violence against others, to welcoming violence against themselves. Like Tyler Durden in *Fight Club* (Fincher, 1999), they embrace an ethos of masochism, not sadism. These films identify the use of (or wish for) violence against others as a potentially dangerous (and perhaps deficient) element of apocalyptic. Whereas apocalyptic texts might anticipate a time of triumph and divine vindication, these films advocate accepting death instead.

Repudiating apocalypticism is evident in the choice of Jesus in *Last Temptation* and Donnie to reject the divine messenger who saves them from death. Unlike biblical apocalypses, these films depict divine guides as possible impostors whose messages must be carefully discerned. While someone threatens Donnie and holds a knife to his neck, Donnie whispers, "Deus ex machina, our savior." Donnie, however, ultimately chooses not to place himself in the hands of a divine deliverer. There is no God "outside of the machine" who saves him; Donnie is a savior *intra machina*, from within the machine.

DOGVILLE

Dogville (von Trier, 2003) features Grace Mulligan, a fugitive who enters Dogville, a small, rural town in the Rocky Mountains.[7] The townspeople begrudgingly accept her offers to help, and her days become filled with chores. The townspeople grow more suspicious when the mob and police start looking for Grace. Her hours of labor are doubled, and her wages are withheld.

Grace is raped by Chuck, and her attempt to flee Dogville is thwarted when Ben rapes her and returns her to town. A metal collar is fastened around Grace's neck and chained to a steel wheel which she drags around. Every man (except Tom, Jr) rapes Grace. Children ring the town bell during each assault. The moral descent is savage and thorough. When they tire of Grace, Tom informs the mob where she is. The gangsters arrive, demand Grace's release, and take her to the head gangster, who turns out to be Grace's father. After a conversation with him, Grace decides to annihilate the town. A massacre ensues in which her father's henchmen burn Dogville to the ground and execute every man, woman, child, and even an infant.

Many hints suggest Grace is a Jesus figure, including her name, which she embodies by displaying (until the end) mercy, compassion, and forgiveness throughout and despite her abuse. She gives her time, energy, and all that she has. She serves in innumerable ways. Everyone benefits from her presence. She affirms others, offers forgiveness, and removes shame from Ben who visits a brothel. She is an agent of truth, challenging a man to admit he is blind. Tom Jr., her closest supporter, is a Judas figure who betrays her. The chain around her neck and steel wheel is her cross. Throughout her persecution she offers no physical resistance. Divine vindication arrives in the form of her father, a God figure. He is called the "Big Man" in the screenplay, and referred to as the "Boss" in the film. His face is hidden from the townspeople until the town's annihilation—a divine judgment of fire. The film's opening and closing camera shots are from a "God-like" point of view, and the narrator is omniscient.

Aside from using a woman Jesus figure (von Trier does the same in *Breaking the Waves* [1996] and *Dancer in the Dark* [2000]), the most startling aspect of Grace-as-Jesus is her proposal to annihilate the town. Her conversation with her father illuminates her conversion from mercy to judgment:

Father: You don't pass judgment because you sympathize with them. The only thing you can blame is circumstances. Rapists and murderers may be the victims, according to you. But I call them dogs and if they're lapping up their own vomit, the only way to stop them is with the lash.

Grace: But dogs only obey their own nature, so why shouldn't we forgive them?

Father: Dogs may be taught many useful things but not if we forgive them every time they obey their own nature.

Grace: So I'm arrogant because I forgive people?

Father: You have this preconceived notion that nobody can possibly attain the same high ethical standards as you, so you exonerate them. I can't think of anything more arrogant than that. You, my child, my dear child, you forgive others with excuses that you would never permit for yourself.

Grace: Why shouldn't I be merciful? Why?

Father: You should be merciful when there's time to be merciful. But you must maintain your own standards. You owe them that ... The penalty you deserve for your transgression, they deserve for their transgression.

Grace: They're human beings, dad!

Father: Does every human being need to be accountable for their actions? Of course they do, and you don't even give them that chance. And that is extremely arrogant. I love you. I love you. I love you to death. But you are the most arrogant person I've ever met ...

Grace: The people who live here are doing their best under very hard circumstances.

Father: If you say so, Grace, but is their best ... really good enough? I do love you.

As Grace exits the car and walks around the town, the narrator explains:

Grace looked around at the frightened faces behind the windowpanes that were following her every step, and felt ashamed of being part of inflicting that fear. How could she ever hate them, for what was at bottom merely their weakness? She would probably have done things like those that had befallen her if she had lived in one of these houses. To measure them by her own yardstick, as her father put it. Would she not have done the same as ... all these people?

An abrupt alteration in music and lighting portends an ominous shift within Grace:

It was as if the light previously so merciful and faint finally refused to cover up for them any longer. The light now penetrated every unevenness and flaw in the buildings and in the people. And all of a sudden she knew the answer to her question all too well. If she had acted like them she couldn't have defended a single one of her actions and could not have condemned them harshly enough. It was as if her sorrow and pain finally assumed their rightful place. No! What they had done *was not good enough* and if one had the power to put it to rights it was one's duty to do so, for the sake of other towns, for the sake of humanity, and not least for the sake of the human being that was Grace herself.

Grace returns to the car and announces, "If there's any town this world would be better without, this is it." The townspeople are executed, and Grace shoots Tom herself. Grace transforms from an advocate of mercy to a champion of apocalyptic judgment. She joins her father's (God's) "band of thugs." The film illustrates the deficiencies of grace. Rather than heralding mercy and compassion as virtuous, the film demonstrates how insidious they are. Grace's grace enables and encourages vile abuse. The only creature that survives the apocalyptic judgment of Dogville is the dog Moses, and his name suggests that people need law, not mercy.

Dogville and the parable of the Sheep and the Goats (Matthew 25:31–46) share many similarities. Both feature an apocalyptic judgment by a (semi-)divine agent. In each case, aiding the poor or vulnerable is the sole criterion determining how one is judged. Like Jesus, Grace is the "least of these"; she is hungry, thirsty, naked, a stranger, sick, and in prison. In both cases, the "least" (Jesus and Grace) become judge at the final judgment; the judge unleashes— or is complicit in—violence. Although *Dogville* reviles those who actively harm Grace, it joins the parable in reserving its harshest condemnation for those (like Tom Jr.) who fail to act. Passivity in the face of injustice is the ultimate sin.

Figure 5.2 Grace and her father debate the merits of mercy versus justice in *Dogville* (2003).

Grace's conversion from mercy to violence parallels the shift of the nonviolent Jesus of the Sermon on the Mount/Plain (Matthew 5–7; Luke 6) into the violent and apocalyptic Jesus (Mark 12:1–9; Matthew 18:23–35; 25:31–46; Revelation 19:11–21). How to explain the transformation from the "love your enemies" Jesus to Jesus the Judge who uses a sword in his mouth to vanquish his enemies (Rev 19:11–21)? This is the Jesus figure *Dogville* presents—one who transitions from grace into wrath. Unlike Donnie Darko and Scorsese's Jesus, Grace evolves *from* mercy to embracing apocalyptic violence and damning the wicked. *Dogville* illustrates the biblical portrayal of a schizophrenic Jesus, and the transformation of Jesus from a pacifist to an apologist for—and wielder of—violence.

Grace's desire to protect the vulnerable fuels her defense of violence. She explains, "It could happen again, somebody happening by, revealing their frailty. That's what I want to use the power for, if you don't mind. I want to make the world a little better." Her motive is not rooted in revenge (as it appears in the Sheep and Goats parable), but in an effort to shield the defenseless. Divine violence in Matthew 25 (and other biblical apocalypses) punishes the wicked, but in *Dogville* it is employed to protect future victims. Grace's violence is primarily protective, not punitive. The film offers an ethic of violence as a force for good, rather than (as in the Sheep and the Goats) violence as punishment. The parable's rhetorical function, of course, can be to use the threat of a violent judgment to persuade people to care for vulnerable victims.

Ofelia, the main character in Guillermo del Toro's *El laberinto del fauno* (*Pan's Labyrinth*, 2006), conforms to and subverts traditional cinematic Jesus figure tropes.[8] As a young girl, Ofelia arrives with her mother at a military outpost in 1944 Spain to join captain Vidal, her stepfather. A faun visits Ofelia, informing her she is a princess from the underworld where her true father reigns as a king. To demonstrate her identity as the princess—and return and be reunited with her father—she must pass three tests. The film's magical realism weaves together the "real" and the "fantasy" world, and in each, Ofelia must overcome brutal monsters.

Ofelia is most similar to the Jesus in John's gospel. Like John's Jesus, she is the child of an otherworldly father who loves her. She comes from this father and has become flesh in the world and dwells among humanity. The faun tells Ofelia, "You are not born of man." (As in the gospels, otherworldly beings know her true identity.) Ofelia's father waits for her return, as John's Jesus expects to return to his father. Like Jesus, Ofelia is given tasks to complete. The scriptures testify about Jesus, and the Book of Crossroads instructs Ofelia and foreshadows her fate. Jesus is associated with life and giving and raising life, and Ofelia enlivens others. Del Toro notes, "The girl saves so many things."[9] Ofelia also has similarities with the synoptic Jesus; she refers to "my kingdom" (*mi reino*) and she tells parable-like stories.

Ofelia's most overt parallel to Jesus is sacrificing her life to protect another; her violent death; and resurrection and reunification in the otherworldly Kingdom with her (divine) father and mother. Del Toro describes this latter scene as "a Trinity in the other world."[10] As in John, Ofelia's father "raises" her to this eternal life. He tells her, "You have spilled your own blood rather than the blood of an innocent. That was the final task, and the most important." Her blood is salvific; its dripping into water triggers her entrance into the afterlife. As in Mark's gospel, the film begins by foreshadowing Ofelia's death (the opening shot shows her on the cusp of death).

At the film's end, Mercedes holds Ofelia's body in a pietà pose. The film ends with the narrator's voiceover: "And it is said that the Princess returned to her father's kingdom. That she reigned there with justice and a kind heart for many centuries. That she was loved by her people. And that she left behind small traces of her time on earth, visible only to those who know where to look." Ofelia's eternal reign restores life, and her presence is visible only to those with eyes to see. Del Toro remarks: "I think the girl really becomes immortal."[11]

Ofelia is associated with eternal life early in the film in a story she tells:

> Many, many years ago, in a sad, faraway land, there was an enormous mountain made of rough, black stone. At sunset, on top of that mountain, a magic rose blossomed every night that made whoever plucked it immortal. But no one dared go near it because its thorns were full of poison. Men talked amongst themselves about their fear of death, and pain, but never about the promise of eternal life. And every day, the rose wilted, unable to bequeath its gift to anyone ... forgotten and lost on top of that cold, dark mountain, forever alone, until the end of time.

Ofelia later enacts this fairy tale within a fairy tale; the path to eternal life is narrow because it paradoxically requires risking death.

Ofelia departs from traditional Jesus figure tropes in many ways. A young Spanish girl is worlds away from the typical adult, male, white Jesus figure. She comes to earth not from "above," but below, and her resurrection is a *descent*. Unlike John's Jesus, but like Scorsese's, Ofelia must discover her true identity. Jesus curses a fig tree (Mark 11:12-21), but Ofelia succeeds in her first task, which is restoring a dying fig tree to life.

Unlike a Jesus who endorses (Mark 12:1–9; Matthew 18:23–35; 25:31–46) and uses violence (Mark 11:12–17, 20; Revelation 19:11–21), Ofelia is consistently nonviolent. She does not harm anyone. She resists, but does so nonviolently. The vision of a non-violent Messiah is at odds with some cinematic Jesus figures (*The Matrix*, *Dogville*) and more similar to Jesus figures in *The Iron Giant* and *Donnie Darko* who ultimately reject violence. Ofelia's nonviolence is a reminder that nonviolent Messiahs are possible, and that the presentation of a violent Jesus in parts of the New Testament is not inevitable.

Unlike John's Jesus, Ofelia models an ethic of *dis*obedience. In John, Jesus consistently obeys God and demands obedience from his followers. The submission to authority that John's gospel aims to inculcate in its audience is anathema to the entire ethical vision of *Pan's Labyrinth*. Disobedience is Ofelia's defining character trait. She refuses to call Vidal "father" as her mother requests. She disobeys Vidal by putting a sedative in his whiskey, and refusing his demand to return his son. Ofelia disobeys the faun's instruction to not eat any food in the pale man's lair. Like Eve, however, she succumbs, and as in Genesis 3, this eating has deadly consequences. Ofelia's final and most consequential act of disobedience is during the third task, when the faun tells her that if she hands over her baby brother, the portal to return to her father will open. Holding a dagger, he explains that the portal will only open "if we offer the blood of an innocent. Just a drop of blood. A pinprick, that's all. It's the final task." She refuses, despite his repeated insistence: "You promised to obey me! Give me the boy!" The faun is shocked at her refusal: "You would give up (*Sacrificaréis*) your sacred rights for this brat you barely know? "Yes, I would (*lo sacrifico*)," she replies. The faun asks, "You would give up your throne for him? He who has caused you such misery, such humiliation?" "Yes, I would," Ofelia says.

Ofelia's disobedience leads to her death and resurrection. Vidal arrives, takes his son, and shoots her in the abdomen. She collapses, forming an inclusio with the film's opening shot. Del Toro describes the film as "a fairy tale about choice, and about disobedience, and about a girl who needs to disobey anything but her own conscience, her own soul."[12] It is through disobedience and defiance that Ofelia reveals herself to be the Princess and the daughter of her (divine) father. In *Pan's Labyrinth*, disobedience is the cardinal virtue; obedience is the deadly sin. Monsters (like Vidal) demand obedience, and heroes (Ofelia, Mercedes, the doctor) disobey. In light of the film, biblical texts (like Romans 13) that demand obedience are potentially monstrous. Similarly, Jesus and God (in John) can be viewed as potentially monstrous in demanding obedience from their followers. Ofelia's heroic disobedience recalls the Hebrew midwives, Moses'

Figures 5.3 and 5.4 After refusing to hand over her baby brother, Ofelia is reunited with her father and mother in *Pan's Labyrinth* (2006).

mother, and Pharaoh's daughter, all of whom disobey Pharaoh's law (Exodus 1).

In refusing to endanger her baby brother, Ofelia relinquishes her longing to reunite with her father. Surrendering this dream enhances the tragedy of her death. Her choice is a contrast to John's Jesus who lays down his life, but does so knowing that he will return to his Father. Ofelia's death is less selfish, and more noble than Jesus' (in John). Del Toro remarks, "I always think of that beautiful quote by Kierkegaard that says the tyrant's reign ends with his death, but the martyr's reign starts with his death. I think that is the essence of the movie: It's about living forever by choosing how you die."[13] Ofelia lives forever by choosing to die nonviolently, disobediently, and in selfless abandonment of her deepest longing, all in order to protect another. In these ways she offers a more compelling Jesus figure than the Jesus in the gospels.

SUMMARY

Just as there are multiple Jesuses in the New Testament (diverse and sometimes conflicting portraits of him in the gospels), and multiple Christs in the Bible, so too are there diverse depictions of Jesus and Christ figures in cinema. As in the Bible, the term "Christ"—when describing Christ figures in films—is polyvalent. The multiple meanings attached to the term "Christ" (figure) and its broad semantic range are illustrated by the variety of traditional and atypical Jesus and Christ figures in film. Although there is a danger of baptizing films and imposing foreign meanings on them by seeing Jesus figures where they are not, there remain clear examples of films featuring Jesus figures. *The Green Mile*, *The Matrix*, and *Jesus of Montreal* offer fairly traditional Jesus figures. The unusual Jesus figures in *Donnie Darko* and *Dogville* respectively highlight Jesus' mental illness and capacity for brutal violence. Although unusual in Jesus films or Jesus figures, these traits are associated with Jesus in the gospels. These films therefore help in drawing attention to aspects of Jesus that are noted in the gospels, but that are regularly neglected in cinematic treatments of Jesus or Jesus figures. *Pan's Labyrinth* offers a Jesus figure who—in some ways—ethically and morally surpasses the Jesus of the gospels.

NOTES

1 So Deacy (2006).
2 Walsh (2013).
3 King (2000), 197.
4 Dargis (1992).

5 Some of this material on *Donnie Darko* appeared in an altered form in Rindge (2016b). Used with permission. Many of my views on the links between *Donnie Darko* and *The Last Temptation of Christ* are influenced by Walsh (2013).

6 All quotations are from the DVD version of the film's theatrical release, not the director's cut.

7 Some of this material on *Dogville* appeared in an altered form in Rindge (2018). Used with permission.

8 Some of this material on *Pan's Labyrinth* appeared in a modified form in Rindge (2021a). Used with permission.

9 Del Toro (2019).

10 Del Toro (2007b).

11 Del Toro (2007a).

12 Del Toro (2007b).

13 Rodriguez (2007).

FOR FURTHER READING

Lloyd Baugh, *Imaging the Divine: Jesus and Christ-Figures in Film* (Kansas City, MO: Sheed & Ward, 1997).

Christopher Deacy, "Reflections on the Uncritical Appropriation of Cinematic Christ-Figures: Holy Other or Wholly Inadequate?" *Journal of Religion and Popular Culture* 13 (2006).

Christopher Deacy, *Screen Christologies: Redemption and the Medium of Film* (Cardiff: University of Wales Press, 2001).

Adele Reinhartz, "Jesus and Christ-Figures," in *The Routledge Companion to Religion and Film* (ed. John Lyden; London: Routledge, 2009), 420–39.

Richard Walsh, "A Modest Proposal for Christ-Figure Interpretations: Explicated with Two Test Cases," *Relegere* 3:1 (2013): 79–97.

BIBLE IN FILM

Many films incorporate the Bible by citing or alluding to specific biblical texts, including a biblical character or image, or featuring a physical Bible as a prop. This chapter explores some of the various ways in which biblical texts, characters, images, and Bibles appear in cinema. The focus will be on how films appropriate and reconfigure material from the Bible, how a film's inclusion of biblical material shapes a film and contributes to its meaning, and how the use of such material might help people rethink and reconsider the meaning of biblical texts. This chapter examines six films: exploring the powerful role of sex and gender in Jesus' movement, *Mary Magdalene* (Davis, 2018) portrays a Mary who departs from her typical depiction in most Jesus films. *Pulp Fiction* (Tarantino, 1994) illustrates how a film (mis)quotes, interprets, and reinterprets a biblical text. The use of a biblical text in *Magnolia* (Anderson, 1999) illuminates central themes of the film, and invites reconsideration of the text's potential meanings. *Dead Man Walking* (Robbins, 1995) and *Hacksaw Ridge* (Gibson, 2016) highlight debates over how to understand and apply the Bible to contemporary and contested ethical issues. *The Book of Eli* (Hughes, 2010) illustrates different ways in which the Bible operates and functions as a physical object.

BIBLICAL CHARACTERS IN FILM

GOD

God often appears as a character in comedies as a benign deity. In *Oh, God!* (Reiner, 1977) and *Oh God! Book II* (Cates, 1980), God is an elderly, white man who recruits people to spread his message to the world. In *Oh, God! You Devil* (Bogart, 1984) George Burns reprises his role as God and plays the devil. In *Bruce Almighty* and *Evan Almighty* (Shadyac, 2003, 2007), God is an elderly Black man whose main job is answering peoples' prayers, and helping people, animals, and nature. In *Dogma* (Smith, 1999), God is a woman, full of grace and also capable of wrath. *The Shack* (Hazeldine, 2017) depicts God as a Black woman who consoles a man facing trauma by helping him to forgive himself and others. In *The Brand New Testament* (Van Dormael, 2015), God lives in a Brussels apartment, and his abuse of his wife and ten-year-old daughter mirrors his contempt for humanity.

Films also feature God figures. In *The Truman Show* (Weir, 1998), Christof is the creator of a pseudo-reality television show whose star—Truman Burbank—is the only one unaware that his entire life is broadcast to the world. Christof orchestrates every detail of Truman's life (the death of his father, whom he dates and marries, etc.), and Christof opposes efforts to enlighten Truman that he is a pawn in this elaborate scheme. Christof manipulates Truman's life because he is convinced that such a life is safer for Truman and more entertaining for the audience. Truman breaks free of Christof's benign tyranny when he departs the safety of Seahaven for the real world. *Stranger than Fiction* (Forster, 2006) features a woman author as a God-like figure whose protagonist in her current novel is a real person. In *Pleasantville* (Ross, 1998) the God figure is a repairman who wants to protect the ordered and decent world of Pleasantville from sexuality, art, books, and emotions.

SATAN

Satan in films usually lurks offscreen. Aside from the dream in *Rosemary's Baby* (Polanski, 1968) in which Satan appears to impregnate Rosemary, the film focuses on Satan's devotees and their attempts to facilitate Rosemary's birth of Satan's spawn. The demon who possesses Regan in *The Exorcist* (Friedkin, 1973) claims to be Satan, but only in order to fool a priest into thinking the girl is not possessed. In *The Omen* (Donner, 1976), *Damien: Omen II* (Taylor, 1978) and *Omen III: The Final Conflict* (Baker, 1981), Satan helps the antichrist Daniel Thorn, but does so from off screen. Satan in these films—*The Witch* (Eggers, 2015) is another example—is a kind of *diabolus ex machina*.

In some films, Satan is incarnate. *Satan* (Murnau, 1920) is no longer fully available, but in the third of three stories, Satan (in human form) coaxes a revolutionary into violence. *Leaves from Satan's Book* (*Blade af Satans Bog*, Dreyer, 1920) imagines Satan's involvement in four different historical periods. In *The Devil's Advocate* (Hackford, 1997), Satan uses an attorney's desire for fame to lure him into having sex and siring the antichrist. *End of Days* (Hyams, 1999) depicts Satan taking control of a man's body in order to have sex with a woman and father the antichrist. In *Devil* (Dowdle, 2010), the titular figure is disguised as an old woman who, trapped with several people in an elevator, kills them one by one. Based on Stephen King's novel, *Needful Things* (Heston, 1993) portrays the devil as shopkeeper Leland Gaunt who sells customers the one item they most desperately want. In exchange, they must do him a favor, which entails some kind of harm against another town member. By the story's end, the town is engulfed in flames. Satan uses consumer capitalism to turn people against one another and destroy their town.

MARY

Mary Magdalene (Davis, 2018) presents Mary as the apostle closest to Jesus and his most authentic representative. Mary resists her family's insistence that she wed and become a mother ("I'm not made for that life"). Her family nearly drowns her in an attempt to exorcise her. Jesus, summoned to help, finds no demon in her. After watching Jesus teach and heal, she leaves her family to follow him. When Mary is told that she will be lost amidst all the men around Jesus, she replies, "I'm lost here." Peter, reluctant to accept a woman follower, says that Mary "will divide our community." This line anticipates

Mary's later discovery that the patriarchal control of her family will also be exercised against her by Jesus' disciples.

Mary becomes Jesus' first woman follower, and her presence is soon felt. She baptizes other women, repeating the same formula Jesus used with her ("I baptize you with water to cleanse you. I baptize you with light and with fire. I baptize you to be born anew, awake, and ready for the day to come"). She corrects the male disciples' expectation that Jesus will launch some kind of revolt against Rome, telling them (and citing Isaiah), "I didn't know we were to be soldiers ... The Prophet spoke of Peace—a prince of peace." Mary tries to correct Judas' belief that Jesus will usher in a kingdom that will resurrect his dead daughter. Jesus is flanked by Peter and Mary when he enters Jerusalem. She sits by him at the Last Supper. While Jesus prays in Gethsemane, Mary rebuts the efforts of his other followers to return Jesus to Cana to protect him from danger.

To Peter's chagrin, Mary's influence leads Jesus to begin teaching other women. When Jesus asks what he should teach them, Mary replies, "Are we so different from men that you must teach us different things?" Jesus promotes a certain kind of gender equality, telling a woman who says, "We're women. Our lives are not our own," that, "Your spirit's your own. And you alone answer for that. And your spirit is precious to God. As precious as that of your husband or your father." When she asks, "Then who should we obey if God commands one thing, but our husbands, our fathers, tell us another?", Jesus answers, "You must follow God." Mary inquires, "So are we to defy them and leave our lives behind?" Jesus answers, "Yes. Though they judge you, persecute you, you must forgive them." "Forgive them?" one woman asks, and then describes an honor killing in which a woman who had cheated on her husband was raped and drowned. Jesus asks her, "How does it feel to carry that hate in your heart? Does it lessen as the months go by? It seeps into your days, your nights, until it consumes everything you once were. You are strong, sister, but you must forgive. There is no other way to enter the kingdom of God. Will you join us, will you be born anew?" Many women answer by joining Jesus' movement.

Jesus and Mary form an intimate, *asexual* bond. In contrast to most depictions, Mary is not sexual with anyone. (The film notes that Pope Gregory claimed in 591 CE that Mary was a "prostitute, a misconception that remains to this day.") The film explicitly rejects this misperception. Mary and Jesus are tender and caring with each other, but they do so platonically. Even Peter, Mary's main opponent, acknowledges her tenderness. In Samaria, he and Mary find a village massacred by the Romans. Among the few remaining survivors, Mary acts as a Mother Teresa figure, offering solace to the dying. To one woman on the cusp of death, Mary says, "You are seen and heard in every act of care. You answer to God with every act of love." Mary's compassion moves Peter, who says of her care, "Mercy. That was mercy."

Mary's devotion to Jesus entails a willingness to be with him while he suffers. Mary washes Jesus' feet, and on two occasions promises to be, and walk, with Jesus while he enters his path of darkness. "I'll be with you. I won't leave." This vow is tested when she sees Jesus struggling under the cross. After running away and collapsing, she ultimately rises and returns to sit at the foot of the cross. With tears in her eyes, she and Jesus gaze at each other. He dies a somewhat subdued death absent of melodrama.

The film's main conflict erupts after Mary tells Peter and the other (male) followers about seeing Jesus after his death. Peter doubts this given the continued existence of oppression, poverty, and suffering in the world. Mary tells him, "We've been looking for a change in the world, but it's not what we thought. The kingdom is here, now." The kingdom is "not something we can see with our eyes. It's here within us" (echoing Luke 17:21). "All we have to do is let go of our anger, our resentment, and we become like children, just as he said." The kingdom "can't be built through conflict, not by opposition, not by destruction. It grows with us, with every act of love and care, with our forgiveness. We have the power to lift the people, just as he did, and then we will be free just as he is."

In response to Peter's insistent doubts, Mary asks him, "How does it feel to carry that anger around in your heart? Does it lessen as the days go by?" With these and other words, Mary becomes Jesus' mouthpiece, replicating his words verbatim. Jesus' presence remains after his death through Mary's words. Peter rejects Mary's view of the kingdom, but she insists, "We have the power to relieve their suffering. It is up to us … The world will only change as we change."

Peter's intolerance of Mary leads to schism. He tells her, "It's not right that you come here now to tell us that he has chosen you before us, that he has brought you some special message." Mary reminds him, "We were all his apostles," and she tells Peter that his message and Jesus' message are not the same. Peter retorts, "You have weakened us, Mary. You weakened him." Mary states, "But I will not stay and be silent. I will be heard." She exits, meets with Jesus once more, her freely blowing hair symbolizing her newfound freedom. Jesus asks her if this is what she thought the kingdom would be like, and Mary's voiceover of the parable of the Mustard Seed follows, forming an inclusio (along with an image of Mary in water) with the film's opening. Unlike the synoptic gospels, in this version of the parable, a woman sows the seed. Mary may be this very woman, or at least function in this same capacity in planting seeds of the kingdom. The film suggests that the Mustard Seed parable in the synoptics was changed to replace the original version of a woman sowing the seed with a man. Mary speaks the parable (at the beginning and end of the film), and this is another instance of her functioning as the authentic voice of Jesus.

The film ends with Mary walking determinedly towards other women followers of Jesus. An image of her underneath the water (from the film's opening) begins to include other women underwater as well. Jesus' vision will be continued most authentically through Mary and these other women followers, and not through Peter or any of the other male disciples. Mary (and the women with her) will carry on Jesus' true legacy.

Scholars speak of the existence of multiple Christianities in the early church (rather than a monolithic Christianity), and this film illustrates the significant role of sex/gender in the emergence of diverse and conflicting Christianities. In casting Mary aside, the male disciples marginalize Jesus. Mary's confrontation with Peter depicts the infant church as no different from the patriarchy in Mary's family. Both spaces silence women who do not acquiesce to men. The film indicts such patriarchal systems that use women as instruments for the purposes of men. The film does not, however, examine the extent to which Mary, in becoming an instrument of Jesus, is at the film's end still ensconced in the same type of patriarchy modeled by her family and the early church. For Mary is still an instrument of a

Figure 6.1 Mary Magdalene meets with the resurrected Jesus in *Mary Magdalene* (2018).

man. This time, however, it is Mary's choice and perhaps therein lies the crucial difference.

PAUL

Although Paul appears in films such as *The Robe* (Koster, 1953) and *Quo Vadis* (LeRoy, 1951), he is the focus of relatively few films. Pasolini wrote a screenplay about Paul, but was murdered before filming began.[1] In *The Last Temptation of Christ*, Paul makes two brief appearances. As Saul (the pre-Paul zealot) he kills Lazarus after Jesus has raised him from the dead because Saul wants to eliminate evidence of Jesus' miracles. During his "temptation" period, the adult Jesus hears Paul preaching about the risen Christ. Jesus introduces himself to Paul, and points out that he is in fact alive, and neither died on the cross nor rose from the dead. Paul tells Jesus, "If I have to crucify you to save the world, I'll crucify you." Paul adds, "My Jesus is much more real and much more powerful." Paul prefers his Christ of faith to the historical Jesus.

Writer and director Andrew Hyatt's *Paul: Apostle of Christ* (2018) portrays Luke (as the author of the third gospel) seeking advice and inspiration from an imprisoned Paul in Rome in order to help the fledgling church there. Some of Paul's dialogue comes from his (authentic and disputed) letters. Paul provides a postmortem voiceover from excerpts of (the disputed, but in the film authentic) letter of 2 Timothy. In conversations with Luke about debates occurring in the church in Rome, Paul says, "We cannot repay evil for evil; evil can only be overcome with good" (Romans 12:17, 21); he shares with Luke portions of the love poem in 1 Cor 13:4–13. After asking Luke if he understands, Paul tells him, "Then write it down." Anchoring Paul's writings in a dialogical encounter rooted in a lived experience matches scholarly views that his letters represent responses to specific problems facing different churches.

Poignant conversations occur between Paul and Ananias (after Saul/Paul is blinded) and (a deleted scene of) Saul and his teacher Gamaliel. The film proposes that Paul's enigmatic "thorn in the flesh" (2 Cor 12:7) was guilt over persecuting and killing Christians. After he dies, Paul has a postmortem vision of reuniting and reconciling with these Christians he persecuted. The film illustrates Paul's adept communication skills in a scene of dialogue with a Roman soldier, and—through Luke's care for this soldier's daughter—how Romans may have been attracted to this new religious movement.

BIBLICAL TEXTS IN FILM

Films that cite or allude to biblical texts are legion. In *X-Men 2* (Singer, 2003), Nightcrawler cites Psalm 23 and the Lord's Prayer. At his bar mitzvah in *A Serious Man*, Danny reads a selection from Leviticus 25:1–26:2. *3:10 to Yuma* (Mangold, 2007) quotes excerpts from Proverbs.

Some films take their titles from biblical texts. *The Sun Also Rises* (King, 1957) is a line in Qoheleth 1:5. Qoheleth wrestles with life's meaninglessness, and meaninglessness pervades the characters' lives in the film. *A Time to Kill* (Schumacher, 1996) is from a poem in Qoheleth (3:3), and it raises the question of the moral appropriateness of Carl Lee's vengeful murder of the men who raped and killed his daughter. *As It Is in Heaven* (*Så som i himmelen*) (Pollak, 2004) is from Matthew's version of the Lord's Prayer (Matt 6:10), and suggests that the communal life among residents of a Swedish village reflects God's will and kingdom on earth. *There Will Be Blood* (Anderson, 2007), from Exodus 7:19, anticipates the film's finale.

Citations of biblical texts can illustrate a film's key theme. In *Footloose* (Ross, 1984), Ren cites portions of the poem in Qoheleth 3 to defend his argument that there are appropriate times to celebrate life, and that now "is our time to dance" (Qoheleth 3:4). On three occasions a journalist in *The Year of Living Dangerously* (Weir, 1982) asks, "What then must we do?" This quotation of Luke 3:10 connects the focus in Luke 3 on caring for the poor with the film's concern for social justice. Jeremiah 11:11, which appears a few times in Jordan Peele's *Us* (2019), connects the verse's warning (that God will "bring disaster upon them that they cannot escape; though they cry out to me, I will not listen to them") with peoples' terror when attacked by their underground doppelgängers.

Scorsese's *Raging Bull* (1980) concludes with an onscreen citation of John 9:24–25, inviting viewers to (re)consider how Jake LaMotta's life relates to a shift from blindness to sight. In *The Mission* (Joffé, 1986), Rodrigo's dual conversion to Christianity and becoming a Jesuit priest is accompanied by his reading of 1 Corinthians 13:4–13. This text suggests that love will play a crucial role in the Christianity and Jesuit identities he adopts. It also implies that his choice to use violence against the Portuguese soldiers—in direct violation of his superior's orders—is an act of love. The film concludes with a citation of John 1:5: "The light shines in the darkness … and the darkness has not overcome it." This verse, juxtaposed with the final image of young Guarani children who survived a Portuguese assault, offers a sliver of hope that the genocide of the Guarani will not be total.

Biblical texts are often used to inspire or justify abuse. In *Intolerance*, Catherine Medici cites **lex talionis** to justify her violent persecution of the Huguenots. *The Girl with a Dragon Tattoo* (*Män som hatar kvinnor*, Oplev, 2009) (and its Hollywood remake) features a serial killer whose murders are influenced by verses in Leviticus. In *Cape Fear* (Scorsese, 1991), Max Cady (imprisoned for rape) quotes the Bible, compares his own sufferings to those of the apostle Paul, and many of the tattoos that adorn his body are biblical references. He tells the attorney whose life he is ruining to read the book of Job, implying that Cady will make the lawyer suffer as Job did. In *12 Years a Slave* (McQueen, 2013) two white enslavers quote biblical texts to their enslaved Africans. Ford cites Luke 17:2, and Epps reads Luke 12:47 ("And that servant which knew his lord's will and prepared not himself, neither did according to his will, shall be beaten with many stripes"). He concludes by holding up the Bible, and declaring,

"That's Scripture." In *Malcolm X* (Lee, 1992), Malcolm scours the Bible to find examples of men (such as David) who committed adultery in order to defend Elijah Muhammad, leader of the Nation of Islam, against charges of inappropriate sexual relationships.

Some films play imaginatively with biblical texts. In *The Shawshank Redemption* (Darabont, 1994), Andy (imprisoned for a crime he did not commit) tells the warden that his favorite biblical passage is "Watch ye therefore for ye know not when the master of the house cometh" (Mark 13:35). The warden says he prefers "I am the light of the world; he that shall followeth me shall not walk in darkness, but shall have the light of life" (John 8:12). Andy, who spends years tunneling through his prison cell wall to escape, has good reason to "watch" for when the master might appear. Unlike Mark 13 and John 8, however, Andy wants to *avoid* the master's arrival, and *wants* to walk (or at least work) in darkness. *Gattaca* (Niccol, 1997) opens with a quotation from Qoheleth 7:13 ("Consider God's handiwork; who can straighten what he hath made crooked?"). The film's dystopian society divides people into a caste system based on God's handiwork (in the form of genetics). The main character demonstrates that it is possible to transcend the limitations of "God's handiwork," and that through diligence and commitment one can "straighten" a genetic makeup that God has made crooked.

Verses from the book of Revelation (whose original Greek title is *apokalypsis*) are fodder in many horror and apocalyptically oriented films such as *The Omen, Children of the Corn* (Kiersch, 1984), *The Seventh Sign* (Schultz, 1988), and *End of Days. Stigmata* (Wainwright, 1999) is one of the few films to cite an extracanonical text; it combines and paraphrases two sayings from the Gospel of Thomas (3, 77).

PULP FICTION

Quentin Tarantino's *Pulp Fiction* (1994) includes a well-known instance of a biblical citation. Crime boss Marsellus Wallace dispatches Jules and Vincent to kill a man named Brett. Before Jules shoots Brett, he delivers a speech:

> You read the Bible, Brett? Well there's this passage I've got memorized; sorta fits this occasion. Ezekiel 25:17. "The path of the righteous

man is beset on all sides by the iniquities of the selfish and the tyranny of evil men. Blessed is he who in the name of charity and goodwill shepherds the weak through the valley of darkness, for he is truly his brother's keeper and the finder of lost children. And I will strike down upon thee with great vengeance and furious anger those who attempt to poison and destroy my brothers. And you will know my name is the Lord when I lay my vengeance upon thee."

Shortly after, a man bursts out from a hiding place and fires multiple shots at Jules and Vincent. Every shot misses, and they return fire, killing him. This moment marks a turning point for Jules who believes that what occurred was miraculous. He rejects Vincent's view that they were merely lucky. "No, no, no, no, that shit wasn't luck … This was divine intervention." He claims, "God came down from heaven and stopped these motherfuckin' bullets… What just happened here was a fuckin' miracle." Jules is so moved that he decides he will resign from his life of criminality that very day.

This choice is later tested when at a restaurant he and the other customers are robbed at gunpoint by Ringo and Honey Bunny. Jules refuses to hand over a briefcase that belongs to his boss, and he pulls his gun. Pointing it at Ringo, Jules says that he happens to be in a "transitional period" and wants to help him and Honey Bunny. He asks, "You read the Bible Ringo? Well there's this passage I got memorized. Ezekiel 25:17…" With only two minor changes in the final sentence (and less bravado), Jules delivers the same speech he gave earlier to Brett. Upon finishing, he tells Ringo:

I've been saying that shit for years. And if you heard it, that meant your ass. I never gave much thought to what it meant. I just thought it was some cold blooded shit to say to a motherfucker before I popped a cap in his ass. I saw some shit this morning that made me think twice. See now I'm thinking maybe it means you're the evil man and I'm the right-eous man and Mr. Nine Millimeter here, he's the shepherd protecting my righteous ass in the valley of darkness. Or it could mean you're the righteous man and I'm the shepherd, and it's the world that's evil and selfish. I'd like that, but that shit ain't the truth. The truth is you're the weak and I am the tyranny of evil men. But I'm trying Ringo. I'm trying real hard to be the shepherd.

Jules does not actually quote the text he claims to quote. Ezekiel 25:17 reads: "I will execute great vengeance on them with wrathful

Figure 6.2 Jules reconsiders his interpretation of Ezekiel 25:17 in *Pulp Fiction* (1994).

punishments. Then they shall know that I am the Lord, when I lay my vengeance on them." Only the last two sentences of his speech are from this verse, and Jules changes even these lines. Jules handles the biblical text with a degree of fluidity. The biblical text is as fluid as chronological time is in the film. Also fluid is Jules' understanding of the text; he offers possible interpretations of (his version of) the text, and reinterprets the text in light of (what he considers to be) a miracle earlier that day. The power of context in shaping the interpretation of a text is evident in the different ways the authors of Matthew (18:1-14), Luke (15:1-7), and Thomas (107) make sense of Jesus' parable of the Lost Sheep.

MAGNOLIA AND EXODUS

Near the end of Paul Thomas Anderson's *Magnolia* (1999), there is a bewildering scene of frogs raining upon the streets of southern California.[2] This mysterious descent is partially explained by the biblical text Exodus 8:2 ("But if you refuse to set them free, I will strike your whole country with frogs"). Apparently unaware of this biblical reference when writing his screenplay, Anderson became obsessed with Exodus 8:2 after being informed of the frog plague in Exodus.[3] References to Exodus 8:2 pervade the film. The numbers "8" and "2" appearing together are ubiquitous; the film's Prologue contains at least eight of them. On at least three occasions the entire phrase "Exodus 8:2" appears—a bus stop sign, a street billboard, and a placard held up in a game show studio audience (a sign Anderson himself removes in a brief cameo). Due to their brevity, these references are usually missed by most first-time viewers, signaling an interpretive gap between the film text and the viewer's understanding of that text.

The warning in Exodus 8:2 occurs within a broader context of oppression and slavery. The warning about the plague of frogs follows Moses' demand that Pharaoh free God's people from slavery. Like Exodus, *Magnolia* juxtaposes oppression and hope for liberation. Most characters' relationships in the film are characterized by

Figures 6.3 and 6.4 Some of the many references to Exodus 8:2 in *Magnolia* (1999).

oppression and (in some cases) attempts at liberation. Whereas this oppression in Exodus is ethnically based, in *Magnolia* it is familial. Parents play the role of Pharaoh and their children are cast as the Hebrew slaves.

Four oppressive parent–child relationships take center stage in the film: (1) Earl Partridge abandons his first wife Lily as she succumbs to cancer, leaving their 14-year-old son, Frank, to care for his dying mother; (2) Jimmy Gator cheats on his wife Rose and likely molested their daughter Claudia; (3) Donnie Smith's parents stole the proceeds from their son's quiz show success; (4) Stanley Spector's father blames his son whenever things go awry, and he treats his son, the current quiz show champion, as a means to his own financial gain.

Parental oppression scars these children. The destructive influence of parents is illustrated by a second citation from Exodus. Donnie whispers, "The sins of the fathers … lay upon your children … Exodus 20:5." In this text Adonai promises to punish children for the iniquity of their parents. Such punishment in *Magnolia* is manifest in the childrens' inability as adults to form healthy relationships. Frank only relates to women as sexual objects. His childhood is so painful he fabricates an alternate version of it. Claudia numbs her pain with a cocaine addiction and anonymous sexual encounters. Donnie has failed financially, vocationally, and relationally. His apex of excitement is trying to procure braces, hoping they will make him attractive to Brad, a bartender who also wears braces. Stanley knows that he functions as a pawn, manipulated by adults who use him to make money; he admits to feeling like a freak. The song playing over the montage introducing the nine main characters— Aimee Mann's "One Is the Loneliest Number"—epitomizes their loneliness and relational dysfunction.

A tragedy of *Magnolia* is that the oppressed can become oppressors. In *Pedagogy of the Oppressed*, Brazilian educator Paolo Freire describes such a transition as almost inevitable for any group of people who have been subject to oppression.[4] Frank epitomizes this. He is the architect and chief evangelist of "Seduce and Destroy," whose aim is to teach men how to seduce women. He conceives of women as prey who are to be hunted and conquered. His life is void of life-giving relationships.

Liberation is fragile and fleeting. What liberation Frank does experience comes in the film's final moments as he sits at the bedside of his dying father whom he hasn't seen in years. Frank's initial rage at his father eventually softens and (with frogs falling in the background) he weeps over his father's death. The liberation of Frank and his father Earl is genuine and poignant, but brief. Claudia's liberation comes in two brief scenes at the film's end: her mother arrives (during the reign of frogs) and embraces her, and policeman Jim Kurring pledges to accept and love her. Aimee Mann's song "Save Me," which plays over Jim's monologue, captures Claudia's yearning for relational connection that is not predicated on being treated as a sexual object. In response to Jim's offer of grace, Claudia smiles (for the first time in the film) and *Magnolia* ends.

Magnolia argues that relational liberation requires confession, and that such confession facilitates the possibility of forgiveness. Earl's moment of liberation (with his estranged son Frank crying at his bedside) comes after he confesses to Phil his regret over cheating on, and abandoning, Lily. Jim Kurring forgives Donnie (instead of arresting him) after Donnie confesses to stealing money to pay for braces. Jim's offer (as a policeman) of forgiveness to Donnie provides a glimmer of liberation for the former quiz show champ. Jim reflects: "Sometimes people need a little help. Sometimes people need to be forgiven. And sometimes they need to go to jail. And that is a very tricky thing on my part, making that call. You can forgive someone. … Well, that's the tough part … What can we forgive?" Jim receives grace from Claudia after he confesses to her his shame over losing his gun while on duty. Linda's confession of her adultery paves the way for her subsequent reconciliation with Frank. It is unclear what kind of liberation Stanley may (or may not) find. He acts as his own Moses, telling his father, "Dad, you have to be nicer to me." His dad, lying on his bed, merely shrugs his shoulders. Stanley repeats himself, and his father turns his head and tries to fall asleep.

Jimmy Gator experiences no liberation because he refuses to confess that he molested Claudia. Forgiveness, extended as a vehicle of liberation to other characters (notably from Frank to Earl), is off limits to Jimmy. Anderson notes, "It's the first time when I've been able, at the end of a film, to hate one of my characters. There truly is a sense of moral judgment at work with this character. I can't even let him kill himself at the end—he's got to burn … With this character, I'm saying 'No.' No to any kind of forgiveness for him."[5] Like Pharaoh, Jimmy's heart is hardened to liberative possibilities. *Magnolia* suggests that liberation—in the form of forgiveness and grace—is possible but only for some and for them only briefly. The main requirement for this limited liberation is confession.

Just as Exodus can illuminate *Magnolia*, so too can the film enlighten our reading of Exodus. The limited liberation that characters in *Magnolia* experience invites us to consider the nature of liberation of the Hebrew slaves in Exodus. As the Hebrews depart Egypt, they "plunder" the Egyptians, taking jewelry of silver and gold and clothing (Exodus 12:35–36). This is the first hint of the Hebrews imitating the behavior of their oppressors. The newly "liberated" Hebrew community is composed of male and female Hebrew slaves, bound and hired servants, the "poor," and widows, orphans, and aliens (Exodus 12 and 21). These social-economic strata, not specified prior to the departure from Egypt, point to a potentially new type of oppression experienced by the Israelites.

Before the Hebrews flee Egypt, God often calls them *ami* ("my people"), a term never applied to the Egyptians. In the conflict between Egypt and the Hebrews, Adonai identifies and sides with the Hebrews, and against the Egyptians. However, after Israel's departure from Egypt, God never again in Exodus calls all the Hebrews "my people." When God does next use the term "my people," it refers not to all of Israel, but to the poor among Israel (Exodus 22:25). Adonai calls the poor "my people" in his warning that Israel not exact interest from them. The identity of Adonai's people changes, but the principle underlying this shift remains consistent. In a conflict between oppressors and oppressed, Adonai is in solidarity with the oppressed. The God who sided with the Hebrews against Pharaoh now is aligned with poor Israelites and is opposed to Israelites who oppress them. In addition to the poor, Adonai's commitment to the newly oppressed encompasses aliens, widows, and orphans. Adonai's solidarity with these oppressed groups entails the same commitment that was expressed on behalf of the Hebrews. If widows or orphans are abused by Israelites and cry out to God,

Adonai will heed their cry and kill their Israelite oppressors with the sword (Exodus 22:21–24).

Opposition develops between Moses and the Hebrews that echoes Pharaoh's oppression of the Hebrews. On three occasions the Israelites complain against Moses (Exodus 15:11–2; 16:3; 17:2–3), and such complaints mimic their prior cries to God against their Egyptian enslavers. As punishment for worshiping a golden calf, Moses has 3,000 Israelites killed, not by Egyptians, but by fellow Israelites. Moses commands those "on Adonai's side" to take the sword and kill brother, friend, and neighbor (Exodus 32:24–27). Moses becomes a new Pharaoh, dispensing his version of justice which includes eliminating fellow Israelites. Moses is not alone. The "sons of Levi," in killing their fellow Israelites, also make the shift, described by Freire, from oppressed (under Pharaoh) to oppressors. The Israelites thus exchange oppression under the Egyptians for oppression under Moses. Albeit of a different sort, the Israelites under Moses experience hunger, thirst, fatigue, homelessness and (for some) execution by the sword. The "liberation" of the Hebrews must be qualified as partial or limited. Israelites continue to be oppressed; what changes is the location of their oppression and the name of their oppressor.

DEAD MAN WALKING

Based on Helen Prejean's memoir, *Dead Man Walking* (Robbins, 1995) follows Sister Prejean's relationship with Matthew Poncelet, a death row inmate sentenced for murder and rape.[6] The Bible plays a key role in their relationship, and in the film's dialogical argument about capital punishment.

Prejean employs biblical texts to comfort and challenge Matthew, telling him that "there are some passages in there about when Jesus was facing death and lonely you might want to check out." During his final walk to his execution, she cites Isaiah 43:1–2. This same text is the basis of a hymn ("Be Not Afraid") she sings to Matthew shortly before his execution. Prejean encourages Poncelet to take responsibility for his crimes, suggesting that he "look at the gospel of John, chapter 8, where Jesus said, 'You shall know the truth, and the truth shall make you free'" (John 8:32).

Biblical texts are primarily cited to support opposing views on capital punishment. Death penalty supporters twice refer to *lex talionis* in the Hebrew Bible. During an execution protestors hold signs reading "An eye for an eye" and "A life for a life." A preacher—carrying a large Bible—proclaims, "Jesus also said, 'He who lives by the sword shall die by the sword'" (Matthew 26:52). A protestor against the execution holds a sign that reads, "Jesus said, 'Let he who is without sin cast the first stone'" (John 8:7). These clashing signs reflect the film's dialogical portrayal of conflicting biblical perspectives regarding violence and the death penalty.

The film highlights the importance of understanding a biblical text in its broader literary context. A prison guard tells Helen, "You know how the Bible says, 'An eye for an eye?'" Helen replies, "You know what else the Bible asks for? Death as a punishment for adultery, prostitution, homosexuality, trespass upon sacred grounds, profanin' the sabbath, and contempt to parents." By (re)contextualizing *lex talionis* within its broader literary context, Prejean undermines the officer's selection of only one of many prescriptions for the death penalty.

The film never specifies which *lex talionis* statement in the Torah (Exodus 21:22–25; Leviticus 24:17–22; Deuteronomy 19:16–21) is the intended referent, perhaps reflecting an American cultural familiarity with the principle of *lex talionis*, but an ignorance regarding its original literary function(s). *Lex talionis* is twice applied in specific cases: any harm committed against a pregnant woman is to be visited upon the injurious party ("life for life, eye for eye ...") (Exod 21:22–25), and anyone who gives false testimony shall receive the same punishment that would have been applied to the defendant ("life for life, eye for eye ...") (Deut 19:16–21). The function of *lex talionis* here as a *protection* for defendants in a legal setting contrasts sharply with its use by characters in the film as a warrant to *harm* defendants.

The one use of *lex talionis* in the Torah as a general principle concludes with an emphasis on its equitable application: "There shall be one law for you, for the alien and for the native there shall be: for I am YHWH your God" (Leviticus 24:22). Such a consistent enforcement of capital punishment diverges from the film's depiction of the death penalty's discriminatory application. An attorney notes,

"You're not going to find many rich people on death row; Matthew Poncelet's here today *because he's poor.*" He suggests that Poncelet's accomplice—convicted of the same crimes—only avoided a death sentence because he had a better lawyer. Prejean's book details the tendency for the death penalty in the US to target poor people and people of color.

In the Ancient Near East, violence could beget escalating cycles of violence; *lex talionis* could minimize such violent spirals by limiting punishment to match the crime. One was forbidden, for example, to respond to bodily injury with murder. Characters in the film who cite *lex talionis* do so, however, not to reduce violence but to perpetuate it.

The film illustrates conflicting voices (biblical and contemporary) regarding capital punishment. Chaplain Farley rebukes Helen for protesting against an execution, asking: "Are you familiar with the Old Testament? 'Thou shalt not kill?' 'If anyone sheds the blood of man, by man shall his blood be shed'" (Genesis 9:6). Helen retorts, "Yes, Father. Are you familiar with the New Testament, where Jesus talks about grace and reconciliation?"

Contextualizing Genesis 9:6 within a broader canonical perspective problematizes Farley's citation of one biblical text as decisively authoritative on capital punishment. So too, however, does Farley's citation demonstrate Helen's perspective as reflective, not of "the Bible," but of one specific biblical voice out of a diverse chorus. Her reference to the New Testament and Jesus suggests her own "**canon within the canon**," one that is Christocentric. The (stereotypical) contrast regarding the disparate attitudes toward violence in the Hebrew Bible and New Testament is unfortunate, given the conflicting perspectives on violence in both testaments.

Farley's citation omits the conclusion of Genesis 9:6 and—therefore—the stated reason for applying the death penalty to murderers: "for in God's image [God] made humanity." Omitting this *imago dei* reference is significant given the film's tension regarding the (divine) humanity of Poncelet. Disregard for Poncelet's humanity surfaces in accusations that he and his ilk are "mad dogs, maniacs." A radio host mocks those who suppose Poncelet is "a child of God." A father of one of the victims calls Poncelet "an evil man" and "scum." Another victim's father insists, "This is not a person! This is an animal! No, I take that back; animals don't rape and murder their own kind. Matthew Poncelet is *God's mistake*." Prejean's affirmation of Matthew's humanity (and divine imprint) is symbolized by the gradual reduction in the physical barrier between the two, and physical contact (placing a hand on and kissing his shoulder). Her affirmation culminates in declaring—in explicit contrast to the radio host—"You are a son of God, Matthew Poncelet."

Farley's neglect to reference the *imago dei* is noteworthy given the correlation between perceptions of Matthew's humanity and attitudes toward his execution. The assistant DA, persuading the pardon board not to grant clemency, remarks, "Matthew Poncelet is not a good boy; he is a heartless killer." Matthew's lawyer tells him, "What we have to do is present you as a person, as a human being … it's easy to kill a monster, but it's hard to kill a human being." Helen tells Matthew that his rants "are making it so easy for them to kill you, coming across as some kind of crazed animal, Nazi, racist mad dog who deserves to die." Whereas *imago dei* is a warrant in Gen 9:6 for capital punishment, it functions in the film as an argument for mercy and clemency. The film's balance of conflicting views is evident in also applying *imago dei* to Walter and Hope, Poncelet's two victims. Interspersing flashbacks to their brutal rape and murder enhances empathy for them. Walter and Hope are humanized as Helen listens to the stories and grief of their parents.

The film acknowledges the Bible's inclusion of conflicting sociopolitical perspectives. After rebuking Helen for protesting against the death penalty, Farley opines, "Look at Romans: 'Let every person be subordinate to the higher authorities; for there is no authority except from God, and those who oppose it will bring judgment upon themselves.'" Farley uses this text (Rom 13:1a) both to legitimize his participation in a system that kills people, and to fault Prejean for protesting the same system.

Helen's opposition to state-sponsored execution is partially rooted in her perception of Jesus as someone who was executed by the state because he posed a threat. She calls Jesus a rebel and a dangerous man. When Matthew asks, "What's so dangerous about 'love your brother?'" she replies, "Because his love changed things … All those people who nobody cared about, the prostitutes and beggars and poor, finally had somebody who respected and loved them, made 'em realize their own worth; they had dignity, and they were becoming so powerful that the guys at the top got real nervous so they had to kill Jesus." The social disruption Jesus models for Helen diverges sharply from the submission to authority Farley finds in Paul's letter to the Romans.

The film invites and rejects comparisons between Poncelet and Jesus. Helen rejects Matthew's suggestion that he and Jesus were killed for similar reasons: "No, Matt, no, not at all like you. Jesus changed the world with his love; you watched while two kids were murdered." Several details do, however, portray Poncelet as a Jesus figure. He is called "son of God" shortly before his execution (Mark 15:39; Matthew 27:54), and he asks Helen to care for his mother, just as Jesus does when he is on the cross (John 19:26–27). Matthew is executed in a vertical cruciform position, his arms extended perpendicularly from his body, and this altered pose (lethal injection victims lie horizontally) invokes the crucified Jesus.

Such parallels signal a similarity between Jesus and Poncelet: state execution as a criminal. Matthew's poverty is a reminder of Jesus' status as a poor, marginalized figure, and how his socioeconomic status contributed to his crucifixion. Jesus' execution is a reminder of America's status as an Empire that does to poor (mostly Black) men what the Roman Empire did to marginalized people deemed to be dangerous (and disposable).

Reminders of Jesus as a crucified criminal pervade the film in the form of the crucifix. Helen wears a crucifix in at least 26 different scenes. In the first of these, a metal detector goes off during her initial visit to Matthew, and the camera zooms in to reveal Helen's crucifix as the source of the noise. This audible alarm anticipates the subsequent conflict Helen will embody in her solidarity with Matthew and her resistance to execution. Her familiarity with this image of an executed criminal leads her not to legitimize violence but to oppose it.

HACKSAW RIDGE

Hacksaw Ridge (Gibson, 2016) depicts the story of Desmond T. Doss (1919–2006), a conscientious objector and Medal of Honor recipient.[7] Doss saved 75 servicemen during the World War II Okinawa battle, all while refusing to touch a weapon. The Bible plays a prominent role in shaping Doss' moral commitment to pacifism.

Doss views the Bible as an ethical blueprint for how to live. A childhood memory of hitting his brother with a brick includes recalling a picture hanging on their wall illustrating the Ten Commandments. The sixth commandment, "Thou shall not kill," accompanied by a picture of Cain and Abel, captivates Doss. When his girlfriend Dorothy remarks that killing is acceptable in warfare, he asks, "What about His commandment?" When an Army psychologist asks him if it was God who told him not to touch a rifle, Doss replies, "God says not to kill. That's one of His most important commandments."

Most of the film's biblical allusions and citations in support of pacifism are from the Hebrew Bible. The film refers to the New Testament only twice. This near exclusive focus on the Hebrew Bible is noteworthy since most defenses of pacifism (as in *Dead Man Walking*) cite New Testament texts. Gibson subverts an inaccurate stereotype that imagines a stark dichotomy between the Hebrew Bible's violence and the New Testament's pacifism. Doss's reliance on the Hebrew Bible for his nonviolent stance is significant given the criticism Gibson received for what many considered to be antisemitic elements in *The Passion of the Christ*. The film's one stereotypical contrast between the Hebrew Bible and New Testament occurs when an Army psychologist tells Doss that King David "was a warrior king and much loved by God." Doss replies, "That's the Old Testament! Jesus said, 'A new commandment I give unto you that you love one another.'" Unlike *Dead Man* Walking or *The Mission*, the film fails to wrestle with the conflicting perspectives in the Bible regarding pacifism and violence.

Befitting his Protestant identity, Doss employs a *sola scriptura* approach to his faith. Nothing is more authoritative (in his mind) than certain biblical texts; his non-violent commitment is due not to Church teaching or tradition, mystical visions, or critical thinking. Doss's Protestantism is also evident in the authoritative weight of his personal interpretation of the Bible. It is his perception of the biblical text that shapes his conviction that pacifism is God's will for him. Unlike Mennonites (and Amish), Quakers, and the Church of the Brethren, Seventh-day Adventists (Doss's church) are not an historic peace church, and do not have a denominational policy of pacifism. If they had, then Doss' pacifism could be due to Church teaching (as is the case with his vegetarianism and Sabbath observance).

Dorothy critiques Doss's reliance on his personal interpretation of the Bible, warning him, "Don't confuse your will with the Lord's." Doss assumes that he is not interpreting the biblical text, but merely recognizing what the text "says." His conscience becomes his ultimate authority. This ethos of (usually rugged) individualism is a cardinal virtue in US culture, and it is a paramount theme in many of Gibson's films (*Braveheart* and *The Patriot*).

Based on a World War I episode, *Sergeant York* (Hawks, 1941) portrays the Bible's influence in shaping York's commitment to pacifism. He exclaims at one point, "I ain't a-goin' to war. War's killin', and the book's agin' killin'! So war is agin' the book!" He declares, "You see I believe in the Bible and I'm a-believin' that this here life we're a-livin' is something the Lord done give us and we got to be a-livin' it the best we can, and I'm a-figurin' that killing other folks ain't no part of what He was intendin' for us to be a-doin' here." After his request to be considered a conscientious objector is denied three times, York cites Jesus' remark ("render unto Caesar the things that are Caesar's, and unto God the things that are God's") to justify his military service.

BIBLICAL IMAGES AND BIBLES IN FILM

Amistad (Spielberg, 1997) recounts the legal aftermath of an 1839 revolt aboard a slave ship. After the ship reached the US, the Africans kidnapped from Mendeland were imprisoned while their case wound its way to the Supreme Court. Two of the men in jail, Cinque and Yamba, converse in Mende about a Bible Yamba peruses. Pointing to an image in the Bible, Yamba tells Cinque, "Their people have suffered more than ours. Their lives were full of suffering." Yamba shares about Jesus: "Then he was born and everything changed." "Who is he?" Cinque asks. "I don't know, but everywhere he goes he is followed by the sun. Here he is, healing people with his hands. Protecting them. Being given children. … He could also walk across the sea. But then something happened. He was captured. Accused of some crime. Here he is with his hands tied." Cinque exclaims, "He must have done something," but Yamba replies, "Why? What did we do? Whatever it was, it was serious enough to kill him for it. Do you want to see how they killed him?" Cinque tells him, "This is just a story, Yamba." "But look," Yamba says, "That's not the end of it. His people took his body down from this ... thing [he signs a cross] ... They took him into a cave. They wrapped him in a cloth, like we do. They thought he was dead, but he appeared before his people again and spoke to them. Then, finally, he rose into the sky. This is where the soul goes when you die. This is where we're going when they kill us. It doesn't look so bad."

Unable to read English, Yamba's knowledge of Jesus comes entirely from 13 black and white images, each of which he shows to Cinque, along with an explication of the image. The scene illustrates the power of the Bible's images, not the written word. The Bible here is an imagistic text; the word has become image.

THE BIBLE AS A PHYSICAL OBJECT

In many films the Bible's importance is due less to its content and more to its role as a prop or physical object. In *The Omen*, for example, a priest covers his bedroom walls with hundreds of pages from the Bible, believing that these pages will protect him from evil.

The Bible plays an important role as a prop in *Hacksaw Ridge*. Connecting his two great loves, Doss's Bible has a picture of Dorothy and a love note from her. When Dorothy gives him the Bible, she says, "You keep it right here [indicating his heart] where I'll be." The Bible comforts Doss. He reads it while awaiting his court martial trial and before the Okinawa battle. While carried on a stretcher from the battlefield, a distraught Doss utters, "My Bible, my Bible, my Bible." A soldier leaves, retrieves it from the battlefield, and hands it to Doss, who clutches it gratefully. As Doss is lowered from the cliffside on a stretcher, the camera lingers on him holding his Bible on his chest.

In *The Shawshank Redemption*, a Bible is an essential tool in Andy Dufresne's multidecade prison escape effort. It is within his Bible that Andy hides his rock pick, a tool he uses nightly to chip away through his cell wall. The Bible conceals Andy's criminal activity and aids in liberating an innocent man. This twin symbolism signals how the Bible can function in diverse ways.

THE BOOK OF ELI

The Book of Eli (Hughes brothers, 2010) offers an extensive treatment of the Bible as a prop. For 30 years Eli has walked West through a post-apocalyptic landscape, with a book hidden in his backpack. This mysterious book is revealed to be a leather bound Bible, with a cross on its front. It is the last remaining Bible, and Eli is on a mission to transport it safely to the West coast of the US.

For most of the film, Eli has a twofold orientation toward the Bible: reader and protector. He reads it every night before going to sleep. When asked if he truly reads the same book every day, he replies, "Without fail." Reading it is a ritual that involves removing it from his backpack, unwrapping the mesh cloth it is wrapped in, and unlocking a device that keeps the book closed. He kisses the Bible before putting it away. This ritualized activity reflects the book's significant (sacred?) status for Eli. When Solara, his walking companion, dismissively says, "It's just a book," he retorts, "It is *not* just a book." He later explains that part of its unique significance is that it is the only copy remaining.

Eli's time spent reading the Bible is reflected in how readily he quotes from it. While preparing to fight a large crowd, Eli announces, "Cursed be the ground for our sake. Both thorns and thistles, it shall bring forth for us. For out of the ground we were taken for the dust we are. And to the dust we shall return." His paraphrase of Genesis 3:17–19 appropriates the "curse" God gives Adam and Eve, and applies it to Eli and those whom he is about to combat. When Solara asks if he can share something with her from the book, he cites Psalm 23. Impressed with the language, she asks Eli if he wrote it. Eli's final line ("I fought the good fight, I finished the race, I kept the faith") is a quote from 2 Timothy 4:7. In response to Solara's question about where they are traveling, Eli says, "Walk by faith not by sight," a paraphrase of 2 Corinthians 5:7. The Bible also influences a part of Eli's moral code. After slamming a biker's head into a bar, Eli tells him, "You are gonna be held to account for the things you've done." Eli's own name is significant since in Hebrew it means "my God."

The film's main conflict develops when Carnegie, a small town despot who has been searching for a Bible for years, realizes Eli has one. Both men are obsessed with it, Eli with concealing and protecting it, Carnegie with obtaining it. When a gang leader tells him to open his backpack, Eli simply replies, "Can't do that." He even refuses to intervene when a woman is going to be raped, telling himself, "Stay on the path. It's not your concern." He will not allow Solara to touch the Bible. Carnegie, desperate to procure it, threatens to kill Solara if Eli does not turn over the book. The function of the Bible as a source of conflict parallels its previous association with a former war; all the Bibles were destroyed after this war, and Eli says that many people believed the Bible "was the reason for the war in the first place."

Carnegie's lust for the Bible is rooted in his conviction that it will help him consolidate political control. "I know its power," he exclaims. "I don't have the right words to help them, but the book does." When Carnegie's henchman dismisses the importance of pursuing Eli "for a fucking book," Carnegie erupts, "It's not a fucking book! It's a weapon. A weapon aimed right at the hearts and minds of the weak and the desperate. It will give us control of them. If we want to rule … we have to have it. People will come from all over. They'll do exactly what I tell them if the words are from the book. It's happened before and it'll happen again. All we need is that book." Carnegie's reference to what happened before is unspecified, but one can imagine that the use of the Bible to justify enslaving other people might be the type of activity he has in mind. Carnegie is deliriously happy when he obtains the Bible; he clutches it to his chest as his most prized possession, and utters, "Ask and you shall receive" (Matthew 7:7).

Eli's third and final orientation toward the Bible, and one marking his character development, is living by its content. He reluctantly gives the Bible to Carnegie only after Solara's life is threatened. She later comments, "I didn't think anything could make you give up that book. I thought it was too important." He replies, "All the years I've been carrying it and reading it every day—I got so caught up with keeping it safe I forgot to live by what I learned from it." When

Figure 6.5   Eli recites from memory the entire Bible in *The Book of Eli* (2010).

she asks, "What's that?" he replies, "Do for others more than you do for yourself." Eli's paraphrase of Matthew 7:12 ("Do to others as you would have them do to you") intensifies Jesus' command. By calling for a higher standard, Eli does to Jesus' words what Jesus does to laws in the Torah (Matthew 5:21–48). The film thus elevates the Bible's content above its representational value—whatever that may be—as a physical object.

Three surprises are revealed when Eli and Solara arrive at Alcatraz, where people are accumulating the world's lost books: Eli's Bible (which Carnegie now has) is in Braille; Eli is blind; and Eli has memorized the entire Bible, word for word. As someone transcribes his words, Eli recites from memory, "The first book of Moses called Genesis. Chapter one. Verse one. In the beginning God created the heavens and the earth. Verse two. And the earth was without form and void. And darkness was upon the face of the deep. And the spirit of God was hovering over the face of the waters. Verse three. And God said, 'Let there be light.' And there was light."

These surprises convey insights. This Bible is not accessible to everyone. Because it is in Braille, Carnegie cannot read it. Claudia, his woman companion, happens to be blind, and she tells Carnegie she can no longer read Braille. A deleted scene shows her sitting in bed and tracing her fingers over the Bible's Braille text. Only those with a certain *dis*ability (blindness) have the ability to access the Bible. Of course, Eli and the folks at Alcatraz want to make the Bible broadly accessible, and this is what Eli's memorization and recitation enable. A printing press begins to print the Bible (the King James version). After it is printed, it is placed in a library shelf alongside the Tanakh, Torah, and Qur'an.

The concept of what the Bible is shifts from that of a book to a person. In his treatment of others, his citation and paraphrasing of it, and in his memorization and recitation of it, Eli becomes the Bible. In Eli, the text of the Bible becomes a living thing; the word of the Bible becomes flesh in the form of Eli. The film's ambiguous title carries potentially diverse meanings: is the "book of Eli" the leather-bound Braille King James Bible in Eli's backpack, is the book "God's book" (since Eli in Hebrew means "my God"), or is Eli *himself* the book? The latter appears to be the case when Eli, arriving at Alcatraz, tells a guard that he has brought with him a King James Bible. The physical Bible is in Carnegie's possession, and so the "book" of which Eli speaks here is *not* (or no longer) a physical object. The film thus transforms the notion of the Bible from a physical object to something human.

SUMMARY

Films can utilize, incorporate, and interpret biblical characters and texts in multiple ways. The process of appropriating biblical texts and characters within the film's narrative and aesthetic world invariably and inevitably involves reconfiguring and reframing them. Biblical texts and characters take on a new life of their own when they appear in cinema. The Bible itself engages in and models this type of reframing and reconfiguring prior biblical texts (precursors). Films also make creative use of biblical texts and characters as precursors. Our understanding and interpretation of a film such as *Magnolia* is deepened and enriched upon recognizing the significant role that Exodus 8:2—and the broader Exodus narrative—plays in the film. *Magnolia* similarly enriches our ability to (re)interpret the Exodus story. *Pulp Fiction* illustrates the fluidity of the biblical text in the hands of its interpreter, and how the text's interpretive adaptability can influence character development. *Dead Man Walking* and *Hacksaw Ridge* demonstrate the potential power of biblical texts to shape—in diverse and divergent ways—peoples' moral values and ethical commitments, and the important role personal interpretation plays in shaping one's understanding of the Bible.

Rather than focusing solely on the Bible's content, *The Book of Eli* illustrates conflicting perspectives regarding the various functions of the Bible as a physical object. *Mary Magdalene* suggests that the powerful role of sex and gender in sidelining women leaders in the early church is something that lurks behind the explicit biblical text.

NOTES

1 Pasolini (2014).
2 Some of the material on *Magnolia* appeared in a modified form in Rindge (2016b).
3 Anderson (2000), 206–7.
4 Freire (2000).
5 Anderson (2000), 201.
6 Some of the material on *Dead Man Walking* appeared in an altered form in Rindge (2012). Used with permission.
7 For a fuller treatment of *Hacksaw Ridge,* see Rindge (2021b).

FOR FURTHER READING

Rhonda Burnette-Bletsch, "God at the Movies," in *The Bible in Motion: Biblical Reception in Film* (ed. Rhona Burnette-Bletsch; Berlin: De Gruyter, 2016), 2: 299–326.

Adele Reinhartz, *Scripture on the Silver Screen* (Louisville, KY: Westminster John Knox Press, 2003).

FILM AS BIBLE

The previous chapters have examined films about biblical texts/characters, films that reimagine biblical texts/characters, and films that cite, allude to, or incorporate biblical texts/characters. Films can also, however, function like biblical texts by replicating certain biblical genres. Films do not, in other words, have to cite a biblical text in order to operate in similar ways as biblical texts. This chapter examines how films can function like biblical laments, prophecies, parables, and apocalypses. Exploring films in this manner shifts in some ways the focus away from questions about the film's content—"does the film cite (or allude to) the Bible?"—to *what* the film is doing and *how* the film is doing it. This focus on a film's rhetorical texture reflects Roger Ebert's insightful remark, "It's not what a movie is about, it's how it is about it."[1]

CINEMATIC LAMENT

The biblical genre of lament (appearing most often in the psalms, but also in Job, Lamentations, and Jesus' cry from the cross in Mark and Matthew) expresses anger and disappointment to God, blaming God for suffering that people endure. Laments typically question God and accuse God of absence, abandonment, apathy, or cruelty. A lament articulates painful emotions and experiences that are often otherwise silenced or ignored. Some laments complain to God about other people, while other laments complain to God *about God*, bringing accusations against God *to* God.

Many films incorporate aspects of lament. In *The End of the Affair* (Jordan, 1999) Maurice Bendrix announces, "I hate you, God. I hate you as though you existed." The film ends (giving the title a dual meaning) with his prayer: "Dear God, forget about me ... leave me alone forever." Ostensibly an alien invasion film, *Signs* (Shyamalan, 2002) follows the spiritual development of Episcopal priest Graham Hess. After an automobile accident kills his wife, Hess leaves the priesthood and abandons his faith in God. His (new) perspective on faith is clear: "There is no one watching out for us ... we are all on our own." After refusing his children's request to pray during what appears to be their final meal together, he holds his young son who is enduring an asthma attack. Using the language of lament, Graham speaks to God for the first time in the film: "Don't do this to me again, not again. I hate you. I hate you." During a later standoff with an alien, the final words Graham's wife spoke inspire him to tell his brother how to defeat the alien. (Graham had previously understood his wife's words as a coincidence arising from random nerve firings, but he now realizes that they saved his family.) Graham also discovers that his son's asthma protected his lungs from inhaling and dying from alien venom. As his son wakes from a stupor, he asks Graham, "Did someone save me?" His father's reply, "I think someone did," suggests a possible return to some type of faith in God. The film's final scene confirms this suggestion by showing Graham emerge from his bedroom dressed in his priest's garb.

TO THE WONDER

To the Wonder (Malick, 2012) is a meditation on the pain and sorrow of love's demise.[2] The film laments the deterioration of romantic and divine love, paralleling both relational dimensions. Shifting from the beauty of the French coast to the toxic pollution in an Oklahoma town symbolizes the relational dissolution between Neil and Marina. Marina laments Neil's increasing silence and emotional detachment: "Why do we come back down?" "How," she asks, "had hate come to take the place of love? My tender heart grown hard?"

The film proposes that the intimacy (human and divine) for which people yearn is—even if experienced—fleeting and unsustainable.

Against Hollywood conventions, and despite their efforts, Neal and Marina are incapable of rekindling their romance. Long camera shots of the characters alone heighten this alienation. Simultaneous shots of Marina on an upper floor, and Neil on the floor below her, make palpable their respective alienation and disconnection. Like the toxic sludge that Neil investigates for his job, there are unseen forces that seem to conspire to keep the couple steadily succumbing to relational death. Neil remains emotionally distant. Marina has a casual sexual encounter which Neil seems unable to forgive, and she returns with her child to France. Not unlike *Run Lola Run* (Tykwer, 1998), the film indicates that one's hunger for love will forever remain elusive.

The silences and distances that haunt romantic relationships have a divine counterpart. Paralleling Neil and Marina's romantic collapse is the despair Fr. Quintana repeatedly expresses to God about God's absence in his life. He offers five prayers throughout the film, and the first four highlight his painful dissatisfaction with this divine distance:

> Everywhere you're present, and still I can't see you. You're within me. Around me. And I have no experience of you. Not as I once did. Why don't I hold on to what I've found? My heart is cold. Hard.
>
> How long will you hide yourself? Let me come to you. Let me not pretend. Pretend to feelings I do not have.
>
> Intensely I seek you. My soul thirsts for you. Exhausted. Will you be like a stream that dries up?
>
> Why do you turn your back? All I see is destruction. Failure. Ruin.

There is a correlation between Fr. Quintana's lament and his actions serving the needy. Despite (or perhaps because of) his longing for the divine presence, Fr. Quintana frequently assists a wide variety of vulnerable populations. He visits the elderly, gives his coat to a poor woman on the street, listens to a deaf woman, cares for the sick at a hospital, gives communion to—and speaks with—prisoners in jail, and cares for those who are poor and developmentally disabled. He embodies Jesus' call to serve the "least of these" (Matthew 25:31–46), the Catholic works of mercy. Such service might be fueled by his recognition that in a world where God is absent, love and justice can only be provided by people. His lament empowers action, catalyzing acts of justice on behalf of the vulnerable.

Fr. Quintana's commitment to action is evident in excerpts from his homilies: "Love is not only a feeling. Love is a duty. You show love. Love is a command, and you say, 'I can command my emotions.' They come and go like clouds. To that, Christ says you shall love, whether you like it or not. You fear your love has died. It perhaps is waiting to be transformed into something higher." Failing to act is what Fr. Quintana condemns most harshly:

> We fear to choose. Jesus insists on choice. The one thing he condemns utterly is avoiding the choice. To choose is to commit yourself. And to commit yourself is to run the risk, is to run the risk of failure, the risk of sin, the risk of betrayal. But Jesus can deal with all of those. Forgiveness he never denies us. The man who makes a mistake can repent. But the man who hesitates, who does nothing, who buries his talent in the earth, with him he can do nothing.

These exhortations apply to the crumbling human and divine relationships in the film. As in Malick's *The Tree of Life*, lament culminates in a twin posture of seeking and surrender. The priest's final prayer, echoing a prayer attributed to St. Patrick, shifts to a request for an unceasing seeking of Christ's presence:

> Where are you leading me? Teach us where to seek you. Christ, be with me. Christ before me. Christ behind me. Christ in me. Christ beneath me. Christ above me. Christ on my right. Christ on my left. Christ in

Figure 7.1 Fr. Quintana laments God's absence, and serves the needy in *To the Wonder* (2012).

the heart. Thirsting. We thirst. Flood our souls with your spirit and life. So completely, that our lives may only be a reflection of yours. Shine through us. Show us how to seek you. We were made to see you.

Seeking thus supplants (or joins) lament. In every lament psalm (with the exception of Psalm 88), there is a shift from lament to praise (or promised praise). For Marina, lament shifts to gratitude; she ends the film praying, "Love that loves us … Thank you."

SILENCE

Based on Shūsaku Endō's novel, *Silence* (Scorsese, 2016) is set in 17th-century Japan, where Christianity is outlawed, and the Japanese government is persecuting and killing Christians. The film's grisly tone is established in its opening shot of two decapitated heads, followed by scenes depicting the torture of Jesuit priests. In this environment, two Portuguese Jesuit priests (Frs. Garupe and Rodrigues) secretly enter Japan to locate Fr. Ferreira, their former teacher and fellow Jesuit who has allegedly apostatized and abandoned his faith.

The language of abandonment is pronounced in the film. A voiceover accompanying the opening scene of the torture of Jesuit priests states, "The officials told our padres to abandon God and the gospel of his love." When Frs. Rodrigues and Garupe first meet Kichijiro, a Japanese man who transports them from China to Japan, he begs them not to abandon him. Kichijiro and his family had been arrested for converting to Christianity, and when Kichijiro's family refused to apostatize, they were burned alive as he watched; he was only spared because he apostatized. Kichijiro reflects, "But I could not abandon them even if I had abandoned God. So I watched them die."

It is God's abandonment, however, that looms large as the film develops, and Fr. Rodrigues laments this divine abandonment. His spiritual journey is a centerpiece of the film. Early on he meditates on an image of Jesus' face, and recalls Jesus telling Peter, "Feed my lambs, feed my lambs, feed my sheep" (John 21:15–17). Rodrigues reflects, "It fascinates me. I feel such great love for it." He later adds, "I felt God Himself was so near." This phase of spiritual bliss is short-lived. After arriving in Japan and witnessing the suffering and misery of Japanese Christians there, Rodrigues asks why God has allowed them to suffer. His empathy for their suffering leads him to tell Mokichi, an arrested Japanese Christian, that it is acceptable to trample on the fumie (an image of Jesus), the public symbol of apostasy. Reflecting on the persecution of Japanese Christians, Rodrigues states, "I began to wonder: God sends us trials to test us and everything He does is good … but why must their trial be so terrible?"

Rodrigues develops a new faith perspective after secretly witnessing Mokichi and two other Japanese Christians lashed to crosses on the beach and drowned as the tide engulfs them. It took Mokichi four days to die. In a letter to his Jesuit superior in Portugal, Rodrigues acknowledges that his superior would say that God heard the prayers of these men as they died. Rodrigues asks, however, "but did He hear their screams? How can I explain His silence to these people who have endured so much?" Lamenting God's silence in the midst of such devastation becomes a defining part of how Rodrigues relates to God. After he discovers that soldiers have decimated the village of Goto (where he and Fr. Garupe ministered), Rodrigues tells God, "The weight of your silence is terrible. I pray but I'm lost. Or am I just praying to nothing? Nothing. Because you are not there."

In some ways, Rodrigues' life begins to mimic that of Jesus. Symbolizing this *imitatio Christi* is Rodriguez staring at his reflection in a stream of water, and seeing his reflected face turn into the same image of Jesus' face on which he formerly meditated. Cementing this identification with Jesus is Rodrigues' immediate arrest by the Inquisitor's soldiers. Kichijiro had betrayed Rodrigues to the Inquisitor, not long after Rodrigues—repeating Jesus' line to Judas—twice told Kichijiro, "Go and do what you must do quickly." Kichijiro calls himself a weak man and asks, "Where is the place for a weak man in a world like this?" Apparently such a place is as a Judas figure.

Much of the remaining film concerns the Inquisitor's efforts to convince Rodrigues to deny his faith and publicly apostatize by stepping on an engraving of Jesus (the fumie). If Rodrigues does so, the Inquisitor will release the captured Japanese Christians, stopping their torture. Rodrigues refuses to apostasize, and is comforted by the thought that he is emulating Jesus' example. Reflecting again on Jesus' face, he prays to God, "I see the life of your son so clearly, almost like my own. And his face, it takes all fear from me. It is the face I remember from childhood. Speaking to me. I'm sure of it. Promising, 'I will not abandon you, I will not abandon you, I will not abandon you.'"

After several of the imprisoned Japanese Christians refuse to step on the fumie, Rodrigues prays, "Thank you, Lord, for hearing my prayer." Yet immediately after his prayer, a soldier decapitates one of these Christians. Rodrigues is brought to a beach where he witnesses four Japanese Christians wrapped in mats of bamboo and dumped into the ocean to be drowned. Fr. Garupe drowns in an effort to save them. That night in his cell Rodrigues laments to God with Jesus' words: "My God, my God, why have you forsaken me? Why have you forsaken me?" (Mark 15:34; Matthew 27:46). Rodrigues continues, recognizing a parallel between God's treatment of Jesus and of himself: "I was your son. Your son was going to the cross. You were silent, even to him." He continues praying over images of a decapitated peasant and Garupe's drowned body: "Your silent, cold son." Rodrigues ascribes God's silence to Jesus as well, perceiving both as unwilling to help him. Rodrigues concludes (referring to either God or Jesus), "He's not going to answer. He's not going to answer."

To apply more pressure to Rodrigues, Inspector Inoue arranges a meeting between him and his former teacher, Ferreira. Rodrigues is dismayed to discover that Ferreira not only publicly apostatized, but that he now studies at a Buddhist temple and is writing a book discrediting Christianity; Rodrigues tells him he is a disgrace. Ferreira encourages Rodrigues to apostatize, which Rodrigues refuses to do. From the confines of his cell later that night, Rodrigues listens to the shrieks of Japanese Christians as they are tortured by being hung upside down in dark pits. He asks God, "Are you here with me?" Ferreira visits Rodrigues in his cell, and implores him, "Do you have the right to make them suffer?" Ferreira chides Rodrigues for being prideful and comparing himself to Jesus. Ferreira asks him, "And what would you do for them? Pray? And get what in return? Only more suffering. A suffering only you can end, not God. I prayed too, Rodrigues. It doesn't help." (Flashbacks show Ferreira being tortured and witnessing the torture and execution of other priests and Japanese Christians.)

As the Japanese Christians continue crying out in pain, Ferreira tells Rodrigues, "You can spare them. They call out for help just as you call to God. He is silent, but you do not have to be … If Christ were here, he would have apostatized for their sake." God's silence, Ferreira implies, does not have to mean that people must also be silent to the sufferings of others. Unlike God—who fails to respond to suffering—people such as Rodrigues can respond and bring an end to such suffering. Ferreira also points out that Jesus' love for the Japanese Christians should compel Rodrigues to publicly deny his faith in order to stop their suffering. Understood in this light, Rodrigues' insistence on not denying his faith is tantamount to betraying Jesus. In order to remain loyal to Jesus (and his ethic of love), Rodrigues must publicly deny him. Since public apostatizing protects others from torture and death, such refutation of one's faith is precisely how one displays authentic devotion to God.

While Rodrigues readies himself to step on the fumie, thus solidifying the public repudiation of his faith, Ferreira tells him, "You are now going to perform the most painful act of love that has ever been performed." Rodrigues looks upon the image of Jesus on the fumie, and hears Jesus speaking to him from it. Jesus beckons him to step on his own image, telling Rodrigues that he (Jesus) is here to share peoples' pain. Rodrigues sees yet again the image of Jesus' face from his childhood, and he steps upon the fumie and collapses. The Japanese Christians are finally released from hanging in the pit. While their bodies are pulled up a crock crows three times (not once as in the novel), alluding to the sound that accompanied Peter's denial of Jesus. In light of the film, Peter's denial can be viewed not as an abandonment of Jesus but rather as remaining loyal to Jesus because of opting to preserve his own life.

Rodrigues spends the next several years working with Ferreira to help the Japanese government identify objects of Christian veneration traders try to smuggle into Japan. He becomes that which he previously detested. Near the film's end, Kichijiro once more asks if he can confess his sins to Rodrigues. This leads Rodrigues to tell

Figure 7.2   Fr. Ferreira tries to convince Fr. Rodriguez to publicly deny his faith in *Silence* (2016).

God, "Lord, I fought against your silence." He hears a voice (presumably God or Jesus) respond, "I suffered beside you. I was never silent." Rodrigues says, "I know. But even if God had been silent my whole life, to this very day, everything I do, everything I've done, speaks of Him. It was in the silence that I heard your voice." Rodrigues shifts from viewing God's silence as indifference to a vehicle through which God somehow speaks. God somehow speaks in silence; *what* God speaks in that silence is unclear.

The most famous lament in the New Testament is Jesus' cry from the cross: "My God, my God, why have you abandoned/forsaken me?" (Mark 15:34; Matt 27:46). What Jesus expresses at the end of his life (in Mark and Matthew)—lamenting God's silence in the midst of his suffering—becomes in Scorsese's *Silence* a crucial developmental stage of Rodrigues' evolving faith. Unlike Jesus—but not quite like lament psalms—Rodrigues passes through lament to an acceptance that God's silence is not tantamount to God's apathy or indifference.

CINEMATIC PROPHECY

Contrary to popular opinion, Hebrew Bible prophetic literature is primarily concerned not with predicting the future, but with communicating God's heart and mind to God's people. While the prophets reveal God's hope for Israel during times of distress and upheaval, they also convey God's judgments against Israel for Israel's failure to care for the poor and oppressed. The prophets often condemn Israel for engaging in religious and spiritual acts of worship while systemically oppressing its most socially and economically vulnerable members such as orphans, widows, foreigners, and the poor (Isaiah 58; Jeremiah 7; Amos 5). Prophets tend to direct their critique at the powerful within their own nation and religion, and advocate on behalf of the powerless. They often seek to elicit empathy for those who suffer. Films can operate or function prophetically by indicting social injustices, constructing alternative social visions, and eliciting empathy on behalf of those who suffer systemic oppression.

Prophetic films articulate social discontent and have the potential to catalyze social-political change. Documentary films are especially conducive to this type of prophetic social critique. Michael Moore's documentaries *Roger & Me* (1989), *Bowling for Columbine* (2002), *Fahrenheit 9/11* (2004), *Sicko* (2007), and *Capitalism: A Love Story* (2009) lament a wide variety of social ills. At the heart of many of these films is an effort to reveal how poor people suffer as casualties of companies' commitment to monetary profit at all costs. *Blackfish* (Cowperthwaite, 2013) draws connections between the abuse of orcas at SeaWorld and attacks by these animals on people.

Ava DuVernay's 2016 documentary *13th* indicts the US prison system for systematically imprisoning Black nonviolent offenders, thereby continuing slavery under a different name. DuVernay's historical drama *Selma* (2014) focuses on the efforts of Rev. Dr. Martin Luther King, Jr. and others in Selma to bring the constitutional right to vote to all Black people in the US. This film is especially pertinent in the aftermath of the US Supreme Court eliminating key parts of the Voting Rights Act for which King and others struggled. DuVernay's historical TV miniseries drama *When They See Us* (2019) profiles five young Black men who spent years imprisoned for a crime they did not commit.

Much of Spike Lee's oeuvre is imbued with a prophetic spirit. *Do the Right Thing* (1989) highlights contemporary racial tensions and racism in New York at a time when many white people in the US believed that racism was something located in the south and relegated to the distant past. *Malcolm X* (1992) is Lee's biopic of the prophetic civil rights leader. Adhering closely to Malcolm's autobiography, the film documents Malcolm's multiple conversions, from criminal to Nation of Islam spokesperson, to Muslim. Malcolm becomes a leading voice in denouncing white America's systemic oppression of Black people. Lee's documentary *4 Little Girls* (1997) recounts the 1963 bombing of the 16th Street Baptist Church in Birmingham, AL that killed three 14-year-old girls and one 11-year-old girl. Lee's fictional film *Bamboozled* (2000) examines racism in the media/entertainment industry. Wanting to leave their jobs at a television studio, two young Black men pitch an idea for a blackface minstrel show. Expecting to be fired for their idea, they are shocked when the studio greenlights it. To the dismay of the two young men, it becomes a ratings bonanza. The film concludes with a montage of film, television, and commercial clips illustrating the overt antiblack racism that has permeated the US media for almost a century. Lee's documentary *When the Levees Broke: A Requiem in Four Acts* (2006) indicts the US government's abysmal response to Hurricane Katrina. *BlacKkKlansman* (2018) is a historical drama based on a 1970s Black policeman who goes undercover and infiltrates the KKK. The film is dedicated to Heather Heyer who was killed while protesting a "Unite the Right" rally in Charlottesville, VA, in 2017. Footage of this incident appears at the end of the film.

The documentary *I Am Not Your Negro* (Peck, 2016) examines James Baldwin's plan to write a book on Malcolm X, Martin Luther

Figure 7.3   Malcolm during a television debate in *Malcolm X* (1992).

King, Jr., and Medgar Evers. Baldwin contends that the sickness of racism in the United States is one which white people must solve, and that any solution must reckon both with the need white people have to denigrate Black people as subhuman, and what this need reveals about white people. Baldwin's incisive analysis of racial politics and racism in the United States is as (or more) relevant in 2021 than when Baldwin was alive.

Many films offer a prophetic critique of issues related to gender and sexuality. *Thelma and Louise* (Scott, 1991) indicts a US culture so steeped in patriarchy that the only way for women to find liberation is to die. Two documentaries by Kirby Dick depict the endemic nature of rape and sexual assault women face in the US military (*The Invisible War*, 2012) and on college campuses (*The Hunting Ground*, 2015). *Boys Don't Cry* (Peirce, 1999) recounts the true story of Brandon Teena, a transgender man who was raped and killed when his biological identity was discovered. It is one of few films to highlight the discrimination and abuse (social, psychological) transgender people can face as they seek to transition into and inhabit their gender identity.

The Girl in the Café (Yates, 2005) is a classic prophetic film. Shortly after Lawrence, a British civil servant, meets Gina, a young woman, he invites her to join him at a G-8 summit in Reykjavik, Iceland. At meals between official meetings, Gina suggests redirecting a larger percentage of the G-8 budget toward poor people in the two-thirds world. Her relentless determination to speak up about this issue is a source of increasing consternation for the G-20 attendees. To Lawrence's great embarrassment, and the annoyance of everyone else, she takes every opportunity, and in a fairly belligerent manner, to press the issue of allocating more funds to poor people. The increasing level of discomfort occasioned by her refusal to be quiet is palpable.

In his toast at one of the dinners, the Prime Minister references the impressive work the summit is doing to combat poverty. Gina interrupts him, murmuring, "That's not true. That's not true." When the Prime Minister admonishes her, and says that heckling is not part of the tradition at the G-20, Gina replies, "What are the traditions, then? Well-crafted compromise and just sort of ignoring the poor?" The Prime Minister asks if they can discuss this later, but Gina says, "I doubt it ... while we are eating a hundred million children are nearly starving. There's just millions of kids who'd kill for the amount of food that fat old me left on the side of my plate, children who are then so weak they'll die if a mosquito bites them. And so they do die. One every three seconds." Three seconds later she snaps her fingers, then continues, "There they go." After another three-second pause, she says, "There they go." She pauses for another three seconds, snaps again, and says,

> And another one. Anyone who has kids knows that every mother and father in Africa must love their children as much as they do, and to watch your kids die, to watch them die and then to die yourself in trying to protect them, that's not right. And tomorrow eight of the men sitting around this table actually have the ability to sort this out by making a few great decisions. And if they don't, some day someone else will. And they'll look back on us lot and say—people were actually dying in their millions unnecessarily, in front of you, on your TV screens. What were you thinking? You knew what to do to stop it happening and you didn't do those things. Shame on you. So that's what you have to do tomorrow. Be great instead of being ashamed. It can't be impossible. It must be possible.

During the end credits, a person snaps their fingers every three seconds. This reminder to the audience—that every three seconds someone dies of extreme poverty—is a summons for viewers to do something to save the lives of people who live in desperate poverty. *The Girl in the Café* is prophetic in depicting someone who challenges those in power to empathize with the suffering of the poor and to act on their behalf. The film exemplifies the rejection prophets experience as a result of provoking those in power to make meaningful changes for oppressed people.

CINEMATIC PARABLES

Jesus' parables are fictional stories that subvert conventional myths. Contrary to the general impression that his parables, like Aesop's fables, transmit morals, lessons or quaint spiritual truths, Jesus' parables often undermine conventional morals. They provoke rather than comfort, disturb rather than appease. In the parable of the

Samaritan, the ethnic and religious enemy is the hero and moral exemplar whom one should imitate, and who will also inherit eternal life (Luke 10:25–37). The parable of the Sheep and the Goats proposes that the sole criterion determining whether a person goes to heaven or hell is whether or not they meet the needs of the hungry, thirsty, foreigner, naked, sick, and imprisoned (Matthew 25:31–46). The parable of Lazarus and the Rich Man suggests that what determines where a person spends eternity is their socioeconomic status; wealthy people who live in comfort spend eternity in agony, and poor people who suffer spend eternity in comfort (Luke 16:19–31). In the parables of the Net, the Wheat and the Weeds, and the Leaven, the kingdom of heaven is presented as a mixture of the pure and the impure (Matthew 13). One of the most perplexing parables is the Dishonest Manager, where Jesus seems to endorse theft (Luke 16:1–8).

Cinematic parables are films that subvert conventional cultural myths. Cinematic apologues, on the other hand, are films that defend such myths. *Top Gun* (Scott, 1986) functions as an apologue in defending and glorifying US military supremacy and morality. The film perpetuates a cherished American myth that success is the only option, and that if the US military uses force, it does so only to protect and defend. *Born on the Fourth of July* (Stone, 1989) is parabolic in its evisceration of many American myths. The film rejects the deeply ingrained myth in America that being a Christian (who abides by the ten commandments) is compatible with serving in the military (and killing others). By illustrating the devastating physiological and psychological trauma of war (e.g., PTSD and moral injury), the film undercuts American myths about the nobility of military service.

Dogville operates as a parable in its subversion of prevailing American myths regarding America's moral goodness. The film skewers the assumption that people, particularly Americans, are good. One of the narrator's opening lines ("The residents of Dogville were good, honest folks") is found sorely wanting, and lacking as much merit as the townspeople. In Dogville, human decency is extinct. The poverty of Dogville's residents also undercuts a myth about the nobility of the poor. The film's final credits play over a montage of photographs, many from *American Pictures* by Danish photographer

Jacob Holdt. These photos depict poor and hungry Americans—many sleeping on the streets and struggling to survive. A fair percentage of them are Black Americans, and many are children. Some photos show poor people who have died. A few display wealthier Americans passing by these poor people living (or dead) on the street. The critique of America is made further evident by scoring the final credits to David Bowie's song "Young Americans."

Following the catharsis many viewers experience during the annihilation of Dogville, the photographic images and music serve a vital rhetorical function. If viewers experience an emotional purgation in Dogville's punishment for their abuse of Grace, the credits seek to convince audiences to apply the condemnation aimed at the townspeople to themselves. The credits are the rhetorical equivalent of the prophet Nathan's retort to King David, "You are the man!" when Nathan succeeds in getting David to condemn himself for his murder of Uriah, Bathsheba's husband (2 Samuel 12:1–7). "*You* are the residents of Dogville!" insist the photographs of poor, hungry, and vulnerable Americans. The film compels American viewers to ponder how their neglect of vulnerable people in their midst is no different than Dogville's abuse of Grace. Identifying sexual assault as the apex of evil, the set's lack of walls invites US viewers to consider their own complicity in sexual violence if they are not actively preventing such abuse.

Figure 7.4   Images and music during the closing credits of *Dogville* (2003) condemn Americans for their apathy toward the poor.

The film also functions as a parable in subverting the (theological) myth that grace and mercy are beneficial virtues. The film uproots this presumption by depicting the unrelentless oppression inflicted upon a person who incarnates and embodies these traits. *Dogville* argues that acting gracefully enables and perpetuates abuse.[3] Grace incarnates her name, serves the townspeople, and refuses to defend herself. She turns her entire body—not only her cheek—when attacked. Grace's acts of grace engender an avalanche of abuse. Her mercy brings out the absolute worst in others. Grace facilitates evil. In a world where people pulverize the weak, mercy merely encourages brutality. Grace's compassion exacerbates her own exploitation. Contrary to James 2:13, *Dogville* insists that judgment must triumph over mercy. As the lone survivor of Dogville's destruction, the dog Moses symbolizes (perhaps with a stereotypical and uninformed view of the Hebrew Bible) that humans require law, not grace, if they are to behave decently toward vulnerable people.

Fight Club (Fincher, 1999), *American Beauty* (Mendes, 1999), and *About Schmidt* (Payne, 2002) function as cinematic parables by subverting myths about America's collective denial of death, and the meaningfulness of the American Dream.[4] Each film features a white man who, despite—or because of—experiencing central pillars of the American Dream, finds his life void of meaning. These films find the American Dream to be existentially bankrupt and spiritually toxic. Each film proposes the countercultural and counterintuitive notion that facing death is an essential step toward meaningful living and spiritual vitality.

CINEMATIC APOCALYPSES

Although the biblical genre of apocalypse is often associated with the end of the world, its literal meaning is "revelation" (hence the title of the last book in the New Testament, whose Greek title is *apokalypsis*). The notion of apocalypse is such a cinematic staple that some films use the term in their titles. *Apocalypse Now* (Coppola, 1979), *Resident Evil: Apocalypse* (Witt, 2004), *Apocalypto* (Gibson, 2006), and *X-Men Apocalypse* (Singer, 2016) reflect shared assumptions of what a cinematic apocalypse will entail (e.g., massive and spectacular violence). Apocalyptic films often reflect (and fuel) social anxieties. Alien and disaster films from the 1950s to the 1970s and beyond played on Cold War inspired fears of nuclear annihilation. Aliens in the original *Invasion of the Body Snatchers* (Siegel, 1956) symbolize communist infiltrators. *The Terminator* (Cameron, 1984) and *The Matrix* films (Wachowskis, 1999, 2003) are steeped in anxieties of technology destroying or enslaving humanity. Fears of global destruction from cosmic collision fuel *Armageddon* (Bay, 1998) and *Deep Impact* (Leder, 1998); anxieties of environmental catastrophe surface in *The Happening* (Shyamalan, 2008), *2012* (Emmerich, 2009), and *Noah* (2014). Post-apocalyptic films such as *28 Days Later* (Boyle, 2002), *The Road* (Coens, 2009), *The Book of Eli* (Hughes brothers, 2010), and *I Am Legend* (Lawrence, 2007) reflect worries about people erasing their humanity in their struggle to survive. Eschatological apocalypses such as *End of Days* (Hyams, 1999), *The Devil's Advocate* (Hackford, 1997), *Noah* (Aronofsky, 2014), and *Children of Men* (Cuarón, 2006) address potential world-ending scenarios.

Film is an ideal medium for the apocalypse genre. Cinema offers a temporary detour into an alternative dimension that—not unlike a heavenly realm—is both distinct from and connected to our own world. As with biblical apocalypses, this "other world" often contains dramatic and violent displays. Such visual spectacles can incorporate the bizarre and grotesque. These graphic displays are not mere aesthetic treats; such films often reveal heavenly mysteries, both to characters in the narrative and to film viewers.

Like many biblical apocalypses, *Donnie Darko, Dogville,* and *Magnolia* view the world as so fundamentally flawed that the only hope of redemption or vindication lies outside of it. This hope must pierce through the world in order to bring salvation. Whereas biblical apocalypses are thought to be produced by oppressed communities longing for a future vindication, apocalyptic films are made by those in the upper socioeconomic echelons. They—and their audiences—have the potential power to alter behavior that is harmful to the environment or the vulnerable in society. Cinematic apocalypses thus occupy a potentially different rhetorical space than their biblical counterparts—one designed not so much to instill hope, but rather to empower change.

In a deleted scene from *Donnie Darko*, Frank tells Donnie about the end of the world by announcing, "God loves his children. God loves you ... I'm here to save you." Richard Kelly deleted this scene because he thought it too clearly conveyed a notion of "divine intervention," and even though Kelly believes this is what the film is about, he decided that it would be "more powerful to leave the mystery intact by not over explaining everything." Kelly would rather leave audiences confused (and possibly mistaken) about his intended message than offer a message that is too easily understood. Reflecting on the Joban film *A Serious Man*, Kelly notes: "[It is] probably my favorite movie of the year. I've seen it three times. When the credits started to roll in that movie, I looked around and everyone in the theater was like, 'What the fuck did I just see?' It was a wonderful feeling. Some of the best memories I have of going to the movies are the WTF movies. Maybe that should be a new genre."[5] Kelly's desire to maintain a sense of unexplained mystery permeates *Donnie Darko*, and is evident in the countless and ongoing efforts of viewers to decipher the film's multiple mysteries. One sign of the film's function as a cinematic apocalypse are these continuing acts of communal interpretation—preserving a textual afterlife—that the film engenders.

Parasite (Joon-ho, 2019) received the Oscar for Best International Feature, and was the first "foreign" film to win Oscars for Best Picture, Best Director, and Best Original Screenplay. Joon-ho's film shines a light on South Korea's unjust socioeconomic stratification, and how the wealthy survive by exploiting the labor of the poor and desperate. Like biblical apocalypses that condemn the wealthy and warn of a divine judgment against them (Revelation 18), *Parasite* depicts a looming (inevitable?) judgment awaiting the wealthy for their existence as parasites on the lives of the poor.

The extracanonical and apocalyptic text of 1 Enoch is a fitting parallel to the film. 1 Enoch contains several divine diatribes of judgment against the wealthy. It proclaims that those who "acquire gold and silver" will quickly perish (94:6–7). To the wealthy, it declares, "Woe to you, rich, for in your riches you have trusted; from your riches you will depart, because you have not remembered the Most High in the days of your riches" (94:8). 1 Enoch associates the wealth of rich people with sins against God, and insists that God will punish the wealthy accordingly (94:10–11; 96:4–97:10). The veneer of righteousness that wealth might provide will not shield the rich, since the deeds of these people are "evil" (96:4). Accusations against the wealthy link their misappropriation of goods with their oppression of the weak. Such people will experience "destruction … in the day of your judgment" (96:8). They will be "destroyed on the day of iniquity" (97:1). Those who acquire gold and silver "unjustly" will be punished for accumulating abundant wealth; their goods will be poured out like water (97:8–9). God's wrathful judgment will be unveiled against the wealthy: "You err! For your wealth will not remain but will quickly depart from you … So you will be destroyed together with all your possessions" (97:10; 98:3). Just as 1 Enoch assures the poor that their suffering and oppression at the hands of the wealthy will not go unpunished, *Parasite* provides a simultaneous challenge to the rich, and a cathartic comfort (albeit faint) to poor people.

SUMMARY

Films need not be explicitly "biblical" in order to generate insight as a result of being placed into dialogue with biblical texts. Similarly, non-explicitly biblical films can often function or operate in ways that resemble biblical texts or genres. Considering how *To the Wonder* and *Silence* function as laments illuminates these films and biblical laments. Thinking of how *The Girl in the Café* and the films of Ava DuVernay and Spike Lee function prophetically offers insight into the rhetorical aims of these films, and helps us appreciate the sociopolitical interests of biblical prophetic texts. Thinking of *Dogville*, *Fight Club*, *American Beauty*, and *About Schmidt* as parables illumines how these films are operating religiously in their critique and subversion of dominant culture norms. Considering films like *Parasite* as apocalyptic illuminates their insistence that the oppression of the poor by the rich demands some kind of dramatic upheaval and judgment. As in biblical texts, boundaries between various genres (cinematic and biblical) can be permeable and porous. Films can participate in multiple genres, and can function as different types of biblical genres. *Dogville* is a film, for example, with a Jesus figure that also functions as parable and apocalypse. *Donnie Darko* has a Jesus figure, and functions apocalyptically.

NOTES

1 Ebert (1997). Ebert designates this "Ebert's law."
2 For a fuller discussion of the film, see Rindge (2020).
3 J. Hoberman notes, "For passion, originality, and sustained chutzpah, this austere allegory of failed Christian charity and Old Testament payback is von Trier's strongest movie—a masterpiece, in fact" (2004).
4 See Rindge (2016a).
5 www.ifc.com/2009/11/richard-kelly.

FOR FURTHER READING

Mary Lea Bandy and Antonio Monda, eds., *The Hidden God: Faith and Film* (New York: The Museum of Modern Art, 2003).

John C. Lyden, *Film as Religion: Myths, Morals and Rituals* (New York: New York University Press, 2003).

Tina Pippin, "This Is the End: Apocalyptic Moments in Cinema," in *The Bible in Motion: Biblical Reception in Film* (ed. Rhonda Burnette-Bletsch; Berlin: De Gruyter, 2016), 1: 405–16.

Matthew S. Rindge, *Profane Parables: Film and the American Dream* (Waco, TX: Baylor University Press, 2016).

Robert Paul Seesengood, "A World of Feeling: The Affect of Lars von Trier and/as Biblical Apocalyptic," in *Close Encounters between Bible and Film: An Interdisciplinary Engagement* (ed. Laura Copier and Caroline Vander Stichele; Society of Biblical Literature, 2016), 209–32.

Robert Paul Seesengood and Jennifer L. Koosed, "Spectacular Finish: Apocalypse in/and the Destruction of the Earth in Film," in *Simulating Aichele: Essays in Bible, Film, Culture and Theory* (ed. Melissa C. Stewart; Sheffield: Sheffield Phoenix, 2015), 143–60.

Richard Walsh, "On Finding a Non-American Revelation: End of Days and the Book of Revelation," in *Screening Scripture: Intertextual Connections between Scripture and Film* (ed. George Aichele and Richard Walsh; Harrisburg, PA: Trinity Press International, 2002), 1–23.

THE FUTURE OF BIBLE AND FILM

The field of Bible and Film is a burgeoning discipline that shows no signs of slowing down. Although it is impossible to predict with certainty how the field will unfold in the future, this chapter examines two areas that will likely receive increased attention within the field of Bible and Film: "non-biblical" films and television.

"NON-BIBLICAL" FILMS

Previous chapters have included conversations between films and biblical texts. With the exception of Chapter 7, these chapters have mostly addressed films that retell, reimagine, cite or allude to biblical texts. Yet much fruitful and insightful work in the field of Bible and Film involves analyzing films that have no explicit references to biblical texts. Robert Johnston's *Useless Beauty: Ecclesiastes through the Lens of Contemporary Faith* does just this, as do many of the essays in both George Aichele and Richard Walsh's *Screening Scripture: Intertextual Connections between Scripture and Film* and Laura Copier and Caroline Vander Stichele's *Close Encounters between Bible and Film: An Interdisciplinary Engagement.* Erin Runions' *How Hysterical: Identification and Resistance in the Bible and Film* also exemplifies this approach.

Films do not have to cite or allude to biblical texts—or function like biblical genres—in order to generate insights when placed into constructive conversations with biblical texts. Innumerable films, for example, share with biblical wisdom literature an interest in existential questions about living meaningfully in a world that may appear meaningless. Like Qoheleth/Ecclesiastes, *Citizen Kane* (Welles, 1941) skewers attempts to find meaning in wealth and success. In *Crimes and Misdemeanors* (Allen, 1989), an argument about whether God is just—given the suffering of the innocent and the prospering of the wicked—mirrors disagreement about this same question in Proverbs, Job, and Qoheleth. *Match Point* (Allen, 2005), revisits these same questions, and offers a more pessimistic vision given the absence of any sort of justice (divine or otherwise) in the world.

Forgiveness is a central motif in films such as *Magnolia* and *Smoke Signals* (Eyre, 1998). The latter film proposes the counterintuitive notion that forgiveness requires accepting and adopting perspectives that clash with one's own. Such an insight, lacking in biblical texts (such as Matthew 6 and 18) that stress the importance of forgiveness, augments these texts in significant ways.

Coping with trauma is a theme at the center of many films and biblical texts (the latter is designated as trauma literature). Like the book of Job, *Life of Pi* (Lee, 2012) laments the injustice of undeserved human suffering. The film offers the provocative suggestion—absent in Job—that just as fiction can function as a coping mechanism for tragedy, so too can belief in God. Religious faith, the film proposes, may be preferable to a harsh reality without God for the simple reason that it is a "better" story. In the film, belief in God is fictitious but preferable (and necessary as a coping mechanism) to life's haunting and traumatic reality. *Pan's Labyrinth* suggests that fantasy may offer a helpful way of coping with trauma as long as that fantasy does not involve an escape from monstrous evil, but gives someone the opportunity to triumph over evil. *Life is Beautiful* (Benigni, 1997) proposes that humor and deceit (in the form of fictional alternatives to reality) may help some people avoid, or at least cope with, trauma. Several M. Night Shyamalan films explore the benefits and dangers of coping strategies people adopt in response to trauma. *The Sixth Sense* (1999) suggests that refusing to face one's trauma prevents one from moving on in the afterlife. *Signs* (2002) illustrates how it can be possible to find meaning within devastating trauma. *The Village* (2004) imagines how trauma can lead a culture to fabricate fictive versions of reality in order to shield themselves from the pain of loss.

All of these films offer proposals for coping with trauma that can be placed into mutually enriching dialogues with biblical texts focused on trauma. *Little Miss Sunshine* (Dayton and Farris, 2006) argues that meaningful living requires embracing failure and weakness. The film is an apt dialogue partner with Paul's argument about the virtue of weakness (1 Corinthians; 2 Corinthians 12:9).

Some films and biblical texts employ similar rhetorical strategies. *Crash* (Haggis, 2004) and the parable of the Unmerciful Servant (Matthew 18:23–35) initially invite their respective audiences to identify with certain characters, and to dislike other characters. Each narrative proceeds to disorient its audience by eliminating their empathy with characters they initially supported, and by establishing empathy with characters they previously disdained. The disruption caused by the frequent subversion of character identification invites the audience to question the validity of their own judgments about fictional characters and persons in their own life.

Some biblical texts and films address similar ethical concerns. Moses' killing of an Egyptian beating a slave, and Jesus' violence at the Temple raise questions about the costs and benefits of using violence as a force for good, and these issues are also at the heart of *The Girl with the Dragon Tattoo*, and the television shows *Dexter* and *24*. Some films and biblical texts utilize similar plot structures. *Boogie Nights* (Anderson, 1997) and Luke's parable of the "Prodigal Son" (15:11–32) portray a young man who departs his family and engages in a life of "sin," has an epiphany about what he is missing back home, and who returns to the gracious embrace of their family.

MOULIN ROUGE! AND SONG OF SONGS

The oft-repeated refrain (and thesis) of *Moulin Rouge!* (Luhrmann, 2001) is: "The greatest thing you'll ever learn is just to love and be loved in return." During the height of the Bohemian revolution in Montmartre, France, a romance blossoms between penniless writer Christian and the courtesan Satine. Recycling pop lyrics, Christian insists that "love is like oxygen," "love is a many splendored thing … love lifts us up where we belong," and "all you need is love." Satine, however, believes that "love is just a game," and she denigrates Christian's romantic rhetoric as "silly love songs."

The film's celebration of love (forms of the word "love" appear 143 times) is a striking similarity with the biblical text Song of Songs. Christian's exaltation of sexuality, sensuality, and romance echoes many central sentiments in Song of Songs. The film and Song of Songs celebrates a love and sexuality that is consensual, mutually enriching, and one that is not restricted to marriage, procreation, or polygamy.

Love, the film asserts, is an art that one must develop, and this education of love entails both giving and receiving love ("to love and be loved in return"). Every character can be evaluated according to their success or failure in learning how to love and be loved. Christian and Satine inhabit the film's thesis, each learning to grow in their capacity to love and be loved. Christian discovers that, unlike his initial idealized vision, love involves sorrow and heartache. When the Duke demands that he and Satine sleep together, Christian is devastated. Satine learns that love can be something other than an economic exchange, that she does not have to be bought, bartered, or sold, and that her worth does not depend on what someone is willing to pay for her. Like Christian, she also learns that love involves pain. She lies to Christian, telling him she does not love him, because she believes that doing so will save him from being killed by the Duke's henchman.

The film associates agony with love in a way that Song of Songs does not. This agony reaches a crescendo when, immediately after Christian and Satine are reconciled to each other, Satine dies in Christian's arms. The love Song of Songs envisions does not involve this depth of heartache. Indeed, Song of Songs insists that "love is as strong as death" (8:6). The film, however, is more bleak; it describes "a force darker than jealousy and *stronger than love* [that] had begun to take hold of Satine." This force is death, and it ends Satine's life. Love, in Song of Songs, is as strong as death, but in *Moulin Rouge!* love succumbs to death's clutches. As in Qoheleth, death in the film is omnipotent and bows to no one.

The film does suggest, however, that it is possible for love to survive death. While Satine dies in Christian's arms, she tells him, "Tell our story, that way I'll—I'll always be with you." Tell their story he does; the final scene shows him typing, concluding their story with the film's mantra, "The greatest thing you'll ever learn is just to love and be loved in return." The vehicle of story enables their love to survive. Indeed, Christian claims that their love will "live forever." Narrative grants their love a kind of immortality, and viewers of the film also encounter Christian and Satine's love through this same vehicle of story.

BIBLE AND TELEVISION

Boundaries between film and television are increasingly blurred, and—as more films are released on streaming services rather than in theaters—will become even more so. Although initially released in theaters, Scorsese's *The Irishman* (2019) was primarily a television event. Zefferelli's *Jesus of Nazareth*, regarded as a "classic" Jesus film, was originally released on television. *The Girl in the Café* was originally a television release. Boundaries between film and television will increasingly become somewhat arbitrary. Considering certain television shows (the criteria for which will have to be determined) as legitimate dialogue partners—in the same vein as films—with biblical texts/genres is desirable given the insights such conversations can generate. Biblical texts appear regularly and frequently in television, and examples are legion. In BBC's *Peaky Blinders*, Irish gangster Thomas Shelby tells his underlings, "Those of you who are last will soon be first." Kevin, the main character in HBO's *The Leftovers*, thoughtfully reads (and reflects on) Job 23:8–17 as he and a minister bury a woman.

THE WEST WING

President Josiah (Jed) Bartlet frequently cites the Bible in NBC's *The West Wing*. (This is not entirely surprising since Bartlet formerly planned to become a priest.) In his first line of dialogue in the series' pilot episode, Bartlet quotes the first commandment ("I am the Lord your God. Thou shalt worship no other God before me"). In a later episode, he argues with a radio talk show host who calls homosexuality an abomination. She clarifies, "I don't say homosexuality is an abomination, Mr. President, the Bible does." He replies, "Leviticus," and she answers, "18:22." Bartlet replies,

> Chapter and verse. I wanted to ask you a couple of questions while I have you here. I'm interested in selling my youngest daughter into slavery as sanctioned in Exodus 21:7. She's a Georgetown sophomore,

speaks fluent Italian, always cleared the table when it was her turn. What would a good price for her be? While thinking about that, can I ask another? My Chief of Staff Leo McGarry insists on working on the Sabbath. Exodus 35:2 clearly says he should be put to death. Am I morally obligated to kill him myself or is it okay to call the police? Here's one that's really important because we've got a lot of sports fans in this town: touching the skin of a dead pig makes one unclean—Leviticus 11:7. If they promise to wear gloves, can the Washington Redskins still play football? Can Notre Dame? Can West Point? Does the whole town really have to be together to stone my brother John for planting different crops side by side? Can I burn my mother in a small family gathering for wearing garments made from two different threads?

Bartlet situates one of the two Hebrew Bible verses that forbid male–male sex (there is no criticism of female–female sex in the Hebrew Bible) within a broader context of laws whose relevance is roundly rejected. By doing so he points out how the insistence on obeying one of these many laws (and disregarding the rest) reflects an inconsistent hermeneutic. Bartlet employs a similar tactic of focusing on a biblical text's broader literary context when he criticizes a preacher's sermon on Ephesians 5:21–27. He faults the preacher for focusing entirely on how husbands and wives should treat one another, when—as he points out—Ephesians 5:21 addresses how all people should submit themselves one to another.

Bartlet interviews Jhin-Wei, a Chinese national seeking asylum in the United States based upon his claim that he is a Christian suffering persecution. Bartlet asks him a series of questions about the Bible to ascertain if the man is indeed a Christian. After answering such queries, Jhin-Wei says, "Mr. President, Christianity is not demonstrated through a recitation of facts. You're seeking evidence of faith, a wholehearted acceptance of God's promise for a better world. 'For we hold that man is justified by faith alone' is what Paul said. 'Justified by faith alone.'" Jhin-Wei demonstrates his knowledge of the Bible and argues that such knowledge is insufficient to determine whether or not one is a Christian.

Bartlet's most authentic display of faith (according to the show's creator Aaron Sorkin) is reflected not in a citation of any biblical text but in an expression and enactment of the biblical genre of lament. After a funeral service for his secretary who was killed by a drunk driver, Bartlet asks to be left alone in the National Cathedral. Walking up the central aisle towards the altar, he tells God:

> You're a son of a bitch, you know that? She bought her first new car and you hit her with a drunk driver. What, was that supposed to be funny? "You can't conceive, nor can I, the appalling strangeness of the mercy of God," says Graham Greene. I don't know whose ass he was kissing there 'cause I think you're just vindictive. What was Josh Lyman? A warning shot? That was my son. What did I ever do to yours but praise his glory and praise his name? There's a tropical storm that's gaining speed and power. They say we haven't had a storm this bad since you took out that tender ship of mine in the north Atlantic last year ... 68 crew. You know what a tender ship does? Fixes the other ships. Doesn't even carry guns. Just goes around, fixes the other ships and delivers the mail. That's all it can do.

As he ascends the stairs to the Inner Sanctuary, he continues:

> Yes, I lied. It was a sin. I've committed many sins. Have I displeased you, you feckless thug? 3.8 million new jobs, that wasn't good? Bailed out Mexico, increased foreign trade, 30 million new acres of land for conservation, put Mendoza on the bench, we're not fighting a war, I've raised three children—That's not enough to buy me out of the doghouse?

Figure 8.1   President Bartlet smokes after lamenting to God in *The West Wing* (1999–2006).

Bartlet pauses at the top of the stairs, holds out his arms, and finishes in Latin:

> Am I really to believe that these are the acts of a loving God? A just God? A wise God? To hell with your punishments. I was your servant here on Earth. And I spread your word and I did your work. To hell with your punishments. To hell with you.

THE HANDMAID'S TALE

Biblical texts are used (and abused) with regularity in the *The Handmaid's Tale*. Their most frequent use is by government representatives to defend their misogyny and brutal treatment of women as sex slaves. In the pilot episode, there are at least five citations or allusions to biblical texts. Women are brought for reeducation to the "Rachel and Leah" center, named after two women in Genesis 29. As part of their reeducation they are told, "Blessed are the meek" (Matthew 5:5). Conveniently omitted is the subsequent promise, that the meek will "inherit the earth." This line also appears in Margaret Atwood's novel, on which the series is based.[1] In a later episode, June dares to repeat this second portion of the verse. "Blessed are they that mourn for they shall be comforted" (Matthew 5:4) is cited to make mourning sound like a desirable state. "If an eye causes you to sin" (Matthew 5:29) is used to justify gruesome physical punishment, including blinding women who transgress the strictures forced upon them. As June notes in the novel, "They can hit us, there's Scriptural precedent."[2]

Preceding each monthly mating ceremony in which the Commander rapes his handmaid, the Commander reads aloud from Genesis 30. This story describes how Jacob's wife Rachel, jealous of his other wife Leah since Leah could bear children and Rachel could not, "gives" her maid Bilhah to Jacob to impregnate—"that she may bear upon my knees and that I too may have children through her" (Genesis 30:3). Jacob impregnates Bilhah and she bears him two sons. When Leah ceases to bear children, she gives her own maid Zilpah to Jacob so he can impregnate her. This scriptural story legitimates the practice in Gilead of forcing handmaids to have intercourse with their commanders while the commander's wife holds them down and watches. *The Handmaid's Tale* invites viewers to understand Jacob's activity with Bilhah and Zilpah as rape, and to see Jacob's two wives as more than complicit in these sexual assaults. Genesis 16 describes a similar scenario in which Abraham's wife Sarai "gives" her maid Hagar to Abraham so he can impregnate her. The television series invites readers of these biblical narratives to imagine these ordeals from the perspective of the handmaid, a victim of rape, rather than from the more common and dominant perspective in the text of the man who rapes her and his wives who propose this activity.

Many names in the television series have biblical roots. "Martha" women, who serve as domestic slaves/servants, comes from an episode in Luke 10:38–42 in which Mary sits at Jesus' feet while Martha does chores. An episode called "Jezebels"—in which June joins the Commander on his trek to a brothel named Jezebel's where women are forced into prostitution—takes its name from a woman in 1 and 2 Kings (and Revelation 2:20). The revolution that brings Gilead into existence has its incipient start among the "Sons of Jacob," a group of men who meet together to discuss the kind of world they want to bring about. Handmaids and Marthas shop at stores with names such as "Milk and Honey" and "Loaves and Fishes."

Gilead, the new name of the former United States, is taken from a place in ancient northern Israel and a person in the book of Judges. Gilead was the father of Jephthah (Judges 11:1), and the name Jephthah means "he opens," a reference to God opening a womb. God is said to open the wombs of Leah and Rachel (Gen 29:31; 30:22). "May the Lord open" is the standard response given by women in Gilead to the greeting "Blessed be the fruit," both of which refer to God "blessing" a woman with pregnancy by opening her womb. Jephthah is also significant because he burns his daughter to death as a burnt offering to God (Judges 11), an act with obvious relevance for the ways women are terrorized in the Gilead of *The Handmaid's Tale*.

The Bible is regarded as a sacred physical object. When a commander reads from it, he first carefully removes it from a container, and unwraps the cloth in which it is held. Serena, Commander Waterford's wife, violates a sacrosanct prohibition when she dares to read from the Bible (John 1) in a public venue. She is punished

Figure 8.2 Serena risks punishment by reading the Bible publicly in *The Handmaid's Tale* (2017).

for doing so by having her finger cut off. Women are to have the Bible read *to* them; they are not to read it themselves. In the novel, the Beatitudes (Matthew 5) are read to the women at lunch; one of them is "*Blessed are the silent.*" June notes, "I knew they made that up, I knew it was wrong, and they left things out, too, but there was no way of checking."[3]

The reason the Bible is utilized so often to justify abusing women is because so many biblical texts do this very thing. As with almost any issue, the Bible contains diverse and conflicting perspectives, and the treatment of women is no different. In addition to texts that seek to liberate and empower women, there are also texts that demean and oppress them. The television series does not even address the most disturbing texts regarding women in the Bible (such as the law for the suspected adulteress in Numbers 5:11–31, allegations of marital fraud in Deuteronomy 22:13–21, and laws about rape in Deuteronomy 22:23–29). In the novel, the Commander reads from 1 Timothy 2:8–15 to defend silencing women, and to stress that their salvation is tied to their childbearing.[4] *The Handmaid's Tale* not only illustrates the (mis)use of the Bible to oppress women but also sheds light on these "texts of terror" (Phyllis Trible's phrase) in the Bible.

JUSTIFIED

In *Justified* (a show whose title echoes a core theological point of the apostle Paul), Boyd Crowder often cites the biblical text word for word, though not always for the most noble of purposes. He quotes the Bible to support his contention that Cain's descendants, the Edomites, are actually the Jews. Raylan Givens fires back, "I think you just use the Bible to do whatever the hell you like." After he is shot by Raylan, Boyd undergoes a conversion (the sincerity of which is debatable), and the Bible plays a significant role in his transformation. When accused of killing someone, he quotes Romans 12 ("beloved never avenge yourself but leave it to the wrath of God") to support his claim that people should not avenge themselves. In response, Art, a US Marshall, slams Boyd's Bible on his hands, yelling, "Will you show me in there where it justifies the killing of innocent people? You really don't know shit about the heavenly Father, do you? It's assholes like you that give Christians like me a bad name." Art's office has a plaque on the wall: "Thou shalt not steal—Exodus 20:15."

Referring to Exodus, Boyd calls methamphetamines a "modern day plague, like locusts, only worse." Boyd launches his own church, and when federal agents appear, he states, "They strike the shepherd so the sheep may scatter," a citation of Zechariah 13:7 that appears in Mark 14:27 and Matthew 26:31. Several of Boyd's followers repeat this same line when they are interrogated. Boyd cites Matthew 11:12 ("The kingdom of heaven suffers violence. Violent men take it by force"), and when he refuses cash from his father, Boyd declares, "Bible tells us a gift blinds the wise and perverts the words of the righteous" (Exodus 23:8; Deuteronomy 16:19). Boyd expels a member of his "church" for being an "Onanist," a reference in some churches to masturbation, even though in Genesis 38:4–10, Onan withdraws (before ejaculating) during intercourse to avoid impregnating Tamar. During a homily at church, Boyd likens himself to Saul on the Damascus Road (Acts 9), cites Jesus' use of violence in the temple (Mark 11:15–17), and quotes 2 Corinthians 5:17 ("Any man be born again in Christ is a new creation"). In a later prayer, he cites part of Psalm 23. He alludes to Matthew 10:28 when he tells his father, "There's more than one way to kill a man.

You can kill his physical body or you can kill his spirit within." Boyd does not only regurgitate biblical texts; he is often seeing carrying his black, leather-bound Bible. By placing the physical Bible in his hands and lacing his dialogue with biblical texts, *Justified* illustrates the moral and ethical complexity regarding the use of the Bible as both a weapon and a tool of redemption.

NARRATIVIZING THE LAW: *DEKALOG*

Polish filmmaker Krzysztof Kieślowski's *Dekalog* (1988) is a series of ten episodes made for Polish television, each of which reimagines one of the ten commandments (Deuteronomy 5). *Dekalog* exemplifies the blurred boundaries between the genres of film and television. All ten episodes were made for Polish television, but two episodes had theatrical releases. Kieślowski refers to the episodes as "films," and when told that a "TV series" would be new for him, he says, "It's not a TV series. Maybe 'a series of films' would be better."[5] He remarks, "I made those films for television but they are not TV films."[6] The series was remarkably successful. It cost $100,000 to make, and made over $3 million; it was viewed in countries around the world. Each episode (filmed by different cinematographers) features different main characters, all of whom live in the same Warsaw apartment complex.

Based on the first commandment ("You shall have no other gods before/besides me" / "You shall not make for yourself an idol"), episode 1 features a professor enamored with computer technology, and his young son Pawel who shares his dad's enthusiasm. As an atheist/agnostic, the father has a materialist view of life. When Pawel asks, "What is death?" the father answers in strictly biological terms. Pawel asks him what is left after people die, and the father says what people remember about the person. He tells Pawel, "There's no soul." Pawel's aunt holds a different worldview. She tells Pawel, "Life is a present. A gift." She claims that God exists, if you believe. When Pawel asks her, "What is God?" she hugs him, and asks, "What do you feel now?" Pawel says, "I love you," and the aunt replies, "Exactly. That's what God is." When Pawel tells his dad that Auntie believes there is a soul, he replies, "Some people find it easier to live if they believe that."

The father believes in the inerrancy of technology. Computers in their home lock and unlock the front door, and turn water faucets on and off. The father uses the computer to calculate if the frozen ice outside their apartment is thick enough for Pawel to skate on. Entering data for the ground temperature and the lake's depth, he determines the ice will hold Pawel's weight, and he tells Pawel he can skate outside. The ice, however, breaks, and Pawel falls through and dies. His despondent father mourns by knocking down an altar in a church that is under construction. Melting candle wax streams down the face of Jesus, making him look like he is shedding tears. The father rubs holy water (in the form of ice) on his forehead.

This episode illustrates and reconfigures the first commandment. Pawel's father violates the command by making technology his god, the computer his idol. He worships his deity with a reliance and dependence upon its version of truth as ultimate. The wages for his sin is the death of his son. (The first commandment claims God will punish children for their parents' iniquity.) The episode interprets the first commandment existentially. Paul Tillich defined religion as "ultimate concern," and the father's reliance upon his computer is religious in this existential sense of finding in it a kind of ultimate meaning. It is unclear if holding the holy water (as ice) reflects a state of repentance. Also unclear is the significance of the inclusio of the aunt viewing Pawel after his death, on a televised local news story; here technology preserves Pawel, albeit fleetingly.

Based on the second commandment (not misusing the Lord's name), episode 2 features a woman (Dorota) whose husband (Andrzej) is on the cusp of death, and who is pregnant with another man's child. She is torn between having an abortion (in case her husband recovers), or keeping the child (in case her husband dies and she can live with the child's father). She asks her husband's physician to share his prognosis, but the doctor refuses to offer any guarantees. He only says that his condition looks bad and he does not know if he will live: "The one thing I know is that I don't know." Dorota explains her dilemma to the doctor: she loves her husband, they were unable to have children, she is three months pregnant with another man's child, and if she has an abortion, she will not have another chance at pregnancy. The doctor is still reluctant to reveal too much, saying only, "All you can do is wait." He does admit that Andrzej's chances of recovery are slim, but says that he cannot guarantee anything.

Dorota makes an appointment for an abortion and breaks off the relationship with the child's father. She chooses her husband, not knowing if he will live. When she tells the doctor she has decided to have the abortion, he tells her not to, and that her husband is going to die. "There's no hope," he says. "Swear to that," she says. He says, "I swear." Her husband, however, recovers. In the final scene, he enters the doctor's office, grateful to be alive, and informs the doctor that he and Dorota are going to have a child. "I'm glad to hear it," the doctor says, not revealing what he knows about the child's paternity. Andrzej asks, "Do you know what that means, to have a child?" The doctor replies, "Yes, I do." The doctor's response is poignant given a prior revelation that his wife and children were killed years ago in a bomb strike during World War II. The episode depicts misusing God's name as declaring with confidence something about which one cannot be certain.

In episode 4 ("Honor your father and your mother") a college-aged woman (Anka) has romantic feelings for her father Michal, whom she suspects may not be her biological father. While he is away on a trip, she finds an envelope of her dad's ("to be opened in the event of my death"). Inside is a letter addressed to her from her mother who died five days after Anka was born. Anka tells Michal that her mom's letter confesses that Michal is not her biological father. She confesses to Michal her feelings for him, and offers her body to Michal, but he does not reciprocate. Anka later admits to Michal that she never read her mom's letter, and lied about its contents. She decides to burn the letter, so neither of them discover what it says. This episode questions the boundaries of what honoring father and mother entail, and whether honoring one parent may constitute dishonoring the other.

Based on the fifth commandment ("Thou shall not murder/kill"), episode 5 focuses on Jacek, a young drifter, who strangles and beats a taxicab driver to death, and Piotr, Jacek's defense attorney, who is opposed to the death penalty. Piotr's lines open the episode: "Punishment is a form of revenge. Especially when it aims to inflict harm and doesn't prevent crime. But in whose name does the law exact revenge? Is it really in the name of the innocent? Do the innocent truly make the laws?" Piotr loses his case, but the judge tells him that his summation was "perhaps the most eloquent indictment of capital punishment" he has heard in years. Piotr visits Jacek on the day of his execution, and witnesses how the state's murder of Jacek is as premeditated, horrifying, and inhumane as Jacek's murder of the taxicab driver. Piotr's remark ("Since Cain the world has neither been intimidated nor ameliorated by punishment") reflects the episode's indictment of capital punishment as an act as heinous as the types of murders it claims to punish and prevent. Perhaps unknowingly, the episode reflects ambiguity regarding whether the Hebrew in this commandment should be translated as "thou shall not *murder*" or "thou shall not *kill*."

The sixth episode ("You shall not commit adultery") follows 19-year-old Tomek, whose obsession with older neighbor Magda leads him to spy on her with a telescope, send her fake post office notices so she will visit him at his job, and get a second job as a milkman so he can deliver milk to her. He eventually confesses all this to her, and when she asks why he watches her, he says that he loves her. They go to a café where he again declares his love for her, but she insists there is no such thing. She says that making love has nothing to do with love. At her apartment, she initiates a sexual encounter, but after only seconds, he ejaculates prematurely; ashamed, he flees to his own apartment where he attempts suicide by slitting his wrists. Magda is told, "He slit his wrists. A broken heart it seems." For days Magda searches for him, and when she finally finds him, he tells her, "I don't watch you anymore." This episode broadens the concept of adultery (from having sex with another man's wife) to focus on potential dangers in other types of sexuality and sexual relations.

Episode 7 ("You shall not steal") features a 22-year-old woman (Majka) who gave birth to Ania when she was 16. Since then Ania has been raised by Ewa, Majka's mother and Ania's grandmother. Everyone is complicit in a ruse that Ewa is Ania's biological mother. When Ania is 6, Majka decides she wants to take Ania and live with her as mother and daughter. She "kidnaps" Ania, spiriting her away, and tells Ania that she is her mother. Majka calls a forlorn Ewa and tells her she wants Ania to be hers, but Ewa refuses. Madjka tells Ewa, "You robbed me of my baby, of the fact I'm a mother. Of

love. You robbed me of myself, of the two of you, of everything."
Majka repeatedly pleads with Ania to call her "Mommy," but Ania
refuses. Majka takes Ania to a train station, but they are discovered
by Ewa, to whom Ania runs, calling her "Mommy." A distraught
Majka leaves, by herself, on the train. The episode complicates the
implications of the commandment by depicting a scenario in which
stealing has become unavoidable. Ewa "stole" Majka's baby six years
ago, and either that theft will remain intact, or Majka will choose
to "steal" Ania back. At one point Majka asks, "Can you steal what's
really yours?"

The focus of episode 8 ("You shall not bear false witness") is an
encounter between Zofia, an ethics professor, and Elżbíeta, who visits Zofia's class. During a lesson on "ethical hell," a student describes
the scenario from episode two. Zofia says she knows how the story
ends, that the child is alive, "and that may be what matters most
in this story." Elżbíeta adds, "You said it was the life of the child
that mattered most," and then she offers her own "ethical hell"
scenario: in 1943, a Polish family willing to take in a 6-year-old
Jewish girl requires that she first obtain a certificate of baptism. Even
though a Polish couple is found to serve as the girl's godparents for
the baptism, the Polish couple renege on their promise when the
girl is brought to their home. Elżbíeta explains, "They've decided
they cannot lie before the God in whom they believe, a God who,
it is true, enjoins acts of mercy, but also forbids bearing false witness.
Though they knew the purpose of the lie involved, it was irrecon-
cilable with their principles."

The girl in the story turns out to be Elżbíeta, and the woman
who reneged on her promise is Zofia. Zofia explains to Elżbíeta
that she and her husband reneged on their promise because they
were members of the Resistance, and were told that the people
planning to hide Elżbíeta worked for the Gestapo, and that they
would use Elżbíeta to locate and arrest other Resistance members.
Zofia then admits that this information they had received turned
out to be wrong. With her hands on Elżbíeta's shoulders, Zofia tells
her, "I left you all alone. I sent you to almost certain death. And
I knew what I was doing. Yes, you're right. There's no idea, no cause,
nothing that could be more important than the life of a child."
Elżbíeta clasps Zofia's hands, and they have a genuine moment of

reconciliation. The episode broadens what constitutes bearing false witness, and relativizes the importance of lying in light of the more significant fidelity people owe one another—even strangers—when their lives are in danger.

Episode 9 addresses the commandment to not covet a neighbor's wife (suggesting that *Dekalog* follows the version of the ten commandments in Deuteronomy 5, not Exodus 20). Romek and Hania are married, and Romek discovers he has incurable impotency. He wants to leave Hania, but she insists that she loves him, will stay with him, and (contrary to his claim) does not need another man. He later discovers (through snooping and tapping her phone) that she is having an affair. Hania ends the affair, unaware that Romek knows about it. He tells her he has been aware of the affair, and wants a break from her. While on a skiing trip, she runs into the man with whom she had the affair. She reiterates that it is over and, afraid that Romek will find out, she tries to phone him to tell him she is returning home. Romek, falsely believing Hania is again cheating on him, leaves a note for her, and attempts suicide. Hania returns home, finds the note, and believes he is dead. Romek survives the attempt, and in the hospital receives Hania's earlier message that she is coming home. He has a nurse call her. Hania tells him over the phone, "You're there. God, you're there." He answers, "I'm here." The episode reimagines what constitutes coveting, and illustrates the deep pain caused when someone cheats.

The final episode addresses coveting possessions. When their estranged father dies, Jerzy and Artur inherit his stamp collection which he had obsessively collected and protected for decades. A bewildered Artur asks Jerzy, "What drives people to covet stuff, to possess something at any cost?" Artur answers his own question when—realizing the stamps are worth millions—the two sons become obsessed with them. As Artur admits, "Nothing else matters anymore." Jurek agrees, "You're right. You forget about everything else." When the stamps are stolen, each son suspects the other of having done it, and each informs the police on the other. They eventually confess this to one another, and laugh together in the final scene. The episode illustrates the emotional and relational costs of covetousness.

Dekalog transplants the genre of law to the genre of narrative. By narrativizing the commandments, Kieślowski shifts a terse propositional imperative into the more complex terrain of relationality. Law becomes a lived reality, and the episodes highlight the emotional, relational, and social dimensions of the commandments. The shift from law to narrative parallels Kieślowski's own transition as a filmmaker from documentary films to fiction. Whereas the commandments are (ostensibly) clear, and perhaps convey a sense of certainty, the episodes dwell in ambiguity and generate innumerable questions. When asked if he found "the answers," Kieślowski replied, "They don't exist. No one's found them, and no one will. That's why the questions are interesting."[7]

Some characters appear in more than one episode, and one character, who never speaks, appears in all ten episodes. These subtle links between episodes highlight the interplay and various connections between the commandments. Kieślowski wanted to turn "every commandment into a challenge for a human being. And can a human being meet that challenge? Is it even possible? Is it possible to adhere to these commandments and truly abide by them? Isn't modern man in such a complicated situation that abiding by the Commandments is practically impossible?" When Elżbíeta tells Zofia, "I've never read anything in your works about God," Zofia's response might channel Kieślowski's own approach to the commandments and life in general: "I don't use the word 'God.' But one can believe without having to use words."

GOD ON TRIAL

In the PBS television movie *God on Trial* (de Emmony, 2008), Jewish prisoners in the Auschwitz concentration camp put God on trial, charging God with breaking God's covenant with the Jewish people. Biblical texts play a central role in the various arguments prisoners advance. Rejecting the claim that it would be blasphemous to put God on trial, one prisoner cites the biblical examples of Abraham haggling with God over Sodom, Jacob wrestling with the angel, and the meaning of the name Israel ("he that striveth with God").

One prisoner cites Psalm 89 to suggest the concentration camp is God's punishment for peoples' sins. Another cites the examples of God flooding the world and God telling Abraham to sacrifice his own son to support his claim that God's punishments are not always proportionate to the crime. Job 22 is cited to show that arguments that God is indifferent are not without precedent. A prisoner cites two selections from Job 38 to contend that God is present even in the midst of inexplicable evil.

The trial's concluding speech is delivered by a prisoner who itemizes a devastating litany of disturbing Hebrew Bible texts. Beginning with Exodus, he points out that God brought the Hebrews out from Egypt not by killing Pharaoh, the one responsible for enslaving the Hebrews, but by killing children. "He slew them all. ... slew his children instead. All the children." He notes that instead of closing up the waters of the sea before the Egyptian soldiers arrived, God waited so that the waters would drown the soldiers pursuing the Hebrews. The prisoner asks what happened to the people already living in the "promised land" when the Hebrews arrived. To answer, he cites Deuteronomy 7:1–2: "When the Lord thy God shall bring you into the land you shall cast out many nations before you ... you shall smite them and utterly destroy them ... and show no mercy to them."

The prisoner mentions God's command to king Saul to destroy Amalek (1 Samuel 15). "Was Saul to show mercy?," the prisoner asks rhetorically. Answering his own question, he cites the biblical text: "Do not spare him, but kill. Kill man and woman. Babe and suckling. Camel and donkey." When Saul meets the Kenites and urges them to flee, the prisoner asks if God was pleased by Saul's mercy. "And when Saul decided not to slaughter all the livestock, was God pleased by his prudence, by his charity?" The answer, of course, is no. The prisoner, again, quotes the text: "You have rejected the word of Adonai, therefore he has rejected you as king." The prisoner then cites what the prophet Samuel did to please the Lord: "Samuel brought King Agag and hacked him to pieces before the Lord."

The prisoner cites David's sin of adultery with Bathsheba (2 Samuel 11), and asks, "Did God strike David for this? Did he strike Bathsheba? Adonai said, 'Since you have sinned against me, the child will die.'" The prisoner states,

> You asked earlier who punishes a child. God does. Did the child die suddenly, mercifully, without pain? Seven days, seven days that child spent dying in pain, while David wrapped himself in sack and ashes

> and fasted and sought to show his sorrow to God. Did God listen? Did that child find that God was just? Did the Amelakites think that Adonai was just? Did the mothers of Egypt—the mothers—did they think that Adonai was just? Did God not make the Egyptians, did he not make their rivers and make their crops grow? If not him, then who? Some other God? And what did he make them for? To punish them? To starve, to frighten, to slaughter them? The people of Amalek, the people of Egypt, what was it like for them when Adonai turned against them?

Gesturing at their desolate surroundings in the Auschwitz barracks, he answers, "It was like *this*."

Referring to the selection earlier that same day (in which prisoners were divided into those who would be gassed and those who would continue to work), the prisoner asks, "When David defeated the Moabites, what did he do?" Citing 2 Samuel 8:2, the prisoner answers, "He made them lie on the ground in lines, and he chose one to live and two to die." He adds,

> We are become the Moabites. We are learning how it was for the Amelakites. They faced extinction at the hand of Adonai. They died for his purpose. They fell as we are falling. They were afraid, as we are afraid. And what did they learn? They learned that Adonai, the Lord our God, *our God*, is *not* good. He is not good. He was not ever good. He was only on our side. God is *not* good ... Oh, at the beginning when he repented that he had made human beings and flooded the earth. *Why?* What had they have done to deserve annihilation? What *could* they have done to deserve such wholesale slaughter? What could they have done that was so bad? God is not good. When he asked Abraham to sacrifice his son, Abraham should have said *no*. We should have taught our God the justice that was in our hearts. We should have stood up to him. He is not good. He has simply been strong. He has simply been on our side.

The prisoner concludes that it is this wicked God that the Jews now face in Auschwitz: "He is still God but not our God. He has become our enemy. That's what happened to the covenant. He has made a new covenant with someone else." Unlike biblical laments, this devastating accusation about God's lack of goodness is neither directed to God, nor is there any demand that God change; there is rather a tacit assumption that God cannot or will not change. The

Figure 8.3 A concentration camp prisoner retells violent biblical texts of terror in *God on Trial* (2008).

prisoner's disturbing conclusion is the result of wrestling with many of the Hebrew Bible's unsettling depictions of God.

SUMMARY

The field of Bible and Film need not limit itself to analyzing films that are overtly "biblical" (Bible *on* Film, or Bible *in* Film). Despite not having explicit citations or allusions to the Bible, films such as *Citizen Kane, Smoke Signals, Signs, Crash, Life of Pi, Boogie Nights,* and *Moulin Rouge!* are only a small sample of the kinds of films which can engender significant insights when placed into critical conversation with biblical texts. Nor should the field of Bible and Film dismiss television—despite differences between it and film—as a legitimate dialogue partner with biblical texts. Sufficient similarities exist between film and television (as mediums of moving visual images) that warrant crafting critical conversations between television and biblical texts. *The Handmaid's Tale, Justified, The West Wing, Dekalog,* and *The Leftovers* all benefit from viewing them in light of certain biblical texts, and considering how they appropriate and reconfigure biblical texts. The field of Bible and Film can also benefit from incorporating films that emerge outside of the

Hollywood studio system, and films that diverge from the standard feature format (shorts, indie films, documentaries, etc.).

NOTES

1 Atwood (1986), 64.
2 Atwood (1986), 16.
3 Atwood (1986), 89.
4 Atwood (1986), 221.
5 Kieślowski (1987).
6 Kieślowski (1990).
7 Kieślowski (1995).

FOR FURTHER READING

George Aichele and Richard Walsh, eds. *Screening Scripture: Intertextual Connections between Scripture and Film* (Harrisburg, PA: Trinity Press International, 2002).

Laura Copier and Caroline Vander Stichele, eds. *Close Encounters between Bible and Film: An Interdisciplinary Engagement* (Atlanta, GA: Society of Biblical Literature, 2016).

Robert Jewett, *Saint Paul at the Movies: The Apostle's Dialogue with American Culture* (Louisville, KY: Westminster John Knox Press, 1993).

―――. *Saint Paul Returns to the Movies: Triumph over Shame* (Grand Rapids, MI: Eerdmans, 1999).

Robert K. Johnston, *Useless Beauty: Ecclesiastes through the Lens of Contemporary Film* (Grand Rapids MI: Baker Academic, 2004; reprint, Wipf & Stock, 2011).

Joseph G. Kickasola, *The Films of Krzysztof Kieślowski: The Liminal Image* (New York: Continuum, 2004).

Erin Runions, *How Hysterical: Identification and Resistance in the Bible and Film* (New York: Palgrave Macmillan, 2003).

Bernard Brandon Scott, *Hollywood Dreams and Biblical Stories* (Minneapolis, MN: Fortress Press, 1994).

Sze-kar Wan, "Justice, Empire, and Nature: Deliverance, Covenant, and New Creation in East Asian Cinema," in *T&T Clark Companion to the Bible and Film* (ed. Richard Walsh; London: Bloomsbury, 2018), 93–103.

GLOSSARY

70mm   a film projection format with larger sizes and wider aspect ratios than the more typical 35mm.

act–consequence   a perspective in certain biblical texts (Deuteronomy, Proverbs, Psalms) that a person will be blessed or cursed (by God) based upon whether they are wise/righteous or foolish/wicked.

Akedah   the story of God commanding Abraham to kill his son Isaac (Genesis 22).

allegorical   an interpretive strategy that finds meaning not in a literal understanding of a text, but in a symbolical, metaphorical, or figurative understanding.

alternative wisdom   refers to biblical wisdom texts such as Job or Qoheleth (Ecclesiastes) that tend to have a more complex view of faith and the world; these views are often in conflict with conventional wisdom (e.g., Proverbs).

apocalyptic   a biblical literary genre (Daniel, Revelation, Mark 13/Matthew 24/Luke 21) in which a divine breaking into the world is anticipated in order to right unjust oppression or persecution. Often accompanied by a divine/angelic messenger who reveals insights to the community of true believers. Also a cinematic genre that is usually associated with the end of the world.

auteur   often used to refer to a filmmaker who writes and directs their own films, utilizing a distinctive style, and exercising a significant degree of control over the final shape of their films.

biblical epic   a large budget film (either about Jesus or a Hebrew Bible narrative) with well known actors, lavish and ornate sets and costumes, hundreds or thousands of extras, and scenes of entertainment (e.g., battle sequences).

canon within the canon   a preference for, or reliance upon, certain sacred texts within one's religious tradition as more authoritative or influential than other sacred texts within one's tradition.

canonical   referring either to (1) the "canon," an official and closed list of sacred texts (such as the Hebrew Bible or the Christian Bible); or (2) the view that all the books within a specific canon share a harmonious view or perspective.

Cecil B. DeMille   a film director who is synonymous with the development (and direction) of biblical epics.

Christology   a belief, view, or perspective about Jesus. Also a technical subfield within the field of Christian theology.

cinematography   what the camera sees and displays.

commission   Jesus' call to his disciples (in Matthew 28) that they spread his message throughout all the world.

conventional wisdom   biblical wisdom perspectives (such as Proverbs) that tend to have a more simplistic view of faith and the world.

dybbuk   a spirit in Jewish folklore that causes misery, and a central figure in the opening Prologue of *A Serious Man*.

evangelist   author of a gospel.

extracanonical   a text that, while considered sacred by some, was not included in the final canon of a religious community (e.g., gospel of Thomas).

first creation story   the story of God creating the world in seven days (Genesis 1:1-4a).

gnostic   from the Greek word for "knowledge," an early Christian, possibly pre-Christian belief and practice—reflected in many texts— that salvation was for a select few to whom God would grant a special revelation of knowledge.

harmony/harmonize   the tendency in Jesus films to blend elements from multiple gospels into one coherent narrative.

Hashem   a Hebrew term meaning "the name," used as a euphemism for God.

Hays code   a popular term for the Motion Picture Production Code, in place from 1934–1968, which established a number of different rules forbidding the types of things films were able to show.

hevel   appearing 38 times in Qoheleth (Ecclesiastes), this Hebrew term literally means "vapor, mist, smoke," and is usually translated as "vain," "futile," "absurd," or "meaningless."

Hebrew Bible   the sacred text of Judaism, consisting of the Torah, Prophets, and Writings. Also called the Tanakh, Jewish Bible, or Old Testament.

hermeneutic   a fancy term for interpretation, or for a method, theory, or practice of interpretation of a text.

historical Jesus   a reference to the human person Jesus as distinguished from the Jesus who is described in the gospels.

imago dei   Latin for "in God's image," a reference to the remark in the first creation story in Genesis 1 that God created humankind in God's image.

inclusio   when a piece of art (such as a film or biblical text) begins and ends on the same or similar note (either the same image, sound, line, etc.).

intertextual   any of the various links between one text and a different text. Such links can be in the form of citation, allusion, echo, or sharing similar themes in common.

intertitle   a piece of printed text (usually used in silent films) that provides information or an explanation to the audience.

kerygma   the gospel or preaching message of the early church.

lament   a biblical genre in which a person (or community) experiencing trauma or suffering directs anger, accusations, and questions to God, and pleads with God to end the suffering.

lex talionis   the "eye for an eye" injunction that appears three times in the Torah.

Marcionite   a Christian "heresy" attributed to Marcion that denigrates the value of the Hebrew Bible due to its association with Judaism.

midrash   an ancient Jewish practice of amplifying the biblical text by supplying details not specified in the text.

Nicene   refers to the council of Nicaea (325 CE), at which the Christian church officially declared that Jesus is fully God and fully human.

passion plays   a performance focusing on Jesus' passion (suffering), usually the last week or few days of his life. The basis of many of the early Jesus films.

pericope   a narrative unit in the gospels with a clear beginning and end. The gospels are composed of numerous pericopes, which the gospel authors arranged in different orders.

redaction   the practice in which authors of biblical texts edit (add to, remove, or modify) material in their source material. (Most scholars think the authors of Matthew and Luke use and redact Mark's gospel as one of their sources in the composition of their own gospels).

second creation account   the story of the creation of Adam and Eve, and their expulsion from the garden of Eden (Genesis 2:4b–3:24).

secrecy commands   Jesus' tendency in the synoptic gospels to silence people after he performs miracles or after people call him a significant title (e.g., Christ, son of God).

Shoah   the Holocaust.

synoptic   the gospels of Mark, Luke, Matthew, which despite the many differences among them, are much more similar to one another than they are to the gospel of John.

"talkies"   appearing in the 1920s, these "talking pictures" differed from silent films by integrating sound.

wisdom literature   a genre of biblical literature (Proverbs, Qoheleth/ Ecclesiastes, Job, Ben Sira) that wrestles with questions about how to live meaningfully.

BIBLIOGRAPHY

Aichele, George and Richard Walsh, eds. *Screening Scripture: Intertextual Connections between Scripture and Film*. Harrisburg, PA: Trinity Press International, 2002.

Anderson, Paul Thomas. *Magnolia: The Shooting Script*. New York: New Market Press, 2000.

Atwood, Margaret. *The Handmaid's Tale*. New York: Anchor Books, 1986.

Babbington, Bruce and Peter William Evans. *Biblical Epics: Sacred Narrative in the Hollywood Cinema*. Manchester and New York: Manchester University Press, 1993.

Bandy, Mary Lea and Antonio Monda, eds. *The Hidden God: Faith and Film*. New York: The Museum of Modern Art, 2003.

Baugh, Lloyd. *Imaging the Divine: Jesus and Christ-Figures in Film*. Kansas City, MO: Sheed & Ward, 1997.

Bazin, André. "Cinema and Theology." Pages 61–72 in *Bazin at Work: Major Essays and Reviews from the Forties and Fifties*. Edited and translated by Alain Pierre and Bert Cardullo. New York: Routledge, 1951 (1997).

Bultmann, Rudolf. *Theology of the New Testament*. Translated by Kendrick Grobel. New York: Charles Scriber's Sons, 1951 and 1955.

Burnette-Bletsch, Rhonda, ed. *The Bible in Motion: A Handbook of the Bible and Its Reception in Film*. 2 vols. Berlin: De Gruyter, 2016.

Burnette-Bletsch, Rhonda and John Morgan, eds. *Noah as Antihero: Darren Aronofsky's Cinematic Deluge*. New York: Routledge, 2017.

Cone, James. *The Cross and the Lynching Tree*. Maryknoll: Orbis, 2013.

Copier, Laura and Caroline Vander Stichele, eds. *Close Encounters between Bible and Film: An Interdisciplinary Engagement*. Atlanta, GA: Society of Biblical Literature, 2016.

Dargis, Manohla. "His Bloody Valentine." *Village Voice* 24 (Nov 1992).

Deacy, Christopher. *Screen Christologies: Redemption and the Medium of Film*. Cardiff: University of Wales Press, 2001.

————. "Reflections on the Uncritical Appropriation of Cinematic Christ-Figures: Holy Other or Wholly Inadequate?" *Journal of Religion and Popular Culture* 13 (Summer 2006).

Del Toro, Guillermo. *Pan's Labyrinth* DVD Audio Commentary. New Line Home Entertainment, 2007a.

Del Toro, Guillermo. "The Power of Myth." *Pan's Labyrinth* DVD Featurette. New Line Home Entertainment, 2007b.

Del Toro, Guillermo. "On Pan's Labyrinth." (Sep 30, 2019). www.youtube.com/watch?v=8-G8pKiuG8Q.

Ebert, Roger. "The Last Temptation of Christ." (Aug 12, 1988). www.rogerebert.com/reviews/the-last-temptation-of-christ-1998.

————. *Freeway.* (January 24, 1997). www.rogerebert.com/reviews/freeway-1997.

————. *The Great Movies II.* New York: Broadway Books, 2005.

Emerson, Jim. "Tree of Life: The Missing Link Discovered!" (April 11, 2012). www.rogerebert.com/scanners/tree-of-life-the-missing-link-discovered.

Emmerich, Anne Catherine. *The Dolorous Passion.* www.jesus-passion.com/THE_PASSION.htm#CHAPTER%20I.

Endō, Shūsaku. *Silence.* Translated by William Johnston. New York: Taplinger, 1980.

Exum, Cheryl, ed. *Plottted, Shot, and Painted: Cultural Representations of Biblical Women.* Sheffield: Sheffield Academic Press, 1996.

————. *The Bible in Film—The Bible and Film.* Leiden: Brill, 2006.

Freire, Paulo. *Pedagogy of the Oppressed.* London: Bloomsbury Academic, 2000.

Friend, Tad. "Heavy Weather: Darren Aronosfky Gets Biblical." *New Yorker* (March 10, 2014). www.newyorker.com/magazine/2014/03/17/heavy-weather-2

Gilmore, Richard. *Searching for Wisdom in Movies: From the Book of Job to Sublime Conversations.* New York: Palgrave Macmillan, 2017.

Hoberman, J. "The Grace of Wrath." *Village Voice* (March 16, 2004). www.villagevoice.com/2004/03/16/the-grace-of-wrath/

Jewett, Robert. *Saint Paul at the Movies: The Apostle's Dialogue with American Culture.* Louisville, KY: Westminster John Knox Press, 1993.

————. *Saint Paul Returns to the Movies: Triumph over Shame.* Grand Rapids, MI: Eerdmans, 1999.

Johnston, Robert K. *Useless Beauty: Ecclesiastes through the Lens of Contemporary Film.* Grand Rapids, MI: Baker Academic, 2004. Reprint, Wipf & Stock, 2011.

Kickasola, Joseph G. *The Films of Krzysztof Kieślowski: The Liminal Image.* New York: Continuum, 2004.

Kieślowski, Krzysztof. Interview (1987). *Dekalog* Criterion Collection DVD, 2016.

————. Interview (1990). *Dekalog* Criterion Collection DVD, 2016.

————. Interview (1995). *Dekalog* Criterion Collection DVD, 2016.

Kilbourn, Russell J. A. "(No) Voice out of the Whirlwind: The Book of Job and the End of the World in *A Serious Man, Take Shelter*, and *The Tree of Life*." *Adaptation* 7 (2014): 25–46.

King, Stephen. *On Writing: A Memoir of the Craft*. New York: Scribner, 2000.

Kreitzer, Larry. *The New Testament in Fiction and Film: On Reversing the Hermeneutical Flow*. Sheffield: Sheffield Academic Press, 1993.

———. *The Old Testament in Fiction and Film: On Reversing the Hermeneutical Flow*. Sheffield: Sheffield Academic Press, 1994.

———. *Pauline Images in Fiction and Film: On Reversing the Hermeneutical Flow*. Sheffield: Sheffield Academic Press, 1999.

———. *Gospel Images in Fiction and Film: On Reversing the Hermeneutical Flow*. Sheffield: Sheffield Academic Press, 2002.

Lyden, John C. *Film as Religion: Myths, Morals and Rituals*. New York: New York University Press, 2003.

Orrison, Katherine, *Written in Stone: Making Cecil B. DeMille's Epic* The Ten Commandments. Lanham, MD: Vestal Press, 1999.

Pasolini, Pier Paolo. *Pier Paolo Pasolini—A Future Life*. Edited by Laura Betti and Lodovico Gambara Thovazzi. Rome: Associazione Fondo Pier Paolo Pasonlini, 1989.

———. *Saint Paul: A Screenplay*. London: Verso, 2014.

Pippin, Tina. "This Is the End: Apocalyptic Moments in Cinema." Pages 405–16 in *The Bible in Motion: Biblical Reception in Film*. Edited by Rhonda Burnette-Bletsch. Vol. 1. Berlin: De Gruyter, 2016.

Ranzato, Emilio. *L'Osservatore Romano* (2014). Cited in "In Francis' Church Pasolini goes to heaven." *Vatican Insider – La Stampa* (July 23, 2014). www.lastampa.it/vatican-insider/en/2014/07/23/news/in-francis-church-pasolini-goes-to-heaven-1.35736033

Reinhartz, Adele. *Scripture on the Silver Screen*. Louisville: Westminster John Knox Press, 2003.

———. *Jesus of Hollywood*. New York: Oxford University Press, 2007.

———. *Bible and Cinema: Fifty Key Films*. New York: Routledge, 2012.

———. *Bible and Cinema: An Introduction*. New York: Routledge, 2013.

Rindge, Matthew S. "Dead Man Walking." Pages 84–9 in *Bible and Cinema: Fifty Key Films*. Edited by Adele Reinhartz. New York: Routledge, 2012.

———. *Profane Parables: Film and the American Dream*. Waco, TX: Baylor University Press, 2016a.

———. "Revelatory Film: Apocalyptic Themes in Film and Cinematic Apocalypses." Pages 337–58 in *Apocalypses in Context: Apocalyptic Currents throughout History*. Edited by Justin P. J. Schedtler and Kelly J. Murphy. Minneapolis: Fortress Press, 2016b.

———. "Lars von Trier's *Dogville* as a Cinematic Parable." Pages 260–69 in *T&T Clark Companion to the Bible and Film*. Edited by Richard Walsh. London: Bloomsbury, 2018.

———. "Cinematic Wisdom: Film and Biblical Wisdom Literature." Pages 479–95 in *The Wiley Blackwell Companion to Wisdom Literature*. Edited by S. Adams and M. Goff. Oxford: Wiley-Blackwell, 2020.

———. "Guillermo del Toro's *El laberinto del fauno* (*Pan's Labyrinth*): Subverting the Cinematic Jesus/Christ Figure." In *T&T Clark Handbook of Jesus and Film*. Edited by Richard Walsh. London: Bloomsbury, 2021a.

———. "Protestant Pacifist: War and Pacifism in Mel Gibson's *Hacksaw Ridge*." In *Protestantism on Screen: Religion, Politics, and History in European and American Movies*. Edited by J. Stevens, G. Espinosa and E. Redling. New York: Oxford University Press, 2021b.

Rodriguez, Rene. "Director keeps Hollywood out of 'Pan's Laybrinth.'" *Seattle Times* (Jan 16, 2007). www.seattletimes.com/entertainment/director-keeps-hollywood-out-of-pans-labyrinth/.

Runions, Erin. *How Hysterical: Identification and Resistance in Bible and Film*. New York: Palgrave Macmillan, 2003.

Ryzik, Melena. "Making 'Mother!,' The Year's Most Divisive Film." *New York Times* (Sep 29, 2017). www.nytimes.com/2017/09/19/movies/jennifer-lawrence-darren-aronofsky-mother-explained.html.

Scorsese, Martin. *Scorsese on Scorsese*. Edited by David Thompson and Ian Christie. Boston: Faber and Faber, 1996.

Scott, A. O. "Heaven, Texas and the Cosmic Whodunit." *New York Times* (May 26, 2011). www.nytimes.com/2011/05/27/movies/the-tree-of-life-from-terrence-malick-review.html?pagewanted=all.

Scott, Bernard Brandon. *Hollywood Dreams and Biblical Stories*. Minneapolis: Fortress Press, 1994.

Seesengood, Robert Paul, and Jennifer L. Koosed. "Spectacular Finish: Apocalypse in/and the Destruction of the Earth in Film." Pages 143–60 in *Simulating Aichele: Essays in Bible, Film, Culture and Theory*. Edited by Melissa C. Stewart. Sheffield: Sheffield Phoenix, 2015.

Shepherd, David J. *The Bible on Silent Film: Spectacle, Story, and Scripture in the Early Cinema*. Cambridge: Cambridge University Press, 2013.

———. *The Silents of Jesus in the Cinema (1897–1927)*. New York and London: Routledge, 2016.

Siegler, Elijah, ed. *Coen: Framing Religion in Amoral Order*. Waco, TX: Baylor University Press, 2016.

Tatum, W. Barnes. *Jesus at the Movies: A Guide to the First Hundred Years*. Santa Rosa, CA: Polebridge Press, 1997.

Testa, Bart. "To Film a Gospel ... and Advent of the Theoretical Stranger." Pages 180–209 in *Pier Paolo Pasolini: Contemporary Perspectives*. Edited by Patrick Rumble and Bart Testa. Toronto: University of Toronto Press, 1994.

Trible, Phyllis. "Eve and Adam: Genesis 2–3 Reread." *Andover Newton Quarterly* 13 (1973): 74–83.

Walsh, Richard. *Reading the Gospels in the Dark: Portrayals of Jesus in Film*. Harrisburg, PA: Trinity Press International. 2003.

———. *Finding St. Paul in Film*. New York: T&T Clark, 2005.

———. "(Carrying the Fire on) No Road for Old Horses: Cormac McCarthy's Untold Biblical Stories." *The Journal of Religion and Popular Culture* 24 (2012): 339–51.

———. "A Modest Proposal for Christ-Figure Interpretations: Explicated with Two Test Cases." *Relegere* 3:1 (2013): 79–97. https://relegere.org/relegere/article/view/569.

———. , ed. *T&T Clark Companion to the Bible and Film*. London: Bloomsbury, 2018.

———. "Biblical Coens: Can We Laugh Now?" *Journal of Religion and Film* 23:2 (2019).

Walsh, Richard, and Jeffrey L. Staley. *Jesus, the Gospels, and Cinematic Imagination: Introducing Jesus Movies, Christ Films, and the Messiah in Motion*. London/New York: T&T Clark, 2021.

Walsh, Richard, Jeffrey L. Staley, and Adele Reinhartz, eds. *Son of Man: An African Jesus Film*. Sheffield: Sheffield Phoenix, 2013.

Wan, Sze-kar. "Justice, Empire, and Nature: Deliverance, Covenant, and New Creation in East Asian Cinema." Pages 93–103 in *T&T Clark Companion to the Bible and Film*. Edited by Richard Walsh. London: Bloomsbury, 2018.

Wright, Melanie J. *Moses in America: The Cultural Uses of Biblical Narrative*. Oxford: Oxford University Press, 2002.

Zwick, Reinhold. "The Gospel According to St. Matthew." Pages 109–14 in *Bible and Cinema: Fifty Key Films*. Edited by Adele Reinhartz. New York: Routledge, 2012.

———. "The Book of Job in the Movies: On Cinema's Exploration of Theodicy and the Hiddenness of God." Pages 355–77 in *The Bible in Motion: Biblical Reception in Film*. Edited by Rhonda Burnette-Bletsch. Vol 1. Berlin: De Gruyter, 2016.

FILMOGRAPHY

CINEMA

3:10 to Yuma (Mangold, 2007)
4 Little Girls (Lee, 1997)
12 Years a Slave (McQueen, 2013)
13th (DuVernay, 2016)
28 Days Later (Boyle, 2002)
2012 (Emmerich, 2009)
About Schmidt (Payne, 2002)
Adam and Dog (Lee, 2011)
Adam and Eve (unknown, 1912)
Adam's Apples (*Adams æbler*) (Jensen, 2005)
Adam's Rib (DeMille, 1923)
American Beauty (Mendes, 1999)
Amistad (Spielberg, 1997)
Antichrist (von Trier, 2009)
Apocalypse Now (Coppola, 1979)
Apocalypto (Gibson, 2006)
Armageddon (Bay, 1998)
As It Is in Heaven (*Så som i himmelen*) (Pollak, 2004)
Bamboozled (Lee, 2000)
Big Hero 6 (Hall and Williams, 2014)
Birth of a Nation (Griffith, 1915)
Blackfish (Cowperthwaite, 2013)
BlacKkKlansman (Lee, 2018)
Boogie Nights (Anderson, 1997)
The Book of Eli (Hughes brothers, 2010)
Born on the Fourth of July (Stone, 1989)

Bowling for Columbine (Moore, 2002)
Boys Don't Cry (Peirce, 1999)
Bram Stoker's Dracula (Coppola, 1992)
The Brand New Testament (Le tout nouveau testament) (van Dormael, 2015)
Braveheart (Gibson, 1995)
Breaking the Waves (von Trier, 1996)
Bruce Almighty (Shadyac, 2003)
Cape Fear (Scorsese, 1991)
Capitalism: A Love Story (Moore, 2009)
Children of the Corn (Kiersch, 1984)
Children of Men (Cuarón, 2006)
Citizen Kane (Welles, 1941)
The Chosen Prince, or The Friendship of David and Jonathan (Mong, 1917)
The Chronicles of Narnia: The Lion, The Witch, and the Wardrobe (Adamson, 2005)
Cool Hand Luke (Rosenberg, 1967)
Crash (Haggis, 2004)
Crimes and Misdemeanors (Allen, 1989)
The Crusades (DeMille, 1935)
Damien: Omen II (Taylor, 1978)
Dancer in the Dark (von Trier, 2000)
David and Goliath (David e Golia) (Baldi and Pottier, 1960)
Dead Man Walking (Robbins, 1995)
Deep Impact (Leder, 1998)
Devil (Dowdle, 2010)
The Devil's Advocate (Hackford, 1997)
Diary of a Country Priest (Journal d'un curé de compagne) (Bresson, 1951)
Do The Right Thing (Lee, 1989)
Dogma (Smith, 1999)
Dogville (von Trier, 2003)
Donnie Darko (Kelly, 2001)
E.T. (Spielberg, 1982)
East of Eden (Kazan, 1955)
Ecce Homo (Duvivier, 1935; *Golgotha*, 1937)
The End of the Affair (Jordan, 1999)
End of Days (Hyams, 1999)
Esther and the King (Walsh and Bava, 1960)
Evan Almighty (Shadyac, 2007)
Ex Machina (Garland, 2014)
Exodus: Gods and Kings (Scott, 2016)
The Exorcist (Friedkin, 1973)
Fahrenheit 9/11 (Moore, 2004)

Feet of Clay (DeMille, 1924)
Fight Club (Fincher, 1999)
Footloose (Ross, 1984)
Forbidden Fruit (DeMille, 1921)
From the Manger to the Cross (Olcott, 1912)
The Fugitive (Ford, 1947)
Gattaca (Niccol, 1997)
The Girl in the Café (Yates, 2005)
The Girl with a Dragon Tattoo (*Män som hatar kvinnor*) (Oplev, 2009)
Gladiator (Scott, 2000)
Godspell (Greene, 1973)
The Gospel according to Saint Matthew (*Il Vangelo Secondo Matteo*, Pasolini, 1964)
Gran Torino (Eastwood, 2008)
The Greatest Story Ever Told (Stevens, 1965)
The Green Mile (Darabont, 1999)
Hacksaw Ridge (Gibson, 2016)
Hail Caesar (Coens, 2016)
The Happening (Shyamalan, 2008)
The Höritz Passion Play (1897)
The Hunting Ground (Dick, 2015)
I Am Legend (Lawrence, 2007)
I Am Not Your Negro (Peck, 2016)
I Confess (Hitchcock, 1953)
Indiana Jones and the Raiders of the Lost Ark (Spielberg, 1981)
Intolerance: Love's Struggle Throughout the Ages (Griffith, 1916)
Invasion of the Body Snatchers (Siegel, 1956)
The Invisible War (Dick, 2012)
The Irishman (Scorsese, 2019)
The Iron Giant (Bird, 1999)
Jesus Christ Superstar (Jewison, 1973)
Jesus of Montreal (*Jésus de Montréal*, Arcand, 1989)
Joseph in the Land of Egypt (Moore, 1914)
Judith of Bethulia (Griffith, 1914)
King David (Beresford, 1985)
King of Kings (Ray, 1961)
The King of Kings (DeMille, 1927)
La ricotta (Pasolini, 1963)
Last Days in the Desert (García, 2015)
The Last Days of Pompeii (*Gli ultimi giorni di Pompei*, Caserini and Rodolfi, 1913)
The Last Temptation of Christ (Scorsese, 1988)
Leaves from Satan's Book (*Blade af Satan's Bog*, Dreyer, 1920)

The Sun Also Rises (King, 1957)
The Ten Commandments (DeMille, 1923, 1956)
Thelma and Louise (Scott, 1991)
There Will Be Blood (Anderson, 2007)
A Time to Kill (Schumacher, 1996)
Tommy (Russell, 1975)
Top Gun (Scott, 1986)
The Tree of Life (Malick, 2011)
The Truman Show (Weir, 1998)
To the Wonder (Malick, 2012)
Us (Peele, 2019)
The Village (Shyamalan, 2004)
The Witch (Eggers, 2015)
X-Men Apocalypse (Singer, 2016)
X-Men 2 (Singer, 2003)
The Year of Living Dangerously (Weir, 1982)
The Zero Theorem (Gilliam, 2013)

TELEVISION

24 (Surnow and Cochran, 2001–10)
Dekalog (Kieślowski, 1988)
God on Trial (de Emmony, 2008)
The Handmaid's Tale (Miller, 2017–)
Jesus of Nazareth (Zeffirelli, 1977)
Justified (Yost, 2010–15)
The Leftovers (Lindelof and Perotta, 2014–17)
Peaky Blinders (Knight, 2013–)
The West Wing (Sorkin, 1999–2006)
Westworld (Nolan and Joy, 2016–)
When the Levees Broke: A Requiem In Four Acts (Lee, 2006)
When They See Us (DuVernay, 2019)

INDEX